FOUNDATIONS OF COMPUTER SCIENCE

COMPUTER SOFTWARE ENGINEERING SERIES

ELLIS HOROWITZ, Editor
University of Southern California

CALINGAERT
Assemblers, Compilers, and Program Translation

CARBERRY, KHALIL, LEATHRUM and LEVY
Foundations of Computer Science

FINDLAY AND WATT
PASCAL: An Introduction to Methodical Programming

HOROWITZ and SAHNI
Fundamentals of Computer Algorithms

HOROWITZ and SAHNI
Fundamentals of Data Structures

FOUNDATIONS OF COMPUTER SCIENCE

M. S. CARBERRY
H. M. KHALIL
J. F. LEATHRUM
L. S. LEVY

*All of the authors are on the faculty of the
University of Delaware*

COMPUTER SCIENCE PRESS, INC.

Computer Science Press, Inc.
9125 Fall River Lane
Potomac, Maryland 20854

First Printing

Library of Congress Cataloging in Publication Data
Main entry under title:
Foundations of computer science.

Bibliography: p.
Includes index.
1. Electronic data processing. 2. Electronic digital computer. I. Carberry, M. S. II. Series
QA76.F6373   001.6'4   78-27891
ISBN 0-914894-18-8

Preface

Computer science is a young field which is undergoing rapid change compared to more established academic disciplines. This movement has led to a variety of curricular approaches. Moreover, the different environments in which computer science has grown-up, and the sundry research interests of faculties has encouraged different courses of study, and attempts to define the nature of the science—which is surely a source of confusion to other disciplines.

It is a truism, that like the five blind Indian sages encountering the elephant, different computer scientists have come to different definitions of computer science. Our (first order) definition is that *computer science is the study of the theory and practice of programming computers.* This differs from the most widely used definition by emphasizing programming as the central notion and algorithms as a main theoretical notion supporting programming. The study of heuristic programming is certainly part of our computer science. While it is premature to measure the relative significance of empirical methods in our science, ignoring them would give a distorted view of the science.

This text was designed for the student taking his or her first course in Computer Science. No college level prerequisites are assumed. Where mathematical notions are employed, intuitive discussions are included to help the student relate to and understand the result.

The book is language independent—we present algorithms in flowcharts, pidgin algol, or decision tables. We show algorithmic methods of translating from one form to another (The text has been taught with at least the following languages: Basic, Cobol, Fortran, PL/1, Algol 60, DELISA—a lisp dialect and APL. It has been class-tested in introductory, computer science together with a variety of language primers. The objective of the text is to provide material at a depth such that it can be covered at the rate of one chapter per week in a one-term course. It is suggested that Chapters 1 through 7 be covered thoroughly, and that topics be selected from the remaining chapters according to the interests of the students and the instructor. It is also possible through more intense work in applications (Chapters 8, 9, and 11) to support a full year of instruction.

The core material is contained in the following sections: 1.1, 1.2, 1.3, 2.1, 2.2, 4.1, 4.3, 4.4, 5.1, 6.1, 6.2, 6.3, 6.4, 6.5, 7.1, 7.2, 7.3, 7.4, 7.5. The remaining material in chapters 2, 4, 5, and 6 is optional and may be covered in sequence. Chapter 3 may be covered after chapter 2 or deferred until all of the core material has been covered—at which time the student will surely have a deeper appreciation of the many concepts and techniques relevant to structuring.

Chapters 8–9 and chapters 11–15 may be covered any time after the core material has been covered. The order is also not critical. A second course in general computer science can easily cover all of the remaining material. Chapter 10 may be covered at any time after chapter 1, with additional outside readings recommended, such as Norbert Weiner's *God and Golem.*

Although the complete text is designed for a one year course, we have also taught it extensively as a one semester course using selected material. Students who complete the year course have a preliminary working knowledge of both high level language programming—including recursion and other advanced topics—as well as a knowledge of structured assembly language programming. (Kimura)

Acknowledgements

The authors are particularly indebted to students and reviewers who have provided helpful suggestions in preparing the text. The faculty and administration of the University of Delaware deserve special thanks for their support of the objectives of Foundations of Computer Science and for providing the academic means for encouraging its development. The patience and persistence of Miss Beverly Crowl in typing the text is also gratefully acknowledged. For the understanding and encouragement from our families, no amount of praise or thanks would be sufficient.

Contents

14.   Mathematical Models of Machines

15.   Programming a Pocket Calculator

Chapter 1

Computer Science: Scientific and Historical Perspectives

In commenting about the relation between experience and its assimilation, Frederick the Great is said to have observed that he knew two mules who had been in the army for forty years but were still mules.

This story applies directly to computers and computer science. A computer scientist is one who not only works with computers, but also abstracts the essential principles of the computer and its application. In learning computer science, you will learn to use the computer, but you will also learn a discipline of thought. The methods of formulating and solving problems which are basic to computer science are also applicable to many other sciences, arts, and humanities.

We begin with an overview of the field of computer science. As a young science, it is still rapidly expanding, with constantly shifting frontiers. Still we try to delimit the scope of the science, and give an indication of how it applies to other fields.

The historical background of computer science is also sketched briefly. The history of the subject is often presented purely as a chronology of devices from mechanical to microelectronic. However, there are also general philosophic and scientific roots to the attempted mechanization of mathematics and of thought.

1.1   Overview of Computer Science

Computer science is an emerging discipline of thought and activity which may be dated from the early 1960s, although its historical roots in logic and mathematics go back to the turn of the century. The very newness of the discipline leads to self-consciousness and introspection which is not found in the more classical disciplines of science. The definition of computer science is still an active area of discourse and development from which only a few glimmers of insight have emerged so far.*

The following is a *tentative* definition of computer science:

> Computer science is a discipline concerned with the study of the principles of programming and problem solving via digital computers, and of representing and processing information.

In order to fully understand this definition, the terms "programming" and "digital computer" deserve some analysis. *Programming* is the act of organizing a complex set of related activities into correct, optimal sequences. Thus, the route selection in travel, pattern layout in sewing, and even the strategy

---

*"It is only after long experience that most men are able to define a thing in terms of its own genus, painting as painting, writing as writing."

Ezra Pound, "A, B, C of Reading," 1934, p. 71

used in courting are examples of programming. Some programming principles are:

(1) *Invariant Imbedding:* In solving a programming problem one should seek smaller, simpler programming problems imbedded within the original one.
(2) *Isolation:* Insofar as is possible, a programming task should be isolated
(3) *Generality:* The solution to the programming problems should be applicable to other similar problems.

Exercise 1.1-1

Propose a travel itinerary for road travel from New York to Los Angeles in minimum time. What principles of programming were used in arriving at your solution?

Exercise 1.1-2

Consider the Towers of Hanoi problem which requires that you move the discs in Figure 1.1 from peg No. 1 to peg No. 3, such that
(a) Only one disc may be moved at a time;
(b) No disc may rest upon any other disc of smaller size.

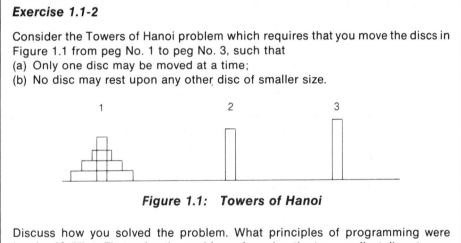

Figure 1.1:   Towers of Hanoi

Discuss how you solved the problem. What principles of programming were involved? (Hint: First solve the problem of moving the two smallest discs to peg No. 2.)

Computers require organization of their activities into correct, optimal sequences. The process of organizing the actions of computers is known as *computer programming.*

A *digital computer* is an electronic device composed of interconnected discrete state elements. The interconnection of these elements permits such actions as counting, arithmetic, logic, and storage. The organization of the interconnections is of considerable scientific and engineering interest, but is of very limited concern to computer science. The relationship of a computer scientist to the organization of a digital computer is analogous to the relationship of an architect to a building. The primary concerns of the computer scientist are (1) the relationships between the major components of the computer and (2) the relationships between the computer and its environment.

Further insight into the definition of computer science may be achieved by considering the theoretical foundations of the science. An outline of the main theoretical areas of computer science was cited by Salton* and attributed to H. Zemanek:

> (1) a *theory of programming,* with emphasis not mainly on the problem of distinguishing the computable from the noncomputable, but rather on a practical theory of algorithms concerned with the construction of economical and efficient programs.

> (2) a *theory of process and processor organization,* which takes into account the finite dimensions of existing memories, the availability of storage hierarchies of varying access speed and costs, and the desire for a reduction in computation and program production time;

> (3) *a theory of description* for processes and computational structures in terms acceptable to the processor; and

> (4) a *theory of computer applications* which would include all features common to most numeric and nonnumeric applications.

The mention of these theoretical areas does not suggest that they are well developed. Computer scientists are actively establishing suitable theoretical foundations of the discipline's primary concerns.

In defining computer science, some things that are not computer science should also be considered. The following are related to but don't coincide with computer science nor are included completely within computer science:

> Digital Electronics
> Mathematics
> Logic
> Mathematical Programming
> Numerical Analysis

If you still feel unsatisfied after learning what is and what is not computer science, then perhaps the chapters that follow will provide that extra "feel" for what computer science is about.** To summarize this first view of computer science, we may say that computer science is now trying to develop programming techniques and significant ways to talk about programs as they relate to digital computers.

---

*G. Salton, "What is Computer Science?" *Journal of the Foundation for Computing Machinery* 19, No. 1, (January, 1972): 1-2. Copyright 1972, Association for Computing Machinery, Inc., reprinted by permission.

**Description would but make it less;
'Tis what I feel, but can't define
'Tis what I know, but can't express"

Beilby Porteus, "On Love"

1.2   Computer Science in Scientific Perspective

Computer science developed into a discipline during the 1950s and 1960s, a period of great emphasis upon technological progress. During this same period, economic and social pressures began to press the computer more and more into the lives of the ordinary people. Much of the interface between computer science and other sciences and humanities is changing very rapidly, but it does deserve some scrutiny in order to view future developments in their proper perspective.

The growth and development of computer science closely parallels that of nuclear science. From the beginning of the so-called "nuclear age" the computer has been relied upon to provide accurate and timely predictions of intensity of nuclear phenomena. From the design of nuclear weapons to the design and control of the most sophisticated nuclear reactors, the digital computer has been indispensable. The technology of computers also underwent rapid development under pressure from nuclear science. The technological activity is still evident in the name of the largest organization of computer-oriented professional people, "Association for Computing Machinery," emphasizing the mechanical or machine aspect of computing. Most computer scientists are now concerned with programming and problem solving.

Close upon the heels of the development of nuclear science came the rapid development of aerospace science in the 1960s. Many of the computer applications developed in nuclear science were readily transferred to aerospace applications. These aerospace applications included guidance and control computations and analysis of radiation effects, both requiring a high degree of numerical accuracy. Many of the reliability problems associated with nuclear science also arose in aerospace science. The most significant new role of the computer in aerospace science was in the area of communication. The computer was called upon to absorb, discriminate, filter, and even improve the features of data being transmitted over interplanetary distances. Instead of being a design engineering tool for a few scientists, the computer became a node in a communications network supporting space travel. Thus, in many ways the aerospace activity gave impetus to the development of the computer.

The rapid growth of population and need for service in the 1960s placed their own unique pressures upon the development of computer science. Businesses, governments, and institutions found that, due to the number of individuals being served, they needed the computer's speed and reliability. New problems arose, however, when it was realized that such applications required storing and manipulating vast amounts of data, most of which was nonnumerical. The technology of data storage underwent very rapid development under this pressure. New problems arose in the areas of data integrity and security, design of interfaces between the nonscientist and the computer, and the elimination of useless data.

Exercise 1.2-1

List the ways you have interacted with a computer in a typical day. List the ways that you suspect you have interacted with a computer but are not sure.

1.3   Computer Science in Historical Perspective

A. Hardware Technology

Most of the concepts implemented in the earliest digital computers built during World War II had been developed by Charles Babbage during the early nineteenth century. However, the technological requirements of the design, precision, and maintenance of tolerances precluded their successful execution. When the technology of scientific instrument design had advanced sufficiently to allow the construction of these complex devices, they were essentially reinvented. It was then that the pioneering work of Babbage was rediscovered.

The principle operation of computers can be understood by referring to Figure 1.2. There are two essential components in Figure 1.2: a storage or memory for numbers or data, and a processing unit. The data to be operated on are introduced initially via the input/output unit into the storage unit. Subsequently, they are routed to the processing unit and back to storage (perhaps several times, depending on the complexity of processing) and finally the (refined) data are routed to the output.

Since the cost of storage increases with the speed of retrieving information, most computing systems use several types of storage. The fastest storage is *main storage* and is often mounted on the chassis of the central processor. *Bulk storage,* typically in the form of tapes or discs, is used to retain large files which would cost too much in main storage and to store data not currently being processed. Often, an initial phase of processing is the transfer of data from a bulk storage file to main storage. The final phase after processing is the return of the updated file from main storage to bulk storage.

In Babbage's early design and in the first implementations, the storage was provided in the form of electromechanical components similar to many office machines, and the sequence of operations on data was preset or externally controlled. The paths of information flow were mechanical linkages. The arithmetic operations were performed in seconds.

By the mid-1940s the much greater speed of electronic circuitry had replaced the electromechanical devices, and the first generation of digital computers to appear commercially in the early 1950s were electronic. These computers

MAIN FRAME

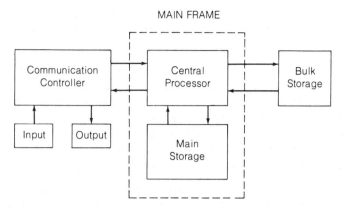

Figure 1.2: *A simplified block diagram of a digital computer*

used vacuum tube circuitry in the processing unit, and a variety of devices for storage. Typical arithmetic operations were measured in tens of micro-seconds, representing a great speed advantage over the electromechanical components. A significant innovation, introduced by von Neumann in the early electronic digital computers, was the control of the central processor activity by data stored in the memory. This *stored program* concept allows programs to be modified, as if they were data, and is used in all subsequent computers.

By the late 1950s, a new generation of computers had supplanted the early electronic digital computers. These new computers used solid state elec-tronics in both the memory and processing units. The transistor, developed in 1948, is a miniature crystalline device functionally equivalent to a vacuum tube. It became the primary active component in the processing unit. The magnetic core memory, composed of myriads of miniature ferrite ceramic cores, became the standard memory component. Typical processing speeds for arithmetic operations were several microseconds (1 microsecond $= 10^{-6}$ seconds).

Today's computers represent the third generation in the evolution of digital computers. Processing units are primarily composed of modules of solid state integrated circuitry. These solid state integrated circuits comprise tens to hundreds of transistors on a small crystalline base. Speed of operation of the processing circuits is measured in nanoseconds (1 nanosecond $= 10^{-9}$ seconds). Memories are primarily magnetic core, but the cores are generally improved, smaller and faster. Solid state memories are becoming more prevalent. Typical processing speeds are of the order of one microsecond or faster for arithmetic operations.

The components we have discussed in this section are generally referred to as the *main frame of the computer*. The complete computer system will in-clude input devices such as punched card readers, output devices such as high speed line printers, and additional storage in the form of magnetic disks and magnetic tape units providing larger quantities of slower but more economical storage. In general, the performance of these auxiliary devices has improved correspondingly.

Finally, as the performance of components has increased, the price has decreased, and the reliability has improved. A good example of the effect of this advance in technology is that today's mini-computers sell for a great deal less than the largest computers of the early 1950s and provide superior performance. On the other hand, the large computers of today that are comparable in price to their predecessors provide significant increases in the size and performance of their storage and processing components.

The improvements in design have altered the use of computers in several ways: (1) A larger class of problems is solved by computers now; (2) A greater emphasis is placed on the use of the computer to simplify problem solving; (3) Some apparently inefficient utilizations are tolerated to make the user's job easier.

In summary, the past several decades have seen a continuing development of computer technology, with the promise of equal progress in the foreseeable future. The improvement in performance is likely to alter the user's view of the computer.

B.   Mathematical Roots

We have a different view of the history of computer science when we look at the development of the mathematical concepts. There is a long history, going back several centuries, of the desire to reduce mathematics to mechanical, routine procedures. With the development of mathematical logic in the last half of the nineteenth century and early twentieth century, this goal began to look feasible. A plan to make mathematical problem-solving routine is attributed to Hilbert. The routine solution of a mathematical problem is known as the *algorithmic method.* Given any pair of numbers, *x* and *y,* we can compute their product, even though we have never performed that particular multiplication before. Likewise, given a theorem of geometry, e.g. $x^2 + y^2 = z^2$ in a right triangle where *x, y* are the lengths of the legs and *z* is the length of the hypoteneuse (Pythagorean Theorem), we would like to have a routine method of generating the proof.

Attempts to achieve the mechanization of mathematics led to some very startling results. The following results were proved in the 1930s: (1) No matter how we develop our mathematical system, there will be true facts which we will never be able to prove (2) Given a sufficiently powerful mathematical system to do arithmetic, we will be unable to automatically ascertain whether a proposed theorem is, in fact, provable.

As a result of these developments and a recognition of the limits of the algorithmic method, logicians and students of the foundations of mathematics began to describe what could be computed—even though there were no automatic computers. The objective was to describe, or characterize, the types of problems which one could solve by a systematic (perhaps manual) computation, and what, in fact, would qualify as a systematic (or *algorithmic*) computation.

Due to the work of these logicians (Turing, Church, Kleene, Post, Markov) we began to develop some concept of an algorithm and a programming language (or language of algorithms). Thus, this work forms some of the theoretical basis of computer science.

C. History of Programming

As we have seen, as computers became more complex and the problems they had to solve became more difficult, the task of programming, or preparing the problem for the computer, grew. Moreover, as the computer technology developed, the number of different kinds of computers grew, making the problem of transferring programs between computers more significant.

The solution to these problems was to program in an algorithmic language and to use the computer to translate the algorithmic language, problem-oriented program to a machine language program.

Fortunately, the field of linguistics was also undergoing a revolution as a result of the same mathematical logic ideas being applied to language. The linguistic developments have made the formal description of the algorithmic languages and the translation from algorithmic to machine language easier.

The earliest algorithmic language of significance was FORTRAN I, developed in the mid-1950s. It is difficult to recreate the atmosphere of only twenty years ago when the feasibility of a machine independent algorithmic language was seriously questioned. Today, FORTRAN is extensively used for scientific computation, with a FORTRAN compiler available for almost every extant computer. (A *compiler* is a program that translates a program from an algorithmic language to a machine language.)

Sammet* discusses some 170 problem-oriented, machine-independent languages. Of these languages, approximately half are specially designed for some limited class of application, but the remaining half are general purpose with more than a dozen enjoying a wide distribution and popularity.

COBOL, developed in 1960, is a business-oriented, machine independent, algorithmic language, and probably the most widely used procedure-oriented language. ALGOL, developed at about the same time, is a language that has had wide influence, especially overseas and in academic environments.

In the mid-1960s, PL/1 was developed to combine many of the features of FORTRAN, ALGOL, and COBOL in a single language. It has not yet succeeded in replacing any of these languages significantly.

---

*Communications of the Association for Computing Machinery (1970).

Other languages of note developed in the 1960s include LISP, a list-processing language used extensively in machine intelligence research such as robot control, and SNOBOL, a string-processing language for text manipulation. Two popular interactive languages, BASIC and APL, have also been developed for communicating with the computer from typewriter-like terminals. The interactive languages may have very significant long-term effects on computer usage because of the ease with which they can be taught at the high school level.

The growth of new languages has had many different motivations (see Sammet, cited previously, for fuller discussion), but two, in particular, will receive some emphasis in chapters 6 and 7: data structures and control structures. *Data structures* refers to the kinds of data that can be conveniently represented, while *control structures* refers to the manner in which the computations can be organized. Both of these aspects of algorithmic languages have been receiving much attention lately. In learning to program, one should be very conscious of how one is solving a problem and the role that these control and data structures play.

Just as there is continuing development in the technological aspects of computers, there is an evolution of techniques and concepts in software, or programming. There is also an interaction between the two as new machine organizations require new programming concepts, and vice versa. You should, therefore, try to cultivate a critical facility to assess which aspects of current programming techniques are desirable and which are not.

Summary

As the symbol-processing power of the computer increases—and this power has been magnified by technological advances so that it is now far beyond what it was in the early 1950s—so does the complexity of the problems which we try to solve using the computer. We are forced to develop more efficient modes of problem reduction, using systematic programming techniques, and employing languages facilitating communication between man and machine.

Computer science is concerned with the problem-solving process. Often the modes of thought induced by abstracting the essence of computer usage give us new perspectives on the problems we are trying to solve. In studying and applying computer science, we should be conscious of solving the problems at hand using the computer and developing concepts and techniques to enhance our problem-solving capability with, or without, the computer.

References and Suggested Additional Readings

(1) Beth, E.W., *The Foundations of Mathematics.* New York: Harper & Row, 1966. Part I, p. 1-81, esp. chap. 3, p. 52-81.

(2) Goldstine, H.H., *The Computer from Pascal to von Neumann,* New Jersey: Princeton U. Press, 1972.

(3) Pylyshlyn, Z.W., ed. *Perspectives on the Computer Revolution.* Englewood Cliffs, New Jersey: Prentice-Hall, 1970. Part I, p. 1-155.

(4) Rosen, Saul, "Programming Systems and Languages; A Historical Survey." In *Programming Systems and Languages.* S. Rosen, ed., New York: McGraw-Hill, 1967.

(5) Salton, G.. "What is Computer Science", Journal of the **Association for Computing Machinery**, 19, 1, (1972).

Problems

1. Try to identify what data should be processed and what a typical computation might be, to establish ways a computer might be useful for the following:
   1) Preparing an income tax return.
   2) Urban planning.
   3) Scheduling airline reservations.
   4) Medical diagnosis.

2. Describe a systematic way for listing all pronounceable six-letter words in English.

3. The score in a football game at half time is 33–0. Assume that a team can score points by touchdowns—6 or 7 points, field goals—3 points, and safeties—2 points. Describe one way of calculating all possible combinations by which the 33 points might have been scored. Example: two 7-point touchdowns, two 6-point touchdowns, one 3-point field goal, and two 2-point safeties.

4. Estimate the number of words in an encyclopedia of your choice, describing how you arrived at your estimate. How many characters of storage would be required to store the encyclopedia in a computer?

5. Using your results from problem 4, assuming an input rate of 500 cards per minute, 80 characters per card, how long would it take to read the encyclopedia into the computer? Assuming a lineprinter rate of 1,000 lines per minute and 130 characters per line, how long would it take to print out the encyclopedia?

6. You are given an 8 qt bucket, a 5 qt bucket, and a 3 qt bucket. The 8 qt bucket is initially full; the 5 qt and 3 qt buckets are initially empty. A single move consists of pouring from bucket A to bucket B until either A is empty or B is full. Describe how you would systematically compute a procedure which would result in exactly 4 qts in the 8 qt bucket. Does your procedure generalize to buckets of other sizes?

7. A large scale scientific computer can do about 10 million additions of ten-digit numbers in one second. Making reasonable assumptions, try to estimate how long it would take a person to do these same 10 million additions. State your assumptions.

Chapter 2

Problem Solving on Computers

In this chapter we introduce the basic concept of problem solving on the computer—the algorithm. Algorithms, which are precisely stated problem solutions, are discussed and characterized. Several examples are given.

The *flowchart*, a graphical notation for the description of algorithms, is introduced next. The major advantage of the flowchart is that it provides a convenient way of visualizing and communicating algorithms. The flowchart can also be used as a basis for programming and, in fact, an algorithm is given for translating a (two-dimensional) flowchart into a (linear) program. The translation algorithm is itself presented as a flowchart. In developing the algorithmic method, we stress the variety of presentations allowable. Different people solve problems in different ways and are comfortable with different styles. The beginning programmer has the unique opportunity to experiment with alternative styles and select the most suitable combination.

The third section introduces two alternative forms of algorithmic description —pidgin-ALGOL and decision tables. Either of these can be used as a basis for programming, or any combination of these plus flowcharts.

The last part of the chapter deals with limitations of the algorithmic method. We first discuss and give two proofs that the "halting problem" has no algorithmic solution—one of the proofs using the flowcharts. The *halting problem* is to determine whether a given program with input data will ever conclude its operation. As an example of a combinatorial problem for which no algorithm is possible, we present the Post correspondence problem—without proof. The Post correspondence problem is a deceptively simple problem involving matching strings of letters. Finally, some consequences of the fundamental limitations of the algorithmic method are given, such as the impossibility of algorithmically determining that two programs are equivalent.

2.1   Algorithms

A.   The Concept of an Algorithm

An *algorithm* is a statement of a systematic procedure for solving a class of problems. An algorithm is a clear, unambiguous description of how a computation is to proceed—a computational recipe. The algorithm tells in detail how to proceed in an organized way through a sequence of elementary steps.

Among the many algorithms with which we are familiar is the procedure for adding a pair of (positive) integers in standard (i.e., decimal) notation. This algorithm is learned early in life and is so familiar that it requires some thought to appreciate its intricacy. Indeed, to appreciate the addition algorithm try to add the following numbers without lining them up: 4,723 + 2,659 = _____ .

A "standard" description of the algorithm for addition is:

Addition algorithm:

(1) Line up the two numbers.

(2) Start with the rightmost column; call it the current column.

(3) Add the digits in the current column.

(4) If the sum of the digits is less than 10, then record the sum in the current column below the line.

(5) If the sum of the digits is greater than 10, record the remainder of the sum when 10 is subtracted from it below the line in the current column, and record a "1" in the column to the left of the current column.

(6) Let the column immediately to the left of the current column be the new current column.

(7) If the current column is empty, *stop.* (The result is available below the line.)

(8) If the current column is not empty, then go to step 3.

This procedure, once it is spelled out in this much detail, can be analyzed to see some of the features common to algorithms. It can also be used as a basis for a computer program for addition. (In most cases, an addition algorithm is built into the computer.) And by changing 10 to 8, wherever 10 occurs in the procedure, we have an algorithm for addition of numbers in octal (base 8) notation. (See chapter 4.) Note that although you may not know the significance of octal numbers, you can follow the computation recipe, i.e., addition algorithm (changing 10 to 8), to add the following octal numbers—2,476 + 3,554. Verify that in base 8 the answer is 6,252.

The algorithm given above has these features:

(1) It starts with a standard description of the input data.

(2) It is organized into a finite sequence of elementary steps, some of which depend on known underlying basic operations.

(3) There are intermediate results to be recorded during the calculation.

(4) The steps in the procedure are to be performed in sequence. The sequence includes data-dependent rules; so 4,523 + 3,554 requires the sequence of steps: 1, 2, 3, 4, 5, 6, 7, 8, 3, 4, 5, 6, 7, 8, 3, 4, 5, 6, 7; while 3 + 4 is done by the sequence of steps: 1, 2, 3, 4, 5, 6, 7.

The study of algorithms is central to computer science, and we shall subsequently consider them from different points of view.

B. Characteristics of Algorithms

Having considered one algorithm in some detail, we now describe some characteristics common to all algorithms. In fact, a procedure not containing any one of these characteristics would not be considered suitable as a description of a computation.

Finiteness of description

The algorithm must be described as a finite (limited) sequence of steps. This description is somewhat stronger than requiring only that the algorithm be stated in a finite description. The standard algebraic series definitions of trigonometric functions, although they are described in a finite number of symbols, contain an infinite number of terms. For example, the sine of an angle θ given in radians may be computed from the series:

$$\sin \theta = \theta - \frac{\theta^3}{3!} + \frac{\theta^5}{5!} - \frac{\theta^7}{7!} + \frac{\theta^9}{9!} - \cdots$$

or more concisely as:

$$\sin \theta = \sum_{k=1}^{\infty} (-1)^{k+1} \frac{\theta^{2k-1}}{(2k-1)!}$$

(this notation is just a mathematical shorthand for the same function). But you cannot use the series as an algorithm because it never terminates. The series can be used as the *basis* for an algorithm if a condition for ending is given—such as "stop when the next term computed is less than 1/100 of the previously computed term."

Preciseness of meaning

Each step in the algorithm must be interpreted in a prespecified way. No semantic difficulties can affect the computation, so different realizations of the algorithm will proceed identically on identical input data. For example, if the algorithm requires division of one number by another, the number of significant places to be computed *and* the rule for rounding or ending the quotient must be understood.

Determinism of execution

At each step of the algorithm, the computation to be performed is uniquely determined by the data, intermediate results, and the procedure. No random choices are allowed. This restriction ensures the computation will be repeatable, and the results obtained will be unique.

Under the determinism requirements, computations that require random samples are not considered to be algorithms. However, there is an extension of the notion of algorithm (called nondeterministic algorithm) which allows choices at various stages of the computation. It can be shown, using methods beyond the scope of this text, that there is an algorithm by which any nondeterministic algorithm can be converted to a deterministic algorithm.

Generality

An algorithm is expected to solve a class of problems. Thus, we do not speak of an algorithm to add three and four but of an algorithm to perform the operation of (decimal) addition. Implicit in the notion of an algorithm is the set of allowable input values—called the *domain*—and the set of allowable output values—called the *range*. Either the domain or the range may be infinite, as indeed is the case with the addition algorithm.

The domain of an algorithm can be sets of names for a sorting algorithm, lists of numbers for complex arithmetic or vector operations, or more general structures. (See chapter 7.) Specification of an algorithm—for example, by a computer program—will identify the domain and range.

Finiteness of execution

Every algorithm must halt with an answer after a finite number of steps. If it does not, then no problem is solved and it is of no value.

Exercise 2.1-1

Consider the problem of finding terms of the Fibonacci sequence:
$$0, 1, 1, 2, 3, 5, 8, 13, 21 \ldots$$
In this sequence of numbers, the first two terms are 0 and 1. After that the terms are such that each new entry in the sequence is the sum of the two preceding ones.

Input: 0 and 1.

Output: The first term of the sequence to exceed 1,000.

Procedure:

(0) In this procedure, two numbers must be retained. These are called *predecessor* and *ancestor*.

(1) Set the predecessor to 0 and the ancestor to 1.

(2) Find the sum, *N,* of the ancestor and the predecessor; if *N* is greater than 1,000; halt.

(3) Set predecessor equal to ancestor and ancestor equal to *N,* and go to step 2.

Clearly this procedure qualifies as an algorithm under our definition. It has a finite set of instructions—three. Each of the steps is simple and can be carried out mechanically. The procedure has two inputs, 0 and 1, and has one output, *N.*

Instead of using the English language exclusively to write out procedure, we may use a combination of mathematical notation and English. Thus, an alternative way of writing the procedure would be:

Procedure:

(1) $P \leftarrow 0$ and $Q \leftarrow 1$.

(2) $N \leftarrow P + Q$; if $N > 1,000$ then halt.

(3) $P \leftarrow Q$; $Q \leftarrow N$; go to step 2.

Clearly this notation is more elegant. The symbol $\leftarrow$ designates replacement; for instance, the statement $N \leftarrow P + Q$ appearing in step 2 indicates that the old value of *N* is to be replaced with the sum of *P* and *Q*.

Complexity of algorithms

Two simple criteria for evaluating the quality of an algorithm are space and time complexity. By *space complexity* we mean the amount of memory required to hold the information generated during the execution of the algorithm as a function of the input. *Time complexity* refers to the number of basic operations generated as a function of input.

Example

By referring to the procedure for computing Fibonacci numbers, we find that step 1 is performed one time while steps 2 and 3 are executed alternately until we reach a halt. We can show that in this case the algorithm halts after 15 executions of steps 2 and 3. The amount of memory used is one computer word for each variable, i.e. *P*, *Q*, and *N*, assuming that each of these numbers can be stored in one computer word.

Exercise 2.1-2

Determine if three numbers are given in order.

Given three quantities *x*, *y*, and *z*; determine whether they are ordered or not. They are ordered if they either increase or decrease in value when listed in the sequence *x*, *y*, *z*.

Input: *x*, *y*, *z*—real numbers.

Output: Yes, if *x*, *y*, and *z* are ordered; otherwise, no.

Procedure:

(1) If $x = y$ then output "yes" and halt.
(2) If $x > y$ then proceed to step 3; else proceed to step 4.
(3) If $y \geq z$ then output "yes" and halt; else output "no" and halt.
(4) If $y \leq z$ then output "yes" and halt; else output "no" and halt.

This procedure involves many simple decisions and nothing else.

Exercise 2.1-3

Find the middle number of three given numbers.

Input: Three integers: *a*, *b*, *c*.

Output: A single integer—the median of the input numbers.

Procedure 1:

(1) Compare *a* and *b*; call the smaller of the two *d*, and call the larger of the two *e*.
(2) Compare *c* and *d*. If *c* is not greater than *d*, then the middle number is *d*.
(3) If *c* is greater than *d*, then the answer is the lesser of *c* and *e*.

Alternatively, we may use:

Procedure 2: (Assumes a primitive operation SWAP to interchange a pair of numbers. Thus, SWAP (*a, b*) gives *a* the value of *b* before the SWAP, and vice versa. For example, if *a* = 5 and *b* = 3 before the SWAP operation is used, then after SWAP (*a, b*) we have *a* = 3 and *b* = 5.)

(1) If *a* is less than *b* then swap (*a, b*).
(2) If *b* is less than *c* then swap (*b, c*).
(3) If *a* is less than *b* then swap (*a, b*).
(4) The result is in *b*.

Example of Procedure 2:

a	b	c	
3	4	5	initial
4	3	5	after step 1
4	5	3	after step 2
5	4	3	after step 3

Exercise 2.1-4

Find the square root of a positive integer, *N*.

Input: *N*, an integer; n_0, an approximation to *N*, a real number; *e*, allowable difference between *N* and n^2, where *n*, a real number, is to be computed.

Output: *n*, the square root of *N*, a real number.

Procedure 1:

(0) $n \leftarrow n_0$
(1) If $|N - n^2| < e$, then the answer is *n*; otherwise continue to step 2.
(2) $n \leftarrow \dfrac{N + n^2}{2n}$
(3) Return to step 1.

IN SOME PROGRAMMING LANGUAGES THIS PROCEDURE WOULD BE WRITTEN MORE CONCISELY AS:

(0) $n \leftarrow n_0$
(1) While ($|N - n^2| < e$) do $n \leftarrow \dfrac{N + n^2}{2n}$

(2) Print *n*.

Procedure 2:

This algorithm is particularly useful for operation on a hand calculator without a built-in square root operation.

(0) Mark off the input number in pairs of columns from the right.
(1) At the most significant column pair start subtracting successive odd integers 1, 3, 5, 7 . . . until such subtraction would yield a negative remainder. The number of subtractions performed is the most significant digit of the partial square root.

2. Moving over one column pair, start subtracting 20 × (partial square root) + j where j is taken as successive odd integers 1, 3, 5, 7 . . . until such subtraction would yield a negative remainder. The number of subtractions performed is the next significant digit of the partial square root.

Example

Find the square root of 18,769 by repeated subtraction (Procedure 2).

	Partial Square Root
1 8 7 6 9	
1	1
8 7 6 9	
2 1	1 1
6 6 6 9	
2 3	1 2
4 3 6 9	
2 5	1 3
1 8 6 9	
2 6 1	1 3 1
1 6 0 8	
2 6 3	1 3 2
1 3 4 5	
2 6 5	1 3 3
1 0 8 0	
2 6 7	1 3 4
8 1 3	
2 6 9	1 3 5
5 4 4	
2 7 1	1 3 6
2 7 3	
2 7 3	1 3 7

Exercise 2.1-5

The Euclidean algorithm finds the greatest common divisor of a pair of integers. By definition if either of the integers is 0, then the other is the greatest common divisor.

In this example, *gcd* is the name of the program to calculate the **g**reatest **c**ommon **d**ivisor.

Input: a pair of nonnegative integers, *m, n*.

Output: a nonnegative integer, *q*.

Procedure:

(1) If $m = 0$, then $q \leftarrow n$; stop.
(2) If $n = 0$, then $q \leftarrow m$; stop.
(3) If $m < n$, then $q \leftarrow gcd(n, m)$; stop.

(4) If $m \geq n$, then $q \leftarrow gcd(m-n, n)$; ⬭stop. *go to (1)*

Example:

$gcd(45, 85)$
$= gcd(85, 45)$ step 3
$= gcd(40, 45)$ step 4
$= gcd(45, 40)$ step 3
$= gcd(5, 40)$ step 4
$= gcd(40, 5)$ step 3
$= gcd(35, 5)$ step 4
$= gcd(30, 5)$ step 4

. . .

. . .

. . .
$= gcd(0, 5)$ step 4
$= 5$ step 1
STOP

Note that in this algorithm, *gcd,* the algorithm is itself used as a component of the computation. Such a computation is well-behaved if there is an "escape" which is always reached after finitely many steps. In this case, the size of the parameters decrease, and steps 1 and 2 provide the escape. This type of algorithm which refers to itself is called *recursive* and the escape is called the *base* of the recursion.   *Def.*

Exercise 2.1-6

Euclidean algorithm—least common multiple

Input: a pair of positive integers *m, n.*

Output: a positive integer, *q.*

Procedure:

$$q \leftarrow \frac{m \times n}{gcd(m, n)}$$

Note that by restricting the domain to exclude 0 inputs, we have eliminated the requirement for testing whether *m* or *n* is 0. If zero values are allowed for inputs, then a test is necessary since division by 0 is undefined.

2.2   Flowcharts

In many cases the nature of the algorithm is more evident from a pictorial representation than from a statement representation. A flowchart is a diagram of directed lines which connect boxes. Each elementary step of an algorithm is placed in a box; the shape of the box defines the type of the process inside.

The directed lines indicate the order in which the various processes are executed.

In this section, we will present a minimal set of flowchart components for the specification of algorithms or programs. These components are a good introductory set to begin programming. In fact, any problem that can be solved by any known algorithmic method can be solved (perhaps less conveniently) with only these simple components. Moreover, no algorithmic method could ever be devised that would be able to solve a problem with a solution that cannot be described in a flowchart.

A. Flowchart Components

We shall use the following flowchart components:

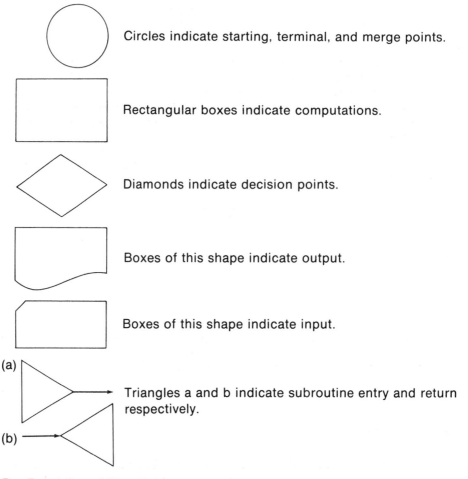

Circles indicate starting, terminal, and merge points.

Rectangular boxes indicate computations.

Diamonds indicate decision points.

Boxes of this shape indicate output.

Boxes of this shape indicate input.

(a)

(b)

Triangles a and b indicate subroutine entry and return respectively.

B. Examples of Flowcharts

Flowcharts to express algorithms will be illustrated by some simple mathematical problems.

Exercise 2.2-1

Draw a flowchart for the Fibonacci sequence algortihm.

Solution: Figure 2.1

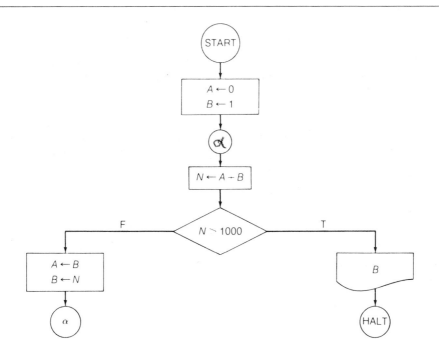

Figure 2.1:   Fibonacci sequence algorithm

Often the data in a problem are organized into a sequential list, so that a data item may be referred to by citing its position in the list. This form of storage organization is called an _array_. For example, if a sequence of five test values, 75, 83, 84, 92, 91 is stored in an array called TEST, then

$$TEST_1 = 75$$
$$TEST_2 = 83$$
$$TEST_3 = 84$$
$$TEST_4 = 92$$
$$TEST_5 = 91.$$

Exercise 2.2-2

Find the average of N numbers stored in an array called A.

Algorithm: Input: $A_1, A_2, A_3 \ldots A_N$

Output: $Avg = (A_1 + A_2 + \ldots + A_N)/N$

Method: Step 1 $S \leftarrow A_1$
            Step 2 $S \leftarrow S + A_2$
            Step 3 $S \leftarrow S + A_3$

            Step $n+1$ $S \leftarrow S + A_N$
            Step $n+2$ $Avg \leftarrow S/N$

We note that step 2 through step n are the same form. Each step is concerned with the current number, the one being processed "now." In other words, we can combine these $n-1$ steps in a step of the form:

Repeat $S \leftarrow S + A_i$ for $i = 2, 3 \ldots N$

However, this instruction requires further decomposition to elaborate its meaning in terms of the primitive flowchart components. One approach would be:

(A) set the count (i) equal to 2.
(B) $S \leftarrow S + A_i$
(C) $i \leftarrow i + 1$.
(D) check count to see if the N numbers have been added, i.e., if $i \leq N$, then go to instruction B.

This set of operations will replace steps two through N. Our method can now be written more concisely as:

Method: Step 1 $S \leftarrow A_1$.
            Step 2 $i \leftarrow 2$.
            Step 3 $S \leftarrow S + A_i$.
            Step 4 $i \leftarrow i + 1$.
            Step 5   if $i \leq N$, then go to step 2
                     if not, go to step 6.
            Step 6 $Avg \leftarrow S/N$.

The corresponding flowchart is shown in Figure 2.2.

The significance of step 3 changes as the value of i changes, to permit sequencing through the entire array. The use of a count associated with an array is termed *indexing*. The index serves as the subscript. We note also that count serves another purpose, testing for the termination of the process.

Exercise 2.2-3

Given a positive number A, find its square root correct to six decimal digits using the approximation.

$$x_{i+1} = 0.5(x_i + A/x_i)$$

where x_i is the ith estimate to the square root.

Solution: Figure 2.3.

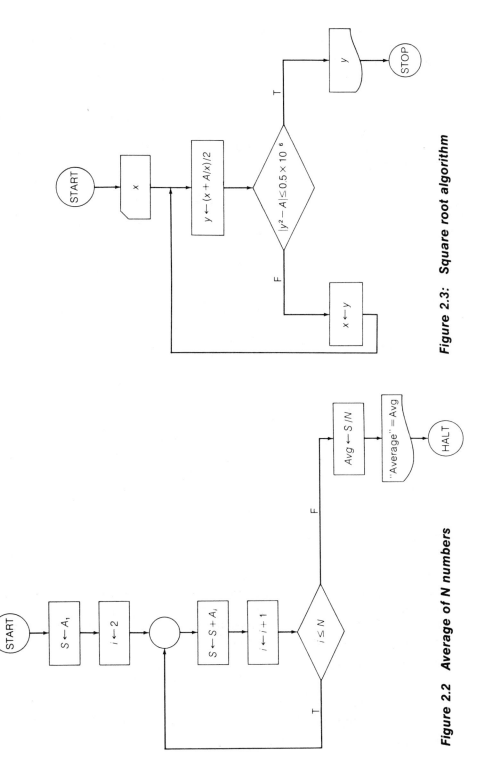

Figure 2.3: Square root algorithm

Figure 2.2 Average of N numbers

Notice that this iterative process (referred to below) is different in several ways from Exercise 2.2-2 in the following respects: a sequence of data is not processed; and the test to decide termination of the computation is not based on the value of the index but on the current estimate of a quantity.

C. Iteration

Iteration is the concept used in revealing the basic structure and simplifying the writing of algorithms. The iterative process consists of four independent components, as shown in Figures 2.4 and 2.5.

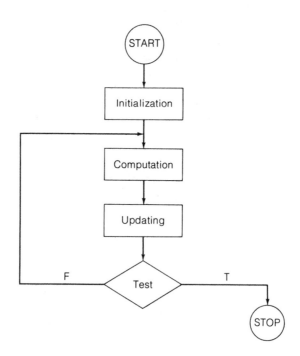

Figure 2.4: Post-test iteration

The initialization, test, computation, and updating actions are all *computations* and may be arbitrarily complex. They may also be merged together in iterations. Thus, the updating may be a side effect of the test or may be merged with or precede the computation.

The function of each component is as follows:

(1) Initialization. During this stage either a variable to be used in the computation stage (Exercises 2.2-1, 2.2-2, 2.2-3) or a control variable to be used as a counter (of Exercise 2.2-2) is set to an initial value.

(2) Computation. This component refers to the steps to be executed during

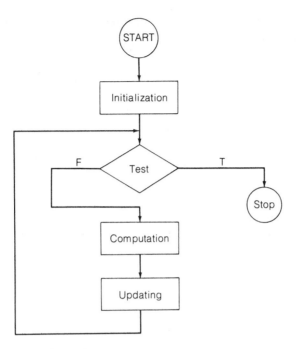

Figure 2.5:   Pre-test iteration

each iteration. These steps may be of any nature, i.e., arithmetic, I/O (input/output), iterative, etc.

(3) Updating. The net effect of doing the computation results in modifying the values of some variables. One of these may be the initialized variable. (This is the case if the initialized variable is a control variable.) Updating may be considered as a reinitialization of a variable for the next repetition.

(4) Testing. Every iterative process must terminate. It must provide a mechanism to allow the program control to exit and execute the statements following the iteration loop—otherwise we will have an infinite loop. Two basic types of tests are available to determine when to terminate an iterative process:

  (a) Tests involving the control variable, in which termination occurs after doing the computation a predetermined number of times.

  (b) Tests involving a specific property of a variable involved in the computation. For instance, one may terminate the computation when a variable changes sign or when the absolute value of a variable exceeds a certain predetermined value. In this case, it is important that an alternative termination procedure be specified in case the condition tested for is never satisfied.

Many authors indicate the use of an iterative statement in their flowcharts by the following symbol:

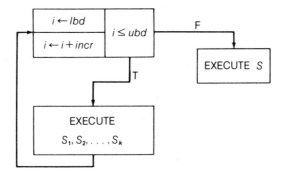

Using this new flowchart component, the algorithm of Exercise 2.2-2 may be expressed as follows:

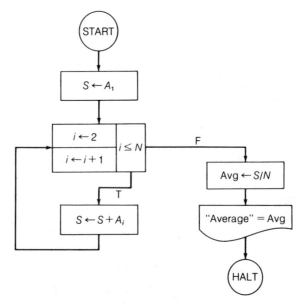

Figure 2.6: Average of N numbers

D. Programming from the Flowchart

The importance of the flowchart is that it provides a picture of an algorithm. The algorithm can be understood from its picture. The flowchart, in turn, can be used directly to produce the program, which can then be run on a computer.

It is essential that a systematic (i.e., algorithmic) method be used to translate the flowchart into the corresponding program that actually performs the

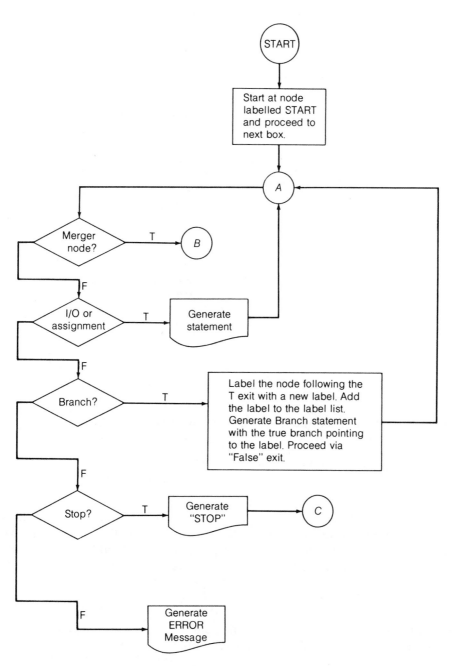

Figure 2.7:   Transcribing a flowchart to a program (Part 1)

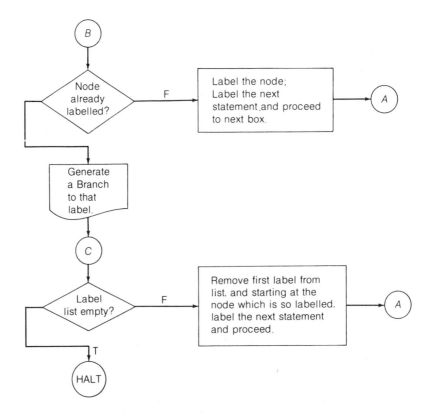

Figure 2.8: *Transcribing a flowchart to a program (part 2)*

intended algorithm. It is very difficult to determine if a program obtained from a flowchart in an unsystematic way actually computes what the flowchart specifies.

We have stressed the importance of proceeding algorithmically from flow-chart to program, and we noted earlier that all computable procedures can be described by flowcharts. This suggests that the method of transcribing a flowchart to a program can itself be shown in a flowchart. This is indeed the case. The flowchart is shown in Figures 2.7 and 2.8.

The purpose of this example is two-fold:

(1) It emphasizes that mapping out the solution to a problem via a flowchart is a primary prerequisite to successful programming.

(2) It illustrates the difference between programming and coding. Once a flowchart is completed, the process of expressing it in any programming language (coding) is simple and straightforward. As a matter of fact, the day may not be far off before we can communicate an algorithm to a computer in the form of a flowchart.

Apply the flowcharting algorithm to the Fibonacci sequence algorithm.

$$A \leftarrow 0$$
$$B \leftarrow 1$$
$$\alpha: \quad N \leftarrow A + B$$
$$\text{If} \quad N > 1{,}000 \quad \text{GO TO } \beta$$
$$A \leftarrow B$$
$$B \leftarrow N$$
$$\text{GO TO } \alpha$$
$$\beta: \quad \text{WRITE } N$$
$$\text{STOP}$$

2.3   Alternative Formulations of Algorithms

The algorithmic method is so central in most of computer science that the student must learn it early in his study of the subject and expand his knowledge of it continuously. One of the main principles of computer science is there is no unique form for expressing algorithms. This is exemplified, in part, in the large variety of programming languages and styles available. In this section, we cannot possibly survey all of the methods and, in fact, many advanced algorithmic and programming techniques are beyond the scope of this text. In later chapters some components of alternative programming methods are presented—data structures and control structures.

The flowchart method that has already been described is one of the ways for describing algorithms. Two more ways are presented below, each one having a certain popularity. The computer scientist should be aware of the different methods, and should select the combination appropriate to his style and problem. In the next chapter, some considerations in developing an appropriate programming style are presented.

A. Pidgin-ALGOL

Pidgin-ALGOL is the generic name given to a style of algorithmic description that is close enough to many programming languages—ALGOL, PL/1, BASIC, FORTRAN—to facilitate the final step of actual program composition. On the other hand, by not specifying what is or is not allowed in pidgin-ALGOL, the pidgin-ALGOL algorithm may contain anything its author feels will be clearly understood. Accordingly, three examples of pidgin-ALGOL programs are presented.

Exercise 2.3-1

Given a text, A, scan it to find the first occurrence of a specified word, B. The assumption is that the programming language does not include an instruction that accomplishes the task in one step. In the program of Figure 2.9, $A[i]$ refers to the ith letter of A, $B[i]$ to the ith letter of B.

32   Problem Solving on Computers

Solution:

```
i ← 1
DO WHILE (i ≤ 1 + LENGTH(A) − LENGTH(B))
      IF A[i] = B[1] THEN DO          ( If 1st letters are same then do )
            j ← 2
            DO WHILE ((j ≤ LENGTH(B)) AND (A[i+j−1] = B[j]))
                  j ← j + 1
                  END
            If j > LENGTH(B) THEN GO TO FOUND;
            END
      i ← i + 1
      END
NOT FOUND:
FOUND:
```

Figure 2.9: *Text-scanning program.*

In Figure 2.9 the program to scan a text to find a specified word is given. In the pidgin-ALGOL program, following each DO there is a sequence of indented lines of text followed by an END. The understood convention is that this block of the program is to be treated as a *unit*. If, in line 3, $A[i] \neq B[1]$, then the program will skip down to line 10 and increase i. If, in line 2, i is greater than $1 + \text{LENGTH}(A) - \text{LENGTH}(B)$, so that B cannot possibly be found in the remaining text as it is too short, the program will skip to line 12, and do whatever follows NOT FOUND. On the other hand, after increasing i at line 10 when the END statement is encountered, the program will return to the second line, since

> DO WHILE condition
>
> ACTION
>
> END

means "test the condition; if it is true, execute the action and return to the beginning; if it is false, go to the point immediately following the statement."

Exercise 2.3-2

List the number of ways to make up a dollar out of half-dollars, quarters, dimes, nickels, and pennies.

Solution: This is an enumeration problem. Each solution is a sequence of five numbers: the number of half-dollars, followed by quarters, dimes, nickels, and pennies. Further, for any two solution sequences, the one that is larger in the first place at which the two solutions differ will be listed first. (0, 2, 1, 2, 5) is a solution with 2 quarters, 1 dime, 2 nickels, and 5 pennies, and will be listed earlier than (0, 2, 1, 1, 10).

The array, A, will be used to store a solution, and the array, W, will be used for the values of the coins: $W[1] = 50$; $W[2] = 25$; $W[3] = 10$; $W[4] = 5$; $W[5] = 1$. The initial solution is $A[1] = 2$; $A[2] = 0$; $A[3] = 0$; $A[4] = 0$; $A[5] = 0$. The program for generating subsequent solutions is shown in Figure 2.10. In the program, INT(x) is the largest integer less than or equal to x, thus, INT(5.4) = 5 and INT(1.3) = 1.

A is vector whose components are the number of each type of coin

Very poor pedagogy. these programs are not easy to figure out; especially if a student has no intuition or experience. Really should show how develop these programs. They are very polished programs and yet they appear out of thin air?

Very Very difficult to read!

```
DO WHILE      (A[5] ≠ 100)
    i ← 4
    DO WHILE      (A[i] = 0)
        i ← i − 1
        END
    SUBTOTAL = W[i] + A[5]
    A[i] ← A[i] − 1
    i ← i + 1
    DO WHILE (SUBTOTAL > 0)
        A[i] ← INT(SUBTOTAL/W[i])
        SUBTOTAL ← SUBTOTAL − A[i] × W[i]
        i ← i + 1
        END
    PRINT A
    END
```

Figure 2.10: **Program for generating subsequent solutions**

The last solution is when $A[5] = 100$, and all the change is in pennies, so this is the test in the outermost WHILE. The first inner loop, lines 3–5, finds the first nonzero denomination, other than pennies. The next solution redistributes the sum of the number of pennies in the previous solution and a unit of this denomination as shown in the loop from lines 9–13.

Exercise 2.3-3

Given three buckets with capacities of eight gallons, five gallons, and three gallons. The eight-gallon bucket is initially full; the remaining buckets are initially empty. A single step consists of pouring from a "source" bucket to a "destination" bucket until the destination bucket is full or the source bucket is empty. Find the minimum number of steps to divide the initial eight gallons equally, so that the eight-gallon container holds four gallons and the five gallon container holds four gallons.

Solution: Note first that the contents of the five-gallon bucket and the three-gallon bucket determine uniquely the contents of the eight-gallon bucket. Accordingly, we need only record the contents of the five-gallon bucket in a variable FIVE and the three gallon bucket in a variable THREE. Our program takes the following form:

Procedure STEPS (current position)
   IF at goal state THEN RETURN (0)
      ELSE RETURN (1 + min (STEPS (new position after action 1),
                     STEPS (new position after action 2),

               .
               .
               .   )

In our problem there are six possible actions:

(1) pour EIGHT into FIVE
(2) pour EIGHT into THREE

(3) pour FIVE into THREE

(4) pour FIVE into EIGHT

(5) pour THREE into FIVE

(6) pour THREE into EIGHT

A program to compute the effects of these actions is:

Procedure: AFTER (FIVE, THREE, i)

```
    IF i = 1 THEN RETURN(5, THREE)
    IF i = 2 THEN RETURN(FIVE, 3)
    IF i = 3 THEN DO
                    TEMP ← FIVE + THREE
                    x ← min(TEMP, 3)
                    y ← TEMP − x
                    RETURN (y, x)
                    END
    IF i = 4 THEN RETURN(0, THREE)
    IF i = 5 THEN DO
                    TEMP ← FIVE + THREE
                    x ← min(TEMP, 5)
                    y ← TEMP − x
                    RETURN (x, y)
                    END
    IF i = 6 THEN RETURN(FIVE, 0)
    END
```

When supplied with the current values of FIVE and THREE and the number of the selected action, AFTER computes and returns a pair of numbers as the new values of the contents of the FIVE gallon and THREE gallon buckets, respectively. Our complete program is:

Procedure STEPS(FIVE, THREE).

```
    IF FIVE = 4 and THREE = 0 THEN RETURN (0)
        ELSE RETURN (1 + min (STEPS(AFTER(FIVE, THREE, 1)),
                              STEPS(AFTER(FIVE, THREE, 2)),
                              STEPS(AFTER(FIVE, THREE, 3)),
                              STEPS(AFTER(FIVE, THREE, 4)),
                              STEPS(AFTER(FIVE, THREE, 5)),
                              STEPS(AFTER(FIVE, THREE, 6)))).
        END
        STEPS(0, 0) now compute the desired result.
```

B. Decision Tables

Another method of specifying algorithms is by *decision tables*. Decision tables are frequently used where a large number of yes—no questions must be answered, and the actions to be taken depend on the set of questions to which the reply is "yes." Decision tables are a complete method of specifying algorithms—every algorithm presented in flowchart form can be presented in decision table form. Similarly, any algorithm presented in decision table form can be described in a flowchart.

Figure 2.11 shows a typical decision table. The decision table is divided into

Table #1

Symptom #1?	Y	Y	Y	Y	N	N	N
Symptom #2?	N	N	N	Y	—	—	—
Symptom #3?	Y	Y	N	—	—	Y	N
Symptom #4?	N	Y	—	—	N	Y	Y
Action #1	X	X		X	X	X	X
Action #2		X	X		X		X
Action #3			X	X			
next-table #1	X			X			X
next-table #2		X	X		X	X	

Figure 2.11: Decision Table

segments by the vertical and horizontal double lines. In the upper left-hand segment are the yes—no questions on which a decision is to be made—these are referred to as *condition stubs*. Below these are *action stubs*. Each column to the right of the vertical double line is referred to as a *rule*. The rules are numbered from left to right. The leftmost, or first, rule is: If the answers to the first and third questions are "yes," and the answers to the second and fourth questions are "no," then perform action # 1, and proceed to the beginning of table # 1. The fourth rule is: If the answer to questions 1 and 2 is "yes," then perform action # 1 followed by action # 3 regardless of the answers to questions 3 and 4. Each dashed—line in the table is referred to as a "don't care."

Advocates of decision table usage stress the transparency of the breakdown of the different possibilities. It is easy to check that a decision table is *complete* and *consistent*. A table is complete if each possible case is dealt with in some rule. (If a case cannot arise, an "error rule" should be provided). A case, *C,* is dealt with (or *covered*) in a rule, *r,* if each occurrence of *"y"* in *C* is matched by *"y"* or *"—"* in *r,* and each occurrence of *"N"* in *C* is matched by *"N"* or *"—"* in *r.*

For example, the case

N
Y
N
N

is covered in the fifth column of Figure 2.11. A decision table is consistent if two different sequences of actions are never specified for the same case.

In our pidgin-ALGOL programs, we have used DO—WHILE statements. Figure 2.12 is a comparison of pidgin-ALGOL, flowchart, and decision table versions of DO—WHILE. (Construct a similar figure comparing IF—THEN—ELSE statements.)

2.4   The Algorithmic Method—Theoretical Limits

Next, we discuss the limitation of the problem-solving capacity of the algorithmic method. The application to computer science is immediate—there are some problems we cannot solve with the computer. The limitation does not appear, however, to derive from the computer or our method of programming, but from the fundamental nature of mathematics, logic, and language. We do not know of any problem-solving technique available to people that cannot, in principle, be programmed, so we tentatively assert that the limitations of the algorithmic method (to be described) are, in fact, limitations on our thought processes.

Two proofs of an unsolvable program

We are familiar with algorithms or programs that take, as their input data, other algorithms or programs. Our flowchart translator is an example of such an algorithm. We can also visualize a recursive algorithm that operates on itself either directly or indirectly. Now we shall try to write a program *P* which can determine if another program *Q* ever reaches a point at which it, *Q*, stops. *P* shall return a value TRUE if *Q* halts, and a value FALSE if *Q* does not halt. Now we ask *Q* to tell us whether the program *R* stops, where *R* is "if *P(R)* then LOOP else STOP" and LOOP is the name of a subprogram with a built-in infinite loop." We see that *P* is confronted with a paradox: if *P(R)* is TRUE, which it should be when *R* halts, then *R* will loop and not halt. On the other hand, if *P(R)* is FALSE, which it should be if *R* loops and doesn't halt, then, in fact, *R* will halt.

The fallacious assumption, leading to the paradoxical behavior of *P*, is that there is a program that can do what is planned for *P;* namely, decide if some arbitrary program ever comes to a halt. The fact that we cannot write a program to perform *P*'s intended function is known as *"the unsolvability of the halting problem."*

The importance of the halting problem result in computer science is such that we now give a second, slightly different, line of reasoning to show its validity.

We assume that:
(1) Every computation is flowchartable.
(2) Every flowchart is programmable.

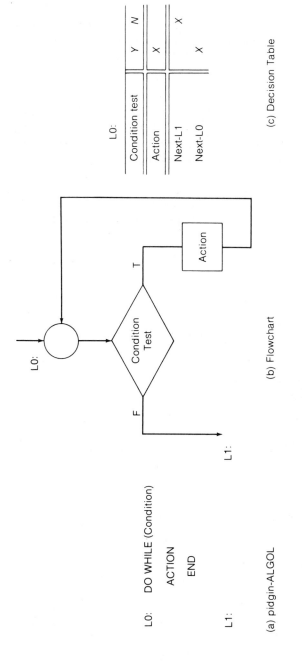

Figure 2.12: *DO—WHILE in different representations*

Assume that there is a program, HALTS, which can do the following: Given a flowchart, F, and the data on which F is to operate, d_F, HALTS can compute whether F will loop on the data d_F. If F will stop when given d_F, then another program, P, which calls on HALTS, is to print 'YES' and stop; if F will not stop with d_F as its input data, then P is to print 'NO' and then stop. P is diagrammed in Figure 2.13.

We may, of course, consider what happens if F is asked to work on its own description. To consider this, we construct a program Q. Q is like P, but given a single flowchart program. Q makes a copy of F and passes the two copies of F as a program and its own data to HALTS for analysis. Q is diagrammed in Figure 2.14.

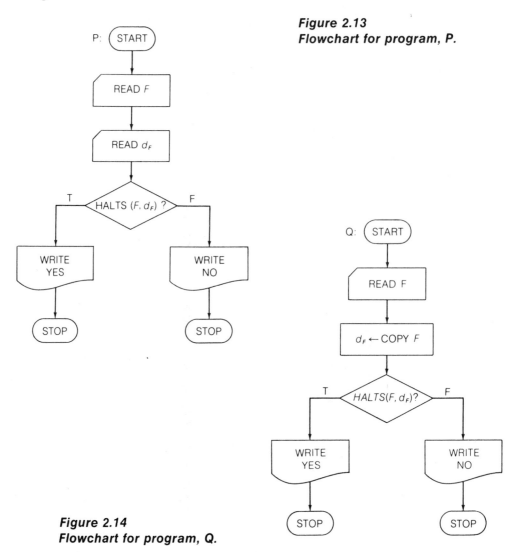

Figure 2.13
Flowchart for program, P.

Figure 2.14
Flowchart for program, Q.

Now Q is a program, which given a program F can tell whether F will halt when working on itself. We may now make a small change in Q and call this new program R; i.e., R is Q with the following change:

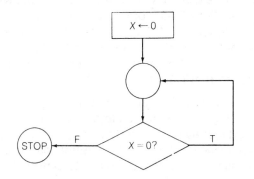

Whenever Q has printed 'YES', R will go to a looping subprogram, e.g.

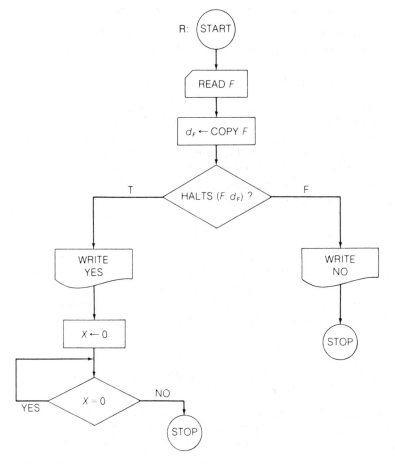

Figure 2.15: Flowchart for program, R.

Now *R,* given any program *G,* will halt, just in case *G* does not halt when working on itself.

What happens when *R* is given itself to work on? *R halts with R* as input just in case *R does not halt with R* as input. Again, we have been led to a paradox by assuming the existence of HALTS. So we conclude that no program can exist that can tell whether another program halts. Our conclusion is proven rigorously. There is no question about not having sought diligently enough for HALTS; it is proven that HALTS does not exist!

We have seen in the preceding section that it is impossible to construct an algorithm to analyze a program and its data and to determine if the program will run forever or ultimately halt. The difficulty is very fundamental to many simply stated problems—no algorithmic solution can ever be constructed. In this section, we describe a simple combinatorial problem that has no algorithmic solution.

A.   What it Means for a Problem to be Unsolvable

Let us consider the following problem, described by Post and known as the Post Correspondence Problem or PCP. Our data consists of a list of pairs of strings; e.g.,
 (*aa;ab*), (*abb;aa*), (*ab;bab*), (*a;b*), (*aa;a*), (*aba;a*), (*ab;b*), (*ba;abba*), (*b;abaa*)

We build pairs of strings using this data by linking the first strings of pairs and the corresponding second strings of pairs. For example, if the first three pairs are chosen in the order 1, 2, 3 then the string formed by the first halves of the pairs is *aaabbab,* while the string formed by the second halves of the pairs is *abaabab.* The Post Correspondence Problem is to find whether there is any way to string pairs together to form the same string from both the first halves of the pairs and the second halves of the pairs. For example, if you chose only the first four pairs as the input list, there would be no solution. With the given data there are solutions.

You might think of many ways to try to program a search for a solution. However, it turns out that *PCP* is unsolvable. (Proof is beyond the scope of this text.) If there is a solution, then a systematic search for a solution will ultimately find it. If there is no solution, the program will never be able to determine this fact and will continue its search.

You might think there would be a way to calculate a number, *N,* possibly dependent on the set of strings, which will fix an upper limit on the number of strings which must be tried to get a solution. There is not because if there were, we would be able to solve *PCP.*

There is no way to bound either the amount of memory needed or the running time required for solving *PCP* for a particular list of input pairs. Again, a bound on running time would provide a means for solving *PCP.*

There is no program that can solve the *PCP* in general. However, it is often possible to solve special cases of problems that are generally unsolvable.

Thus, if we restrict *PCP* to cases where only a single letter alphabet is used in forming the strings, we can obtain a solution.

There is little practical interest in finding solvable cases of *PCP*. However, there are many unsolvable problems which do have some practical significance. Special solvable cases of those unsolvable problems are, indeed, of interest.

B.　Problems Reducible to the Halting Problem and Implications

In this section, we will discuss three more unsolvable problems. We will not prove these problems are unsolvable, but will only indicate that their unsolvability is deduced from a line of reasoning that shows if we could solve one of these problems, we could use that method of solution to solve the halting problem. This line of reasoning about unsolvable problems is known as *reducibility*.

The first problem reducible to the halting problem is the equivalence problem for programs. Given two programs, P_1 and P_2, if P_1 and P_2 with the same input data will always produce the same result, it is unsolvable. Because this is, in general, unsolvable, it suggests that if two programmers, *A* and *B,* write completely independent programs to solve the same problem, it will be very hard—perhaps impossible—to know if they are equivalent. Similarly, if a flowchart and an independent program (i.e., one not systematically obtained from the flowchart) are considered, there is no systematic way to know, in all cases, whether they are doing the same job.

The unsolvability of the equivalence problem does not preclude the study of equivalence of two programs, *A* and *B,* if *B* is obtained in some systematic ways from *A*. We can establish systematic rules for going from one form of a program to another. Compilers do this in going from a source program in a procedure oriented language to a machine language program. In this chapter we presented a systematic way of going from a flowchart to a linear program.

A second unsolvable problem reducible to the halting problem is the unsolvability of the equivalence of grammars specifying programming languages (see chapter 5). Given two *BNF* grammars, it is unsolvable if these two grammars yield the same set of "sentences," in general. This undoubtedly accounts for a great deal of the pragmatic difficulty of trying to read and interpret such a grammar.

A third unsolvable problem is a rather well-known mathematical problem— to find the solution in terms of integers of a simultaneous set of equations with integer coefficients. This problem defied the best efforts of mathematicians for the first two-thirds of the twentieth century until it was, finally, shown to be unsolvable.

Thus, it is certainly not obvious if a mathematical problem is unsolvable. But in programming any problem, the programmer must be aware of the possibility that the problem might be unsolvable.

Summary

The process of solving a problem on a digital computer can be organized conveniently into seven steps:

(1) Obtain a precise statement of the problem.

(2) Determine a method of solution.

(3) Develop an algorithm for the method of solution.

(4) Draw a flowchart for the algorithm.

(5) Translate the flowchart into a programming language.

(6) Test the program with sample data to clear all errors.

(7) Perform a final execution of the program to obtain answers.

In this chapter we have concentrated on items two through five. In later chapters we will discuss the remaining steps.

Particular attention was devoted to the algorithmic method of problem solving. This method, and the terminology related to it, are often referred to as "the computer metaphor." We have shown application of the algorithmic formulation to a collection of different problems.

Finally, the limitations of the algorithmic method were discussed. We have shown several problems, some directly applicable to programming, that have no algorithmic solution.

References and Suggested Additional Readings

(1) Chapin, N. "Flowcharting with the ANSI Standard," *Computing Surveys* 2, No. 2, (June 1970).

(2) Knuth, D.E.. *The Art of Computer Programming, Fundamental Algorithms.* Vol. 1, Reading, Mass.: Addison-Wesley, 1968.

(3) Minsky, M. *Computation, Finite & Infinite Machines,* Englewood Cliffs, N.J.: Prentice-Hall, 1967.

Problems

1. Describe, in detail, the decimal multiplication algorithm.
2. Give an algorithm to determine the number of rate reversals in an array. (If $a_{i+1} - a_i$ and $a_{i+2} - a_{i+1}$ have different signs, then we say that the rate has reversed at a_{i+1}). Does it matter if the array is processed forwards or backwards? Explain.
3. Describe an algorithm to check if $N \leq 10$ is expressible as a sum of squares of 2 integers.

4. Describe an algorithm for computing the solutions to $ax^2 + bx + c = 0$. Cover all cases.

5. Given an array A of 100 numbers and an array B of 10 numbers, describe an algorithm to find the first place, if any, where B is contained in A (i.e., the smallest j so that $A_{j+i} = B_i$; $1 \le i \le 10$).

6. The combinatorial coefficients $C(m, n)$ are defined as

$$C(m, n) = \frac{m!}{n!(m-n)!}$$

   a. Find a recursive formula for computing $C(m, n)$ for nonnegative m and n (0! is 1).

   b. What is the escape in your recursion?

7. Apply the flowchart-to-linear-code algorithm given in the text to derive the linear code corresponding to the square root flowchart.

8. Find any solution to *PCP* for the following list of pairs of strings P. (b, a), (a, b), (ba, aa), (b, ab), (a, ab), (aba, b).

9. Let P_1 and P_2 be two programs consisting of only arithmetic assignment statements. Describe how you would test equivalence of P_1 and P_2. (Note: The equivalence problem for these restricted programs is solvable.)

Chapter 3

Programming Methodology

The methodology of programming has been receiving considerable attention recently. First, while resources expended in programming are growing continually, the same is not true of equipment costs, with the result that the major problem in using computers is the software (programming) problem. (*Software* is the set of programs, procedures, and associated documentation; *hardware* is the set of physical components of the computer system.) Second, some recent insights into the nature of programming show promise of substantial improvement in the quality of programs.

At present, we can describe programming theory as being in a pretechnical phase. Certain qualitative judgments can be made about different programming techniques, and guidelines for writing good programs stated, but there is no set of quantitative measures that can be used to develop good programs.

In general, we describe *programming* as the preparation of algorithmic solutions to problems, i.e., in such a form that they can be carried out mechanically. Experience has shown and theory confirms that programming is a very demanding activity, not unlike playing chess against a strong opponent, except that programs are much more complicated and generally require cooperative effort among groups of programmers.

Moreover, programming is an activity that often extends over periods of time (e.g. months), in which it is impossible to concentrate exclusively on the program. And, even if you could concentrate exclusively on the program, the limitations of an individual's "performance"* would make the process error-prone.

Thus, the programmer must develop an algorithmic solution and document the thinking process, so that he, or another programmer, can pick up the program later and be familiar with its workings. Programming requires communication, and a good program is a clear expression of an algorithm.

Since programming is very difficult, it is also error-prone. Errors occur precisely when the limits of our performance are exceeded. For this same reason, once an error occurs, it is difficult to excise. If we wish to have correct programs, we must find out how to avoid introducing errors.

Methods of writing error-free programs are emerging, but it is too early to tell how effective these are. Some are based on management and documentation techniques, and we will not discuss these here. Others are based on principles of program organization and how to avoid certain devices that strain the programmer's performance. These are under the general heading of *structured programming*. Structured programming will be discussed. Then, for cases where serious errors are made, techniques for diagnosing and removing errors will be discussed.

---

*Performance—The ability of an individual to carry out a specified intellectual activity.

3.1   Writing Correct Programs

A. Philosophy and Attitude

Most practical programs are very complex and make severe demands on the programmer's intellect and power of concentration. At the same time, the social and economic consequences of poor programming present increasing pressure for higher standards of accuracy and correctness.

We can expect that poor or incorrect programs will become quite unacceptable, and standards of accuracy and demonstration of correctness will be required. As programming becomes an applied science with an increasing body of knowledge, we can expect higher levels of training and proven ability to be required for entry into the profession. Certainly, application of computer programs in critical services—e.g. air traffic control, computerized medical data—will be unacceptable unless very high standards of correctness are maintained.

The programmer should anticipate this evolution in the nature of programming and begin to insist on the highest attainable quality of programming. Certainly this high level will not occur if the primary standard of programming performance is to be the number of lines of program written per person-month.*

The computer scientist's image does not depend only on his own self-image, but the general attitude towards programmers is certainly influenced by their conception of themselves and their craft. It is particularly in the area of programming that the disparity between the popular conception and reality is largest.

B. Relationship to Environment

Environment can be defined as the totality of information available to an algorithm. This includes the contents of computer memory and the library of programs available. We use *environment* in this specific technical meaning here.

The programs a programmer writes in a particular environment depend on the user languages available, the machines, and the relationship between the user language and the machines. If we wish to write correct programs, it is necessary to have correct compilers and correct machines and operating systems. In practice, all machines and compilers are released with "bugs." In the course of use, the "bugs" are gradually removed, but of course, "improvements" are occasionally introduced, bringing with them new "bugs." Consequently, the programmer has rarely, if ever, found himself and his pro-

---

*This might be an acceptable measure if two months were added for each error in the program.

grams in a bug-free environment. If we are to write correct programs, the whole environmental "pollution" will have to be decreased. We can, therefore, expect that our ability to write dependable software will evolve over a period of years in which the whole gamut of supporting programs and machinery will be correctly developed.

There is yet another sense in which the environment affects the program and this is a pragmatic aspect of the environment. One aspect of pragmatics is the psychological part of the symbolic process. Programming is an intellectual activity, and it is important that the reasoning done by the programmer be "natural," and that this reasoning be reflected in the program itself. Thus, the method of programming, including the choice of user language, should not require the programmer to resort to artificial modes of thought or expression. Of course, we will retain a variety of programming techniques and languages because not everyone thinks in the same way. But hopefully, the artificiality existing in today's programming language will gradually disappear.

C. Difficulty of Building Correctness in After the Fact

Once a program has been incorrectly written, the best thing to do is start over and construct a new program that is not subject to the difficulties. There are several reasons why this is so:

(1) The occurrence of errors—other than small oversights—is, as we pointed out above, an indication that the program is at the limit of the programmer's performance. Hence, a new way of organizing the program is required that will not impose these difficulties.

(2) It is difficult to feel confident that a program from which you have just removed the one-hundredth error is indeed free of bugs, at last. With such a program, the programmer constantly wonders when the next bug will show up.

Rewriting a program several times to get a satisfactory version is not unusual, and is in fact recommended, especially for the beginner. Each successive rewriting will be found to take considerably less time, and the savings in time in working with a more readable and better organized program will justify the effort. Only when you are satisfied with the correctness, legibility, and efficiency of a program should it be considered complete.

D. Establishing Correctness

(1) *Tracing*
   Tracing is a calculation showing the sequence of intermediate results computed by a program. Consider the program of Figure 3.1. The program has three variables: $I, J, K. I$ is initialized to 0, and the initial values for J and K are the input data for the program. Suppose we wish to deter-

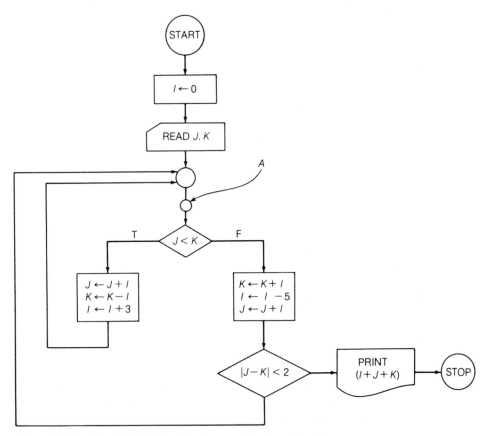

Figure 3.1:   Flowchart used in the example of tracing.

mine the values that should be printed out as a result, so that we can use this as a "check" that the program is correct.

We prepare a chart, as shown in Figure 3.2. The chart contains one column for each variable in the program. On the chart, we enter the new values of the variables as control passes point *A* in the flowchart.

Of course, additional information can be recorded if desired, such as:

(1) The location of the program—to what step the current line in the trace corresponds.

(2) The results of each computed test at each branch point.

It is also possible to do automatic tracing. Many user languages have features that facilitate the tracing. Variations include selective tracing which traces only selected variables over specifically designated portions of the program and tracing of only the results of specific statements or selected tests.

Pass No	*I*	*J*	*K*	
1	0	7	17	Initial values
2	3	7	17	
3	6	10	14	
4	9	16	8	
5	4	20	17	
6	−1	19	21	
7	2	18	22	
8	5	20	20	
9	0	20	25	
10	3	20	25	
11	6	23	22	
12	1	24	28	
13	4	25	27	
14	7	29	23	
15	2	31	30	The result is 63

Figure 3.2: **Trace of values at point A of flowchart of Figure 3.1 using the randomly chosen input data J = 7, K = 17**

However, as you can see from even the simple flowchart we have traced, large quantities of output data can be produced by traces, perhaps too much to be of use to the programmer attempting to analyze. Indeed, since tracing is often used where the program may be erroneous, the program may enter a non terminating computation and continue printing out tracing information until stopped by the computer's clock. As we indicate in the next section, tracing is best used to analyze a suspect portion of a program where it can be used selectively.

(2) *Tracing Proves Nothing*
The flowchart of the previous section is "syntactically" a good flowchart, but it is synthetic and doesn't represent any known problem. Thus, there are many of the characteristics of the algorithmic method here.

We do not know whether this computation terminates for any given pair of inputs *J, K*. We do know that, in general, given a flowchart, we can't tell whether it will always compute an answer—no algorithmic method can determine this. After we have checked that the computation indicated by the flowchart is correct—for any finite number of test cases—there is no guarantee that for any case that has not been tested, the program will behave well.

Suppose, on the other hand, there is an error in the flowchart, and we have an independent algorithm for computing the intended function. While there is no algorithm for determining in a finite amount of computation if our flowchart does what is intended, we can theoretically determine in a finite amount of time if there is an error in the flowchart. (This theoretical result does not mean that the method is practical. Ten million years is a finite amount of time, but is unsatisfactory as the turn-around time on a problem.)

Despite the very weak theoretical basis for tracing and the fact that it can never establish correctness, but only weed out errors, tracing is widely used as a means of analyzing programs. Hopefully, more suitable tools will be used in the future.

(3) *Proving Correctness*
A program is correct if it computes what we intended it to compute. Thus, a proof of correctness can only establish that the program satisfies some *a priori* description of the computed result. Technically, such a description is known as a *predicate*. The predicate asserts that some condition is to hold at the end of the computation.

Usually, the computation may involve some iterative steps. In that case, we describe the conditions (i.e., predicate that holds as we go through an iterative cycle). A predicate that is true as the program goes through a sequence of steps in which many variables change is called an *invariant*.

Let us consider the program shown in the flowchart of Figure 3.3. The object of this program (other than demonstrating a correctness proof) is to multiply two numbers, a and b, by repeated addition of b to the partial product, c, a times. Two temporary registers, x and y, are used to hold the quantities a and b.

At point A, immediately preceding the test on x, we attach a loop invariant.

$$c + x \times y = a \times b \text{ is the invariant.}$$

We claim this condition is trivially true the first time we reach point A, because then $c = 0$, $x = a$, $y = b$. Now let c_n, x_n, y_n, be the values of these variables at a point A after the loop has been traversed n times. We claim that if $c_n + x_n \times y_n = a \times b$, then it must be the case that $c_{n+1} + x_{n+1} \times y_{n+1} = a \times b$, if indeed there is an $(n + 1)^{st}$ traversal of the loop. Note that:

(1) $y_n = y_{n+1} = b$ since y is not changed

(2) $x_{n+1} = x_n - 1$, since in each traversal x is decreased by 1

(3) $c_{n+1} = c_n + b$ since $c_{n+1} = c_n + y_n$, but $y_n = b$. Using these facts, we have:

$$c_{n+1} + x_{n+1} \times y_{n+1} = c_n + b + (x_n - 1) \times b$$
$$= c_n + x_n \times b$$
$$= c_n + x_n \times y_n$$

But, by assumption, $c_n + x_n \times y_n = a \times b$ and therefore $c_{n+1} + x_{n-1} \times y_{n+1} = a \times b$.

Now, using the principle of mathematical induction, we have at once our invariant, $c + x \times y = a \times b$. The principle of mathematical induction says

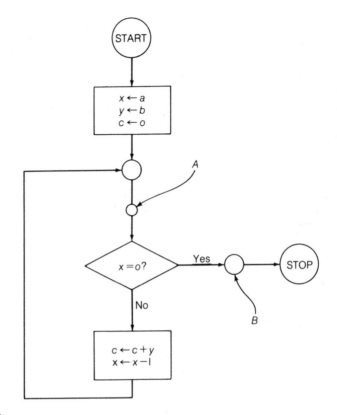

Figure 3.3:

that (1) if an equation is true for the 0th case and (2) given that, if it is true for the nth case, it can be shown to be true for the $(n + 1)^{st}$ case, then it will be true for every case.

Next, having shown that the invariant is true at point A, we can assert at point B that $c = a \times b$, since $c + x \times y = a \times b$ at point A, and transition from A to B changes nothing, but guarantees that $x = 0$.

Finally, we must show that the program does, in fact, reach point B. We have here assumed that A is a nonnegative integer and have used the integer property that if you count down from any nonnegative integer you must reach 0 in a finite number of steps. Thus, we see that the program is correct.

Our example has shown the essential ideas in proofs of correctness. The "creative" part of the proof is the description of the predicates. The remaining parts of the proof can be mechanized, in principle, although the existing automatic theorem-provers are inadequate for proving correctness of reasonable programs.

There is ongoing research and development in computer-assisted proof procedures. Most probably, these proof procedures used from interactive terminals will provide the first practical application of these techniques.

E. Building the Proof into the Program

In the preceding section, we indicated how a proof for an existing program can be developed. The starting point of such a proof is the assertion of the appropriate predicates and invariants. These predicates and invariants represent the semantics of the programs. Hence, the proof of program correctness is almost the opposite of a compilation from user language to machine language, as follows:

In user languages, there are typically declarations, such as type declarations. The declarative assertions are translated by the compiler into inoperative statements—storage allocation, construction of tables, etc. The semantics of the declarative statement is thus taken to be the actions of the compiler.

In proofs of correctness, we proceed in the reverse direction. Starting with action statements in the program, we construct declarative assertions, and these are then taken to be the semantics of the program.

Both points of view can be resolved by adopting a point of view expounded by Chomsky; the semantics of a statement can be represented in the different forms of expression in which it can be stated. For example, the statements "John threw the ball" and "The ball was thrown by John" are different expressions of the same fact. Either of these forms of statement can be viewed as a paraphrase of the other.

The practical application of this symmetric situation is that we may proceed to formulate the declarative statements first and then elaborate these statements into an action program whose effect is to keep the statements valid. When we have elaborated the statements completely, we have a program whose proof of correctness is built-in. The following example illustrates the development of a program from a statement of its effect.

The program to be developed will sort three members, so that at the end of the program we will have $x \geq y \geq z$. Thus, as long as $x > y$ or $y > z$, some action is to be taken by the program. Therefore, our initial version of the program might look like:

> WHILE $x < y$ or $y < z$*
> DO [something to reach the solution]

We can see that when this program terminates, the condition we are trying to satisfy will hold. In more general terms, we could write this form of initial solution as:

> WHILE THE PROGRAM PREDICATE IS NOT TRUE
> DO [something to reach the solution]

---

*WHILE—DO is a stylistic variant of DO—WHILE.

The second step in our program development is to describe how to reach the solution, as follows:

WHILE $x < y$ or $y < z$
      DO [IF $x < y$ THEN EXCHANGE x and y;
            IF $y < z$ THEN EXCHANGE y and z]

This second version of the program, when recast in the syntax of a particular user language, will sort the quantities in question.

An improved version of the program will store the value of the comparison of x and y so that it need not be recomputed. A further improvement is obtained by combining the IF statements to form an IF ... THEN ... ELSE, yielding

WHILE [IF $t \leftarrow (x < y)$ THEN TRUE ELSE $y < z$]
      DO [IF t THEN EXCHANGE x and y ELSE EXCHANGE y and z].

Here, we store the result of the x, y comparison in t, so it need not be recomputed. Considering all possible values of x, y, and z requires an average of slightly less than 4 computed tests.* In chapter 2, we see that this problem was done using only 3 tests:

if $x < y$ then exchange x and y
if $y < z$ then exchange y and z
if $x < y$ then exchange x and y

3.2   Structured Programming

A.   Motivation

Instead of the great number of precepts of which Logic is composed, I believed that the four following would prove perfectly sufficient for me, provided I took the firm and unwavering resolution never in a single instance to fail in observing them.

The *first* was never to accept anything for true which I did not clearly know to be such; that is to say, carefully to avoid precipitancy and prejudice, and to comprise nothing more in my judgment than what was presented to my mind so clearly and distinctly as to exclude all ground of doubt.

The *second,* to divide each of the difficulties under examination into as many parts as possible, and as might be necessary for its adequate solution.

The *third,* to conduct my thoughts in such order that, by commencing with objects the simplest and easiest to know, I might ascend by little and little, and, as it were, step by step, to the knowledge of the more complex; assigning in thought a certain order even to those objects which in their own nature do not stand in a relation of antecedence and sequence.

---

*Note that to compute the predicate $x < y$ or $y < z$ requires only one comparison if $x < y$, and two comparisons otherwise.

"And the *last,* in every case to make enumerations so complete, and reviews so general, that I might be assured that nothing was omitted.*

Structured programming is the name that has been given to a method of program development that attempts to develop correct, readable programs. Structured programming can, of course, be combined with other methods for establishing correctness.

Originally, structured programming received its impetus from an observation of Dijkstra's on the pragmatic role played by the control structures in the program. Dijkstra observed that the presence of GO TO's, i.e., unconditional transfers of control in a program, tended to make for unintelligible programs because the process of keeping track of where we are in the process almost immediately exceeds the competence of the programmer.

Subsequently, other factors were noted that tend to make programs difficult to read, and some positive principles or guidelines for program development also emerged.

The basic philosophy underlying all of the recent rational approaches to programming is probably better categorized under the title "systematic" programming, as used by Wirth, or "disciplined" programming, since there is much more of concern than just the control structures of the program.

B. The Principle of Stepwise Refinement

One of the important ideas in program development that has evolved with structured programming is the principle of stepwise refinement. The principle of stepwise refinement is to state the overall program objective in comprehensible form and to proceed through successive specification of detail to the final program in such a way that:

(1) at each level of additional refinement, the added details can be understood in terms of the small part of the program that is being elaborated; and

(2) the small part being elaborated is independent of other parts being elaborated.

The principle of stepwise refinement is thus a prescription for generating a program with block structure. Block structure is desired because of the relative simplicity of the underlying sequential control within the block.

Consider the following simple example in which the computer is being programmed to play *nim***. The simplest program is:

---

*Descartes, René. "Discourse on the Method of Rightly Conducting the Reason; and Seeking Truth in the Sciences," Translated by John Betch, Chicago: The Open Court Publishing Company, 1920, p. 19.

**Nim is a game played by two players. In *Nim,* one starts with a pile of *N* matches. Players alternate turns and at each turn a player can remove 1, 2, or 3 matches from the pile. The player who takes the last match loses.

PLAY Nim

at the next level of refinement, the program might be:

WHILE GAME IS NOT OVER:
PLAY NEXT MOVE

This can be still further refined to:

WHILE GAME IS NOT OVER:
READ MOVE FROM TERMINAL
COMPUTE MACHINE MOVE
GENERATE OUTPUT TO TERMINAL

Now each of the three portions can be elaborated independently. For example, to develop the input part we might want to:

GENERATE PROMPTING SIGNAL TO TERMINAL
READ INPUT FROM TERMINAL
CHECK LEGALITY OF MOVE
UPDATE NUMBER OF "MATCHES"

At each stage of the program elaboration, the programmer's attention is focused on those issues that need resolution. The attention given to these issues tends to make the programming proceed more smoothly since there are fewer issues to decide at any given time, i.e., while input formats are being considered, other data structures can be ignored.

Top-down vs. bottom-up programming

The principle of stepwise refinement is to some extent an idealization of the programming process. At the top level we understand the algorithm in terms of abstractions to be programmed or elaborated at the next level of detail. However, usually many of the concepts and abstractions needed to complete our program are captured in facilities provided by a high-level language or by programming constructs that we have developed. Examples of such components are data structures, subroutines, and macros, which are often developed as building blocks to provide a general problem-solving capability. These are examples of "bottom-up" program features since they are composed from simpler machine features and are intended to be included in a program at some later time.

You can expect both bottom-up and top-down programming methods will be used in computer science as both methods are used in other types of intellectual activities.

What to avoid

It has been suggested by Dijkstra that the use of certain programming features tends to make programs more difficult to understand and validate. An

example is the GO TO statement of FORTRAN. In general, there is agreement
that the fewer GO TO's a program has, in a language that provides alternate
forms of expression, the easier it will be to follow. Standard FORTRAN does
not provide such alternate forms of expression (DO WHILE, IF . . . THEN . . .
ELSE). Still, even in FORTRAN, programs can be made more comprehensible
by programming in flowchart form where these constructs are available and
using the algorithm for converting flowchart to straight line code.

While the use of GO TO's is to be avoided, in most cases, it is doubtful that
they should be avoided altogether. There does not seem to be an entirely
adequate alternate form of expression for escaping from the innermost
iteration of a nested set of iterations. An iteration is often called a *loop* because a circuit, or loop, is traversed in the flowchart. For example, a program
searching a three-dimensional array, A, for a particular value A might look as
follows:

$i \leftarrow 1$;
DO WHILE $(i \leq I_{max})$;
    $j \leftarrow 1$;
        DO WHILE $(j \leq J_{max})$;
            $k \leftarrow 1$;
            DO WHILE $(k \leq K_{max})$;
                if $A(i, j, k) = A_0$ THEN GO TO FOUND;   *where is FOUND*
                $k \leftarrow k + 1$;
                END   *moved here to explain to student*
            $j \leftarrow j + i$;
            END;
        $i \leftarrow i + 1$;
        END;
    NOT FOUND:

The corresponding GO TO-less code is more complex. (We leave it for the
reader as an exercise. Hint: Include a completion test on each DO . . . WHILE
condition. Be sure to check that you end up with the proper values of i, j, k
for the located element.) This is optional at this point in your reading.

Other features to be avoided are global variables and side effects. Again, use
of these programming constructs makes the programs less readable, in
general.

3.3   Program Debugging

In chapter 2, we stated that the process of solving a problem on the computer
included formulating an algorithm for the problem, drawing a flowchart for
the algorithm, translating the flowchart into a programming language, and
debugging the programming. *Debugging* is the process of converting the

original program into a workable solution for the given problem by removing translation and execution errors.

A. Translation Errors

After preparing a programming problem for computer solution, the program must be entered into the computer. In the computer, the program is translated from the programmer's language to a language the computer can directly execute. The translation process is called *compilation.* The version of the program prepared by the programmer is called the *source* program. The internal program compiled by the computer is called the *object* program.

During compilation, the computer may produce a listing of the source program with an indication of *compilation errors.* These errors are illegal constructions that violate the syntactic or semantic rules of the language and prevent the compiler from translating one or more program statements. Such errors include:

(1) Transfer of control to a nonexistent labelled statement;

(2) Unbalanced parentheses (i.e., an unequal number of right and left parentheses);

(3) Use of an undeclared array.

The error messages appearing on the program listing provide a description of the type of error and the point of its detection. However, the actual error may be located elsewhere in the program and the error message merely notes the computer's first indication of it. For example, an error message will mention the use of an undeclared array in an assignment statement; but the actual error occurs not in the assignment statement itself, but at the beginning of the program, where the necessary declaration is missing. The processor is unable to translate statements in which errors occur; this may result in subsequent error messages caused by the omission of these particular statements.

Translation errors prevent execution of the program; the programmer corrects the appropriate cards in the source deck and resubmits the deck for compilation.

B. Execution Errors

When a successful compilation is obtained, the machine can execute the object program produced by the compilation process. The execution process will be terminated either by successful completion of the program or by an execution error. *Execution errors* are logical errors detected during actual execution of a program statement. Such errors include:

(1) use of an input or output unit that is not available to the program;

(2) division by zero (A/B where B has the value 0);

(3) integer overflow (an integer variable assumes a greater value than can be stored in a memory word);

(4) subscript out of bounds.

The machine again produces error messages indicating the type of error and the point of detection. The absence of execution errors does not guarantee a workable program; errors in program logic may cause the program to be executed successfully but still produce incorrect results.

In order to debug a program, you must test both the program to assure that it agrees with the flowchart, and the flowchart to assure that it specifies a correct solution to the given problem. The process of establishing program correctness was discussed in Section 3.1.

The following is a catalog of execution errors.

(1) Insufficient program initialization—you cannot assume that variables and arrays all contain zeroes at the start of program execution. The memory words referenced by these variables may contain "garbage" (extraneous values) left over from the compilation process or the previous run. Thus, the programmer must assume responsibility for initialization.

(2) Execution of a loop one too few or one too many times—the latter often occurs in conjunction with the reading of input data and results in an END-OF-FILE error indicating that the program attempted to read a nonexistent data card.

(3) Resetting of control index in a loop—the control index is automatically incremented by the loop structure; if this index appears on the left side of an assignment statement within the loop, the index is reset at this point. In most cases, this is an error in logic.

EXAMPLE: SUM:=0;
                FOR I:=1 STEP 2 UNTIL 9 DO BEGIN
                    SUM:=SUM+I;
                    I:=I+2;
                    END

The statement I:=I+2 increments the control index by 2 during each execution of the loop; since the index is also incremented by 2 via the FOR loop structure, the end result is that the numbers 1, 5, 9 are summed rather than the numbers 1, 3, 5, 7, 9.

(4) Improper transfer to beginning of loop—you transfer control to the beginning of the loop only if you want to start execution of the loop with the initial value of the control index; if you are inside the loop and merely want to begin the next pass through the loop with the new incremented value of the control index, then you must transfer control to the last statement of the loop and the loop structure itself will accomplish this.

(5) Inexact values in loop structure—computer arithmetic is carried out in the base 2 number system. Since not every decimal fraction can be represented exactly in base 2 or binary, errors can result. The number 1/10 or 0.1 is an example of a

number that does not have an exact binary representation. Therefore the loop structure FOR $I := 0$ STEP 0.1 UNTIL 1.0 will never terminate since the increment is not exactly 0.1 in the machine's binary memory; I never reaches a value of exactly 1.0. A better way of writing the above loop structure is FOR $I := 0$ STEP 0.1 WHILE $I \leq 1.01$.

(6) Array subscripts out of range—this is often indicated by an error message specifying an invalid index. However, this error can occur in a multidimensional array and be undetected by the system. A mapping function is used to relate elements of a multidimensional array to the one-dimensional computer memory. In the case of a two-dimensional array, ARR, whose lower bounds are 1 and upper bounds are 8 and 3 respectively, this mapping function *may* take the form:

$$ARR \, I, J \leftrightarrow base + 3(I - 1) + (J - 1)$$

where base is the starting location of the array in the machine's memory. A double-headed arrow, $\leftrightarrow$, indicates that either side of the expression can be used to determine the remaining side. Thus, the elements of array, ARR, are associated with 24 successive locations in memory beginning with the location indicated by "base." To determine whether the subscripts of an array element are out of range, the machine may use the mapping function to determine whether that array element is associated with one of the 24 locations reserved for the array. Thus, ARR 1,100 $\leftrightarrow$ base + 99, which is out of range and an error message is generated; however, ARR 1, 10 $\leftrightarrow$ base + 9, which is within the specified 24 locations and the error is not detected.

(7) Parameters in subroutine calls—you must be careful that the formal parameters in the subroutine definition and the actual parameters in the subroutine call agree in number, order, and type.

Annotating a program

A good program is correct and easily understood by others familiar with the problem. In this way, the original programmer can store the program and easily reuse and alter it later; in addition, others can make use of and expand the program for their own purposes.

To facilitate this program readability, you can place the program statements in outline form, indenting loops and subsegments in the same manner as you would indent subitems in an outline. Most languages also provide for some type of program commentary. This commentary takes the form of special statements within the program describing both the overall algorithm and its component parts. Such statements appear on the program listing but are not translated by the compiler.

References and Suggested Additional Readings

(1) Conway, R., and Gries, D. *An Introduction to Programming—A Structured Approach Using PL/I and PL/C.* Cambridge, MA: Winthrop Publishers, 1973.

(2) Dahl, O.J., Dijkstra, E.W., and Hoare, C.A.R.. *Structured Programming.* New York: Academic Press, 1972.

(3) Rustin, E.R.. *Debugging Techniques in Large Systems.* New York: Prentice-Hall, 1971.

(4) Wirth, N.. *Systematic Programming: An Introduction.* New York: Prentice-Hall, 1973.

Problems

1. Trace the program that is traced in this chapter using as input data:
   (a) $j = 1$ $k = 1$
   (b) $j = 5$ $k = 0$
   (c) $j = 6$ $k = 12$

2. Is there any set of input data for which the program referred to in problem 1 loops?

3. How would you arrange to trace a program during its development testing and to bypass or eliminate tracing afterwards? Discuss and compare several possibilities.

4. A proof of correctness is based on some predicted result of the computation, called a *program invariant*. Describe how you might use these program invariants in tracing.

5. Using the flowchart of the Fibonacci sequence program given in chapter 2, prove that the program is correct.

6. Write a program to reverse an array, A, with n elements whose indices run from 1 to n, so that the final value of $A[n - i]$ (i.e., after the program is run) is equal to the initial value of $A[i + 1]$, where $0 \leq i \leq n - 1$. Prove your program correct. Did your proof uncover a "bug" in your program that will sort the elements of an array? Develop the correctness proof at the same time.

7. Using the method of stepwise refinement, develop a sorting program that will sort the elements of a linear array. Develop the correctness proof at the same time.

8. Examine an actual programming language, and list and interpret five error messages that can be produced during the compilation process.

9. Examine an actual programming language, and list and interpret five error messages that can be produced during program execution.

10. Examine an actual programming language to determine how commentary can be placed in the program.

11. Using a working program, write a set of output statements to trace the flow of control through the program and to monitor the value of a particular variable.

Chapter 4

Computer Systems—
An Overview

In chapter 2, the concept of an algorithmic method of problem solving was formalized. The advent of digital computer, capable of performing over a million operations per second, made it practical to apply such mechanical procedures to a vast range of problems.

Digital computers comprise two major components the hardware (electronics) and the software (programs). In this chapter, we shall discuss how the hardware operates, from a programmer point of view, to provide a better understanding of the software discussed in a later chapter. Of particular interest is the means by which a computer communicates with its external environment to receive input data and to transmit computer results, and the way in which this data is represented and stored in the machine. The stored data consists of instructions, numbers and characters. The machine interprets the stored instructions and operates accordingly upon the stored data to perform the desired computation.

We shall commence by considering the representation of data within the machine. Digital computers deal with strings of zeros and ones. Consequently, all data must be transformed into 0's and 1's before they are manipulated by the computer circuitry.

In the second part of this chapter, we discuss a typical organization of a modern computer. In particular, we shall discuss the physical pieces into which a computer may be logically divided and their characteristics. Finally, we touch on microprocessors.

4.1   Number Systems and Representation of Information

Several methods of representing information in the computer exist; most of these rely upon the binary or base two number system.

Number systems

The decimal or base 10 number system with which we are familiar has ten individual digits 0, 1, ..., 9. To represent numbers of magnitude larger than 9, we could have "invented" additional digits, but the concept of representing each number by its own distinct symbol quickly becomes impractical. Thus, the idea of positional notation was introduced, in which the relative position of a digit with respect to the decimal point determines a weighting of that digit. The digit to the immediate left of the decimal point is said to occupy position 0; digits to the left and right of position 0 occupy successively higher positive and negative positions respectively. In the case of the decimal system, the weight of the Kth position is 10^K; the value of a number is equal to the sum of the product of each digit with its respective positional weight.

Example:*

$$456.35 = 4 \times 10^2 + 5 \times 10^1 + 6 \times 10^0 + 3 \times 10^{-1} + 5 \times 10^{-2}$$

The decimal system is called *base 10* or *radix 10* because its positional weights are powers of 10. A number system can be of any base or radix N; a radix N system will contain N distinct symbols as digits 0, 1, ..., $N - 1$ and its positional weights will be powers of N. (Note that the largest value representable by a single digit in a radix N system is $N - 1$; to represent the value N, we require a symbol in the digit position with weight N.)

Example:*

Radix 10 (decimal)	0, 1, ... , 9	$324.2_{10} = 4 \times 10^0 + 2 \times 10^1 + 3 \times 10^2 +$ 2×10^{-1}
Radix 8 (octal)	0, 1, ... , 7	$324.2_8 = 4 \times 8^0 + 2 \times 8^1 + 3 \times 8^2 + 2 \times 8^{-1}$
Radix 2 (binary)	0, 1	$1011.01_2 = 1 \times 2^0 + 1 \times 2^1 + 0 \times 2^2 +$ $1 \times 2^3 + 0 \times 2^{-1} + 1 \times 2^{-2}$
Radix 16 (hexadecimal)	0, 1, ... , 9, A, B, C, D, E, F	$2E8.B_{16} = 8 \times 16^0 + 14 \times 16^1 + 2 \times 16^2 +$ 11×16^{-1}

To work with numbers in the various radix systems, it is necessary to convert the representation of a number in one system to the representation of that number in another system. The easiest way to convert a number from a radix A representation to a radix B representation is to convert the number from radix A to radix 10 and then from radix 10 to radix B.

A radix A number is easily converted to radix 10 by expanding it into the sum of the products of each digit with its positional weight and then evaluating this series using decimal arithmetic. In the previous example,

$$324.26_8 = 4 \times 8^0 + 2 \times 8^1 + 3 \times 8^2 + 2 \times 8^{-1} + 6 \times 8^{-2}$$

$$= 4 \times 1 + 2 \times 8 + 3 \times 64 + 2 \times 0.125 + 6 \times 0.015625$$

$$= 4 + 16 + 192 + 0.25 + 0.09375$$

$$= 212.34375_{10}$$

The following method for converting a decimal number to a radix B representation is more complex. We separate the number into an integer and a fractional part, convert each to radix B, and then combine to obtain the desired radix B representation.

First consider the integer part I; if the number I were represented in base B, evaluation of its positional notation series expansion would yield its decimal

---

*Subscripts are used to indicate the radix being used in writing a number. When the subscript is missing, it should be assumed to be 10.

value, i.e., $I = d_tB^t + d_{t-1}B^{t-1} + \ldots + d_2B^2 + d_1B^1 + d_0$. Note that if I is divided by B, the remainder is d_0, the least significant digit of the base B representation. If the quotient Q_1 of this division is again divided by B, the remainder is d_1, the next least significant digit. Thus, the consecutive remainders, obtained by dividing the consecutive quotients by the radix B, form the digits of the base B representation, from least to most significant. Now consider the fractional part F where $F = d_{-1} \times B^{-1} + d_{-2} \times B^{-2} + \ldots + d_{-s} \times B^{-s}$. Note that if F is multiplied by B, the integer part of the product is the digit d_{-1}. Thus, analogous to the integer case, the digits of the base B representation from most to least significant are the consecutive integer parts of the product obtained by multiplying the consecutive fractional parts by the radix B.

Example:

Convert 212.34375_{10} to octal (radix 8)

$$
\begin{array}{r}
26 \text{ Remainder 4} \\
8\overline{)212}
\end{array}
$$

$$
\begin{array}{r}
3 \text{ Remainder 2} \\
8\overline{)26}
\end{array}
$$

$$
\begin{array}{r}
0 \text{ Remainder 3} \\
8\overline{)3}
\end{array}
$$

$$212_{10} = 324_8$$

$$
\begin{array}{r}
.34375 \\
\times 8 \\
\hline
2.75000 \text{ Integer part 2}
\end{array}
$$

$$
\begin{array}{r}
.75 \\
\times 8 \\
\hline
6.00 \text{ Integer part 6}
\end{array}
$$

$$.34375_{10} = .26_8$$

Therefore $212.34375_{10} = 324.26_8$

The binary of radix 2 system is usually chosen for representation of numbers in computer memory. It is most efficient, and it is simplest to build electronic devices that have only two states, one state for each of the two digits of the binary system.

4.1.1.   Computer Words and Number Representation

Most computers built today use the binary system to represent data. A typical computer may be thought of as having a large number of places in which arrays of bits (digits 0 or 1) are stored. These arrays are often of fixed length, known as the word length of the computer, i.e. a computer word consists of a designated number, m, of bits numbered 0 to $(m-1)$ from left to right. Word lengths are generally in the range 8-64 and are usually a multiple of eight bits. It is possible to interpret the contents of a word in various ways as we shall see in the remainder of this section. We begin by considering their interpretation as numbers: integers and reals (floating point).

It is clear that a string of bits can be interpreted as an integer number. However, these integers may either be positive or negative. The treatment of the sign varies from one computer to another. We shall discuss two methods for treating the sign based on what is known as a fixed-point number representation. This term refers to the fact that the radix point is regarded as having a fixed position in the computer word. Clearly, if the position is immediately to the right of the bit numbered $(m-1)$, all numbers are integers.

1. Sign-magnitude representation. Each integer in this representation system is represented by bits of which the first is the sign bit (0 denotes + and 1 denotes -). The remaining $m-1$ bits represent the magnitude of the integer in the conventional binary system. If $m = 4$, then representation of $+5$ and -5 are, 0101 and 1101 respectively. The range of representable numbers is $-2^{m-1} + 1$ to $+2^{m-1}-1$ with two representations for zero $+0$ and -0.

2. Two's Complement representation. Another representation for fixed point numbers is called two's complement. This form is identical to sign magnitude form for positive numbers so that all nonnegative numbers begin with a zero. A negative number to be stored in an m bit word is represented as 2^m-X where X is the absolute value of the negative number being represented. If $m = 4$ then the representation of $+5$ and -5 are 0101 and 1011 respectively. In this representation, unlike the previous one, zero has only one representation, all zeros. All numbers in the range -2^{m-1} to $(2^{m-1}-1)$ have a unique representation in 2's complement.

Floating point representation

Floating point representation of numbers overcomes the troublesome problems of the fixed point scheme. In a *floating point* system, the sign and K-most significant digits (called the *mantissa*) of the number are stored together with an exponent indicating the relative placement of the binary point. Initially the binary point is assumed to immediately precede the leftmost digit of the mantissa; the exponent designates the power of the radix by which the mantissa must be multiplied to obtain the actual number. Thus, the exponent specifies the number of positions to the right (positive exponent) or left (negative exponent) that the binary point must be moved. Both the mantissa and exponent are represented in the sign magnitude radix system.

Example:

Binary system.

Each word contains 8 bits as shown below:

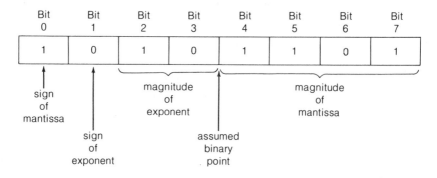

Mantissa is -0.1101_2.

Exponent is $+10_2 = 2_{10}$ indicating that the binary point of the mantissa must be moved two positions to the right.

Thus, the number represented in the above word of memory is
$$-0.1101_2 \times 2^2 = -11.01_2.$$

As described thus far, a number may have more than one floating point representation. For example, the number $3.5_{10} = 11.1_2 = +0.111 \times 2^2$ or $+0.0111 \times 2^3$. Thus, this number could be represented in the system of the previous example with an exponent of $2_{10} = 10_2$ and mantissa of 0.1110_2 or with an exponent of $3_{10} = 11_2$ and mantissa of 0.0111_2, i.e., as

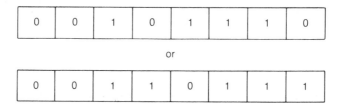

or

In order to have a unique representation for all nonzero numbers, and to have identical representations for zero in fixed and floating-point systems, we require that the leftmost digit of the mantissa be nonzero and that the number zero be represented with a zero exponent. Such a representation is said to be in normalized form. Thus, in the above example, the normalized floating point representation for the number $3.5_{10} = 11.1_2$ is

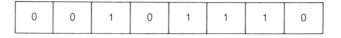

Character representation

Thus far we have only discussed the representation of numbers in computer memory. Many problems require that alphabetic and character information also be stored in memory. An example of such a problem is the sorting of a list of student names into alphabetic order.

If a memory work contains N bits, then 2^N different configurations of the states of these bits is possible. If we let each configuration represent a different character, then 2^N different characters can be represented in a memory word. For example, if $N = 3$, then we might represent the letters A through H as

$$0\ 0\ 0 = A$$
$$0\ 0\ 1 = B$$
$$0\ 1\ 0 = C$$
$$0\ 1\ 1 = D$$
$$1\ 0\ 0 = E$$
$$1\ 0\ 1 = F$$
$$1\ 1\ 0 = G$$
$$1\ 1\ 1 = H$$

On looking at the contents of a memory word, we cannot tell whether the data stored there is a fixed point number, a floating point number, or a character. How the contents of a memory word are interpreted depends on the instruction the machine is executing.

In most cases, the number of different characters representable in a word of memory is much larger than necessary. Thus, we choose a number M, where M bits are sufficient to represent all the characters in our character set, and divide each memory word into $K = N/M$ fields of M bits each. Each field can contain the representation for one character. The representations for K characters can be stored in the K fields of one memory word. This eliminates wasted space in a memory word and provides a more efficient storage scheme.

There are three widely used codes for representing characters: Binary Coded Decimal (BCD), Extended Binary Code Decimal Interchange Code (EBCDIC), and the American Standards Code for Information Interchange (ASCII). BCD requires six bits per field and EBCDIC and ASCII codes require eight. These codes are given in the Appendix.

Each code divides a field into a zone and a numeric portion as shown below.

Six bit format used in *BCD*	zone		numeric			
	0	1	2	3	4	5

Eight bit format
used in *EBCDIC* and
ASCII (Eight bit
formats are often
called *bytes*).

zone				numeric			
0	1	2	3	4	5	6	7

TABLE 1 gives the *BCD* and *EBCDIC* codes and card punches and the corresponding *ASCII* codes.

Example:

Suppose the word contains 18 bits. Using BCD code, the characters forming the name JIM would be stored as follows:

0	1	2	3	4	5	6	7	8	9	10	11	12	13	14	15	16	17
1	0	0	0	0	1	0	1	1	0	0	1	1	0	0	1	0	0

J   I   M

Example:

Suppose the word contains 18 bits. Using BCD code, the characters 121 would be stored as follows:

0	1	2	3	4	5	6	7	8	9	10	11	12	13	14	15	16	17
0	0	0	0	0	1	0	0	0	0	1	0	0	0	0	0	0	1

1   2   1

A memory word containing the representation for the three characters 121 looks different from a memory word containing the number $121_{10} = 171_8 = 1111001_2$. Each of the three characters in 121 is treated individually and their individual representations are packed into one memory word only to effect an efficient storage scheme.

If the BCD, EBCDIC, and ASCII codes for a character are interpreted as binary numbers, then the representation for each alphabetic character is a smaller binary number than the representations for characters following it in the alphabet. This facilitates sorting of alphabetic information by merely sorting its representation into numeric order.

Example:

Word contains 18 bits; using BCD code.

CAT is stored as

0	1	0	0	1	1	0	1	0	0	0	1	1	1	0	0	1	1

DOG is stored as

0	1	0	1	0	0	1	0	0	1	1	0	0	1	0	1	1	1

COD is stored as

0	1	0	0	1	1	1	0	0	1	1	0	0	1	0	1	0	0

If these words are placed in order of increasing binary value, they become:

0	1	0	0	1	1	0	1	0	0	0	1	1	1	0	0	1	1

representing CAT

0	1	0	0	1	1	1	0	0	1	1	0	0	1	0	1	0	0

representing COD

0	1	0	1	0	0	1	0	0	1	1	0	0	1	0	1	1	1

representing DOG

which results in the character words they represent being in alphabetical order.

Arithmetic computations

A computer word can contain a number in either fixed or floating point form; you cannot determine which form has been used by examining the contents of the word. For example, the word 00101110 might represent the fixed point number $56_8 = 46_{10}$ or, using the floating point scheme of the previous example, the floating point number $0.111_2 \times 2^2 = 11.1_2 = 3.5_{10}$.

Thus, when the control unit requests the arithmetic/logical unit to perform an operation, such as addition of two computer words, it must also specify whether the contents of the two words are to be interpreted as fixed or floating point numbers. If both words contain fixed point numbers (integers), then arithmetic operations on the two words proceed the same as these operations on binary numbers.

Example:

Two computer words contain 00111001 and 00011100, representing the fixed point numbers 57_{10} and 28_{10} respectively. Their sum is then computed as

$$
\begin{array}{r}
00111001 \\
+ 00011100 \\
\hline
01010101 = 85_{10}
\end{array}
$$

If the two computer words contain floating point numbers, then an arithmetic operation on the contents of these words proceeds the same as an operation in scientific notation. For example, if you have the numbers 0.432×10^4 and 0.516×10^3 in scientific notation, then addition of the two numbers requires that the smaller of the two first be adjusted so that it has the same exponent as the larger number. Thus 0.516×10^3 becomes 0.0516×10^4 and addition of the two numbers proceeds as follows:

$$\begin{array}{r} 0.432 \times 10^4 \\ + 0.0516 \times 10^4 \\ \hline 0.4836 \times 10^4 \end{array}$$

To add two floating point binary numbers, the mantissa of the smaller of the two numbers is shifted right a number of positions equal to the difference D of the two exponents. This is equivalent to multiplying the smaller of the two numbers by 2^{-D} and thus D must be added to the value of its exponent. Therefore, the two numbers now have the same exponent, the mantissas may be added, and if necessary, the result again adjusted to achieve normalized form.

Example:

Two computer words contain 00111001 and 00011100, representing the floating point numbers $0.1001_2 \times 2^3$ and $0.1100_2 \times 2^1$. The difference between the two exponents is $3 - 1 = 2$, requiring that the mantissa of $0.1100_2 \times 2^1$ be shifted right two positions and two be added to its exponent.

$$\begin{array}{r} 0.0011_2 \times 2^3 \\ + 0.1001_2 \times 2^3 \\ \hline 0.1100_2 \times 2^3 \end{array}$$

Example:

Two computer words contain 00101101 and 00011110, representing the floating point numbers $0.1101_2 \times 2^2$ and $0.1110_2 \times 2^1$. Addition of the two numbers proceeds as follows:

$$\begin{array}{r} 0.0111_2 \times 2^2 \\ 0.1101_2 \times 2^2 \\ \hline 1.0100_2 \times 2^2 \end{array}$$

However $1.0100_2 \times 2^2$ must be adjusted to the normalized form 0.1010×2^3, which is represented in floating point form as 00111010.

Other arithmetic operations are performed on floating point numbers in a similar manner. It is obvious that floating point representation allows a wider range of values to be represented in memory and provides a means of operating on fractional numbers. However, floating point representation retains fewer significant digits than fixed point representation and arithmetic computations and, although performed automatically by the machine, is more time-consuming. Thus, integer or whole numbers are generally represented in fixed point form.

4.2   The Hardware Components of a Typical System

By the hardware components of a computer, we mean its actual physical units. We expect a computer to have some physical means of transmitting information to and from its environment, some structure for retaining this transmitted information for repeated use, a physical mechanism for performing basic computations (such as additions, multiplications, testing for equality), and an overall control mechanism for supervising operation of the other units. A typical system has five such components, usually called INPUT, OUTPUT, MAIN MEMORY, CENTRAL PROCESSOR, and BULK STORAGE units respectively as in Figure 4.1.

The CENTRAL PROCESSOR comprises a control unit and an arithmetic/logic unit. The control unit directs the interaction of the other components; it selects the command to be executed, obtains the required data from memory or the input unit, signals the arithmetic/logic unit to perform a required computation, and sends data to memory for storage or to the output unit for display of results. The *arithmetic/logic unit* performs computations and makes decisions based on data given to it.

The MAIN STORAGE of the machine is usually composed of magnetic core units that facilitate fast access of information stored therein. The main storage unit will be discussed in detail in the next section.

Input and Output Units

INPUT/OUTPUT units transmit information to main memory for processing by the system and from main memory for display of computed results. Many

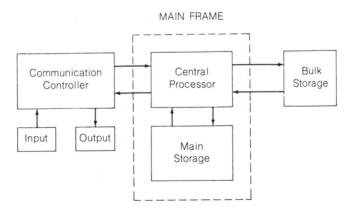

Figure 4.1:   The Main Hardware Components of a Computer

input/output units exist, and new varieties are being introduced in efforts to adapt the computer to a continually wider range of activities.

The traditional form of input is the *punched card*, a thin rectangular card consisting of eighty columns. Each column contains twelve rows in which small holes can be punched; each configuration of holes in these rows represents a different character. For example, using what is called the *Hollerith code*, a column with a hole only in row 2 is interpreted as containing the digit 2 whereas a column with a hole punched both in row 2 and in row 12 is interpreted as containing the character *B*. Thus, each column corresponds to one character and one such punched card can contain up to eighty characters of punched information.

These cards can be manually prepared on a *keypunch machine*. This device resembles a typewriter, except that depressing a keyboard key produces the appropriate configuration of holes in a column of a card rather than producing a character of print. Typically, the user punches his instructions and data on punched cards. These cards are then read as input by a device called a *card reader*. A typical card reader can process approximately 1000 cards per minute. (See Figure 4.2).

The most common form of output is the *line printer*, a device that prints an entire line of 132 characters of output at one time. These operate at a speed of approximately 2000 lines per minute. (See Figure 4.3).

A relatively new form of input is the diskette, a small disk capable of holding as much information as an entire box of punched cards. These diskettes are

Figure 4.2: *Control Data Card Reader*   Courtesy Control Data, Inc.

easily handled and stored. Information is manually inserted via a data station similar to a keypunch console; this information is then converted into a form usable by the computer via a data converter.

Recent advances in the area of man-machine communication have produced input/output units for interactive computing. Such a unit might contain a teletype-writer for data transmitted directly to the machine via the keyboard (see Figure 4.7) and a display unit for presenting computer-generated information either graphically or as a line of print. The graphic data is displayed as a series of points or vectors. The IBM 2250 is this type of remote graphic terminal, and uses a 1024 × 1024 coordinate grid for its display screen. Information displayed on the screen can be altered via the keyboard and a user-held Light Pen.

As computers are used more and more for on-line processing, special purpose input/output units are being developed for remote communication with a central computer. Such applications include banking transactions, supermarket check-outs, and inventory control. (See Figures 4.5 and 4.6).

Bulk storage

The amount of main core storage available on a system is limited and generally insufficient for storage of all required information. BULK STORAGE provides additional memory for large amounts of data at relatively low cost but with a much slower rate of access. This auxiliary memory may be used

Figure 4.3: Honeywell's PRU1200 and PRU 1600 Printer   Courtesy Honeywell, Inc.

both for temporary storage of intermediate results during computation or for long-term storage of information.

Bulk storage can be classified into *on-line* and *off-line* devices. On-line memory is immediately accessible to the computer. One such device is the *magnetic disk drive.* It operates on a disk pack consisting of a stack of circular metal disk plates on which almost 100 million characters of information can be stored. A read/write head moving back and forth over each rotating disk plate can locate an item of information in about 300 milliseconds, and can transfer data to or from main core memory at over 100,000 characters per second.

Off-line memory may not be immediately accessible to the computer. The *magnetic tape unit* is an example of off-line memory (see Figure 4.4). Information is stored on reels of magnetic tape, similar to that used in commercial tape recorders. The tape unit can transfer data between a tape reel and main core memory; however, a particular reel of tape is not available for use unless it has been placed on the tape unit. In addition, an item of information can be accessed only by passing over all preceding data on the reel, and one tape

Figure 4.4: Honeywell Magnetic Tape Unit

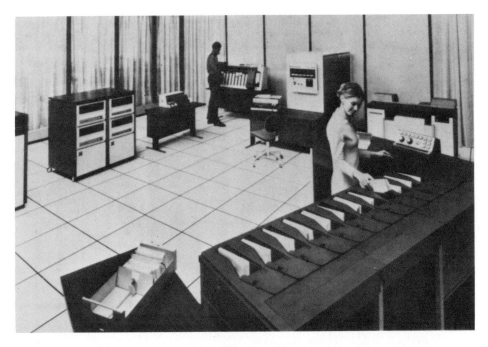

Figure 4.5: **Burrough's B1700 system for use in bank data processing**

Courtesy Burrough, Inc.

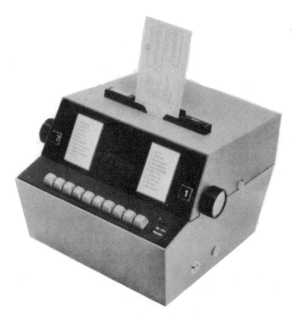

Figure 4.6: **An IBM Remote Data Unit for On-line Processing**   Courtesy IBM

***Figure 4.7:   Control Data Medium Scale General Purpose Computer
System***   Courtesy Control Data, Inc.

reel can store only about 10 million characters. However, magnetic tape is a
very inexpensive form of memory. This slow access rate and low cost result
in magnetic tape being used primarily for long-term storage of data rather
than for auxiliary memory during a machine computation.

Main Storage

Figure 4.8 shows a block diagram of a typical computer memory. It consists
of M words with unique addresses $0,1,...,M-1$, two special registers called the
memory address register (MAR) and the memory data register (MDR), and
three control lines. The GO/IDLE wire can be in either of two states GO or
IDLE. A memory cycle starts when the control line changes from IDLE to GO.

To read the contents of a memory word its address is placed in the MAR,
the read line activated and GO/IDLE line is changed to GO. When the memory
senses the GO, it begins an operation cycle which when completed the contents of the specified word would have been copied in the MDR. The contents of the word is not changed.

To store a word in memory, the word is placed in the MDR and the address
into which it must be stored is placed in the MAR. The write line is activated

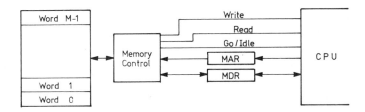

Figure 4.8:   Typical Memory

and the GO/IDLE line is set to GO. When the memory senses the GO it erases the contents of the specified word and then copies the contents of the MDR into the word.

The time taken to read a word from or into memory (i.e. a memory cycle) is on the order of a microsecond. It is obvious that the writing process is destructive while the reading process is non-destructive in the sense that the contents of the addressed computer word is erased or not.

This type of memory is called random access because any address may be read or written in some fixed time.

Control Unit

This unit repeatedly executes the control cycle represented in Figure 4.9.
To execute instructions, the control unit must retrieve them. One of the control unit registers, the program counter (PC), contains the memory address of the next instruction to be executed. To fetch an instruction, the contents of PC is transferred to the MAR and a read operation is performed; the desired

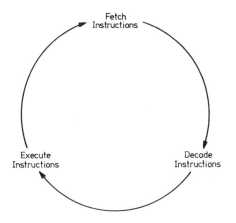

Figure 4.9

instruction appears in the MDR after a fixed delay. The PC is incremented so that the next instruction fetched will come from the next sequential memory location. The contents of the MDR is then transferred to yet another register, the instruction register (IR), where its meaning is decoded. The instruction is then executed; the control passes information to the arithmetic/logical unit for computation and/or memory to obtain or store data whichever the instruction calls for. Facilities are available to change PC so that the numerically sequential next instruction is not always the next one performed.

Arithmetic/Logical Unit

This unit comprises circuits for performing various operations and a limited set of registers. The operations typically include arithmetic and logical ones. The operations take one or more arguments (operands); these operands are contents of memory words found in the unit registers or in memory locations. The results of such operations usually are placed in the unit registers.

Central Processing Unit

The control unit, the arithmetic/logical unit, and the registers are normally grouped together both physically and logically to form the central processing unit. This organization collects together in one module all the physical devices associated with the execution of instructions. Due to more advanced technology in logic design, the CPU is usually the least expensive component of a computer system. It is not unusual to find computers with more than one CPU.

4.3   Microprocessors

The solid state electronic technology that has developed since the invention of the transistor in the late 1940's has produced a range of electronic devices with extremely high density of functional units, known as large scale integration (LSI). A typical LSI component is a wafer of crystalline silicon on which electronic circuits have been impressed, each elemental circuit occupying an area of several $(mil)^2$*. The LSI component known as a chip contains many thousands of circuits. An LSI component is usually encapsulated in a somewhat larger case, providing physical support and convenience in further packaging.

Utilizing the LSI technology, it has been possible to construct a microcomputer from as few as three LSI chips, with a single chip serving as the central processing unit of Figure 4 --. Although progress in the field of microelectronics is quite rapid, and improved chips are announced at frequent intervals, the Intel 8080 may be considered a typical LSI microprocessor.

---

*A $(mil^2$ is an area (.001) inches by (.001) inches.

The 8080 is a 8-bit microprocessor, which means that the word length is only eight bits. All arithmetic operations are, therefore, operations on operands which are eight bits, so that arithmetic operations on longer operands have to be programmed as subroutines. Communication with the memory modules, which are on other chips, is by means of electrical signal lines, known as busses. The 8080 has an eight bit data bus, a sixteen bit address bus, and additional lines for control signals and voltages. The sixteen address bits are used to address memory and input/output devices, so that the maximum random access memory (RAM) that is available with the 8080 is 65,536 eight bit bytes. An additional 65,536 eight bit bytes of read-only memory is available for fixed software.

The typical instruction cycle time is 2 μsec, but, of course, this is only for eight bit operands.

Counts of the number of different instructions vary, but one hundred is a representative estimate. Typically, the instructions are single address instructions in which, as usual, a second address is implied; in arithmetic instructions, the accumulator would be the implied address. The instruction lengths are one, two, or three bytes depending on what is being addressed. A direct memory address instruction is three bytes, since the bit address requires two of the bytes. A register instruction is two bytes. There are three pairs of general eight bit registers in the microprocessor, as well as, several special purpose eight bit and 16-bit registers.

Since the 8080 has been a very popular microprocessor, much of the software (see Chapter 12) that a user expects has been developed for it.

Summary

In this chapter, we have discussed the hardware components of a typical computer system: input, output, memory, and central processor. We have examined the methods by which information can be represented in computer memory. Numbers are represented in either fixed or floating point form. There are several methods of fixed point representation, including sign-magnitude and two's complement. Floating point representation consists of storing a specific number of significant digits along with an indication of the position of the radix point relative to these digits. Character information may be stored in memory according to a character code, among which are the BCD, EBCIDIC, and ASCII codes. We then examined the interaction of instructions and data in memory during execution of a program.

References and Suggested Additional Readings

(1) Gear, William. *Computer Organization and Programming*. New York: McGraw-Hill, 1969.

(2) Stone, Harold. *Computer Organization and Data Structures*. New York: McGraw-Hill, 1972.

Problems

1. (a) If a memory word contains 9 bits, how many distinct binary numbers can be represented in a word?
   (b) What is the minimum number of bits required to represent 200 distinct binary numbers in a memory word?

For each of the following programs, specify the data required for input, the data desirable as output, and the most appropriate input/output devices. (Problems 5-7)

2. A grading program for grading multiple choice exams (each student's answers are marked on an optical scan sheet).

3. An industrial accounting program to maintain and update lists of employees with appropriate personnel information (i.e., social security number, salary, etc.)

4. A chess playing program to compete against human players.

5. A variation of batch processing is the entry of program decks by users from remote stations. The decks are entered successively and form a queue that the operating system must process. The results are then output on a device at the remote station. Indicate some desirable responsibilities of the software support for this type of system.

6. Assume a memory word contains 24 bits.
   (a) Show how the number 362 is stored in memory.
   (b) Show how the number −73 is stored in memory.
   (c) Show how the word *ART* is stored in memory using *BCD* code.
   (d) Show how the word *ART* is stored in memory using *EBCDIC* code.

7. Assume a memory word contains 24 bits.
   Bit 0 = sign of mantissa
   Bit 1 = sign of exponent
   Bits 2-11 = magnitude of exponent
   Bits 12-23 = mantissa
   Show how each of the following numbers is stored in memory in normalized floating point form.
   (a) 126.25   (b) −350   (c) 0.015625

8. (a) Convert the decimal numbers 0 through 20 to base 8.
   (b) Convert the decimal numbers 0 through 20 to base 2, adding leading 0's to represent each as a string of six binary digits.
   (c) Compare your results of part a and b and note the correspondence between each group of three binary digits and a single octal digit—can you formulate an algorithm for easy conversion between binary and octal?

9. (a) Convert the decimal numbers 0 through 40 to base 16.
   (b) Convert the decimal numbers 0 through 40 to base 2, adding leading 0's to represent each as a string of eight binary digits.
   (c) Compare your results of part a and part b and note the correspondence between each group of four binary digits and a single hexadecimal digit—can

you formulate an algorithm for easy conversion between binary and hexadecimal?

Appendix*

Table 1: BCD and EBCDIC Codes and Card Punches and Corresponding ASCII Codes

Character	BCD code	EBCDIC Code	ASCII Code	BCD Cards	EBCDIC Cards
blank	110 000	0100 0000	0100 0000	no punch	no punch
.	011 011	0100 1011	0100 1110	12, 8, 3	12, 8, 3
(	111 100	0100 1101	0100 1000	0, 8, 4	12, 8, 5
+	010 000	0100 1110	0100 1011	12	12, 8, 6
$	101 011	0101 1011	0100 0100	11, 8, 3	11, 8, 3
*	101 100	0101 1100	0100 1010	11, 8, 4	11, 8, 4
)	011 100	0101 1101	0100 1001	12, 8, 4	11, 8, 5
-	100 000	0110 0000	0100 1101	11	11
/	110 001	0110 0001	0100 1111	0, 1	0, 1
,	111 011	0110 1011	0100 1111	0, 8, 3	0, 8, 3
'	001 100	0111 1101	0100 0111	4, 8	8, 5
=	001 011	0111 1110	0101 1101	3, 8	8, 6
A	010 001	1100 0001	1010 0001	12, 1	12, 1
B	010 010	1100 0010	1010 0010	12, 2	12, 2
C	010 011	1100 0011	1010 0011	12, 3	12, 3
D	010 100	1100 0100	1010 0100	12, 4	12, 4
E	010 101	1100 0101	1010 0101	12, 5	12, 5
F	010 110	1100 0110	1010 0110	12, 6	12, 6
G	010 111	1100 0111	1010 0111	12, 7	12, 7
H	011 000	1100 1000	1010 1000	12, 8	12, 8
I	011 001	1100 1001	1010 1001	12, 9	12, 9
J	100 001	1101 0001	1010 1010	11, 1	11, 1
K	100 010	1101 0010	1010 1011	11, 2	11, 2
L	100 011	1101 0011	1010 1100	11, 3	11, 3
M	100 100	1101 0100	1010 1101	11, 4	11, 4
N	100 101	1101 0101	1010 1110	11, 5	11, 5
O	100 110	1101 0110	1010 1111	11, 6	11, 6
P	100 111	1101 0111	1011 0000	11, 7	11, 7
Q	101 000	1101 1000	1011 0001	11, 8	11, 8
R	101 001	1101 1001	1011 0010	11, 9	11, 9
S	110 010	1110 0010	1011 0011	0, 2	0, 2
T	110 011	1110 0011	1011 0100	0, 3	0, 3
U	110 100	1110 0100	1011 0101	0, 4	0, 4
V	110 101	1110 0101	1011 0110	0, 5	0, 5
W	110 110	1110 0110	1011 0111	0, 6	0, 6

Character	BCD code	EBCDIC Code	ASCII Code	BCD Cards	EBCDIC Cards
X	110 111	1110 0111	1011 1000	0, 7	0, 7
Y	111 000	1110 1000	1011 1001	0, 8	0, 8
Z	111 001	1110 1001	1011 1010	0, 9	0, 9
0	000 000	1111 0000	0101 0000	0	0
1	000 001	1111 0001	0101 0001	1	1
2	000 010	1111 0010	0101 0010	2	2
3	000 011	1111 0011	0101 0011	3	3
4	000 100	1111 0100	0101 0100	4	4
5	000 101	1111 0101	0101 0101	5	5
6	000 110	1111 0110	0101 0110	6	6
7	000 111	1111 0111	0101 0111	7	7
8	001 000	1111 1000	0101 1000	8	8
9	001 001	1111 1001	0101 1001	9	9

*Courtesy of Professor C. V. Gear.

Chapter 5

Semiotics: Syntax, Semantics and Pragmatics

Programming is the communication of an algorithmic process to a computer. The computer is "instructed" in detail as to the sequence of steps it is to carry out to solve the problem under consideration and the specific form in which the results are to be presented. Hence, we want our programming language to be clear and capable of efficiently stating the computational plan.

We know that all algorithmic processes can be represented symbolically. Further, the computer is often best understood as a symbol-processing device. The input to the computer is a sequence of symbols, perhaps in the form of holes in a punched card, or in magnetized areas of a surface of tape or disk, or in a string of electrical impulses from a typewriter keyboard. The symbols are used in the computer according to rules built into the machine to generate a new set of symbols that are used as output, again embodied in some physical form, possibly magnetized areas, or printed characters. Accordingly, the notion of symbol manipulation is central to computer science.

Semiotics, or the science of symbols, may be subdivided into three areas:
   Syntax—the grammar, or set of rules, that define the acceptable strings of symbols ("good sentences"), and their grammatical structure.
   Semantics—the "meaning" of a string of symbols—possibly its relationship to other strings of symbols or actions of the symbol interpreter.
   Pragmatics—the practical and psychological part of the symbol communication and computation system.

Syntax describes the organization of sentences. Most of the familiar grammatical terminology (such as "noun," "verb," "adverb") is syntactic. According to the syntax of English, some sentences are well formed (e.g., *I gave the book to John*), while others are not (e.g., *The book I John gave to*). Semantics is concerned with the meaning of sentences and the fact that the sentences *I gave the book to John* and *John was given the book by me* are equivalent statements. Semantics is also concerned with the ambiguities in the meaning of words or sentences. The sentence "I speak to Bill about the book on the train" can either mean (1) that the book was about a train or (2) that my conversation took place on the train. Pragmatics deals with the efficiency of the symbol communication process. Scientific, professional, or technical writing may be poor communication for the nonspecialist, but is often most quickly perceived by its intended audience.

In computer science, our concern with syntax is to insure precise descriptions of the language i.e., sets of symbol strings —that we use to communicate with the computer. A precise syntax facilitates the computer's interpretation of our symbol strings and is almost universally required by the processors. Clear semantics states exactly how the computer is interpreting a given string of symbols, or program, and that the effect of the program is, indeed, as intended. The description of the pragmatics of a computer language allows an assessment of relative efficiency of different symbol strings (which are semantically equivalent).

The state of knowledge of the semiotics of computer language is rather non-uniform. Much is known in methods of syntax description, and a quasi-standard method is established which we describe below. Semantics is currently an active area of research with several different methods being used, so we indicate only briefly some semantic considerations. Pragmatics is virtually a virgin area of computer semiotics, but there is increasing theoretical interest in efficiency (or complexity) of computation.

The status of the formal descriptive machinery in each of the semiotic areas is closely related to our knowledge about the area. Syntax is well-described and mechanized. Semantics is often poorly described—or stated in ambiguous natural language. Pragmatics is mostly ignored.

5.1   A Summary of Important Concepts

A.   Introduction

Concern with semiotics and its central role in computer science arises from a number of motivations:

Precision in the use of language has often been noted as one of the characteristics of person-machine communication. A program of instruction is executed faithfully to the smallest detail—and sometimes yields results that are surprising to the programmer. Subsequent detailed analysis usually shows that the computer was doing exactly what it had been told—not what the programmer may have intended to tell it. The exact use of language is obviously important for most scientific and numerical computation. Equally significant is the fact that careful use of language can sharpen the logic of our thinking, helping us to avoid imprecise concepts, or inconsistent arguments, when we want to be precisely accurate.

Fortunately, modern developments in logic and linguistics have provided us with descriptive tools that enable us to analyze our computer languages, although the linguistic methods are not yet adequate to describe a *natural* language like English. We can describe concisely the exact syntax of a language and know whether a statement or sequence of statements is grammatically acceptable to the computer. We also can describe the precise effect that a statement will have in the computation and avoid any ambiguity.

In the brief history of computers, programming languages have evolved from sequences of machine instructions, through symbolic assembly languages, to procedural languages. The procedural languages, often called ''higher-level'' languages, are much more readable and more easily understood than machine languages—especially when used in well-organized programs. The procedural languages—such as BASIC, FORTRAN, PL/1—are generally translated or compiled into the language of the machine by a program called a *compiler*. The development of computers and their language processors has been and remains a major concern of computer scientists.

In summary, the concern with the semiotic aspects and their development is three-fold. A clear understanding of syntax and semantics enables us to compute what we intend. A good representation of syntax and semantics allows communication among computer scientists and other computer users. An algorithmic description of the semiotics of a language is essential in the development of programs to process the language.

B. Syntax

A simplified discussion of syntax is presented in this section. A more detailed discussion is contained in section 5.2. The objectives of this section are to illustrate how a simple grammatical description is read, to show how the analysis of a statement in the language can be represented graphically, and, finally, to explain how the graphic representation can be used to check grammaticality.

The grammar in Table 5.1 shows the syntax of an arithmetic statement. The first line [⟨arithmetic-statement⟩ :: = ⟨variable⟩ = ⟨arithmetic-expression⟩;] define it to be a variable followed by an equal sign, followed by an arithmetic expression, followed by a semicolon. Items in angular brackets are names of syntactic items, the composite symbol ":: =" is read "as defined to be," and the other symbols denote themselves. The second line [⟨arithmetic-expression⟩ :: = (⟨arithmetic-expression⟩ ⟨binary operator⟩ ⟨arithmetic-expression⟩) | ⟨variable⟩] says that an arithmetic expression is defined to be an open parenthesis followed by an arithmetic expression, followed by a binary operator, followed by an arithmetic expression, followed by a closing parenthesis, or an arithmetic expression is a variable. The only new features in the definition are the use of "|" to separate alternate definitions and the apparent circularity of the first definition. The third line [⟨variable⟩ :: = a | a⟨variable⟩] also has this apparent circularity, but in neither case does it cause any insurmountable difficulty. The first part of the third line says that "a" is a variable and is the first definition of ⟨variable⟩. The remainder of the third line says that an "a" followed by a ⟨variable⟩ is a ⟨variable⟩. Hence, "aa" is a ⟨variable⟩. Now since "aa" is a variable we can use the second definition again to find that "aaa" is a variable. Repeating this process as often as we wish, we find that any string of 1 or more a's is an acceptable variable.

⟨arithmetic-statement⟩ :: = ⟨variable⟩ = ⟨arithmetic-expression⟩;
⟨arithmetic-expression⟩ :: = (⟨arithmetic-expression⟩ ⟨binary operator⟩
⟨arithmetic-expression⟩) | ⟨variable⟩
⟨variable⟩ :: = a | a ⟨variable⟩
⟨binary operator⟩ :: = + | − | × | ÷

Table 5.1: Syntax of ⟨arithmetic-statement⟩

A graphic representation of the syntax of a string of a symbols is called a *derivation tree.* A derivation tree starts with a single node labelled with the name of a syntactic class. Below each node in the graph are a sequence of nodes labelled with the components of one of its definitions. The nodes of the tree having no descendants are, from left to right, labelled with the symbols of the string. In Figure 5.1 the derivation tree of the arithmetic assignment statement "$a = (aa \times a);$" is given, in accordance with the grammar of Table 5.1.

The form of rule used in the grammar of Table 5.1 is called *Backus Naur Form* or BNF. If the grammar is presented in the form of a set of BNF statements, as shown in Table 5.1, then a sentence is grammatical just in case it has a derivation tree. For example, a common error in PL/1 (which has a similar grammar for assignments) is to omit a closing semicolon on an arithmetic statement. If a closing semicolon is not given, there is no way to construct a derivation. Another common error is to omit a parenthesis, especially if there is a string of several parentheses. Again, an attempt to construct a derivation tree will fail.

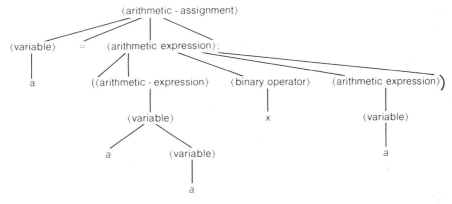

Figure 5.1:   Derivation tree of "$a = (aa \times a);$"

C.   Semantics

Section 5.4 elaborates on this simplified discussion of semantics. In semantics we are concerned with the meanings and possible misinterpretations of programs.

Consider the arithmetic assignment statement:

$$x = A + B \times C \uparrow D - E - F$$

where $\uparrow$ denotes exponentiation.

Given values of the variables A to F, there are many different possible values computed on the right-hand side of this assignment statement. The ambiguity of the right-hand side is due to several sources. The sequence of operations implemented in the compiler is not necessarily the conventional sequence. One possibility is $A + (B + C^{(D - (E - F))})$ a strictly right-to-left evaluation as APL. Another is $(A + (B \times (C^D)) - E) - F$, which is FORTRAN.

Even if the order in which the operations are performed is understood, there is a possible misinterpretation from the fact that computer arithmetic is not exactly the usual arithmetic. Problems, known as *overflow,* arise when intermediate results are larger than the maximum allowable value. For example, in computing the value of $A + B - C$ the addition of A and B may cause overflow and an error, whereas if the subtraction is performed first an overflow might not occur.

While semantic considerations are important, they are often ignored in introductory treatments because the semantics of most programming languages are close enough to the conventional meanings so that the casual computer user is often fortunate enough to avoid semantic problems. Also, there is less uniformity in the discussion of semantic problems, some of the approaches being covered in section 5.4. Finally, the technical concepts required for a complete discussion of semantics are more difficult and are beyond the beginning student.

D. Pragmatics

In pragmatics, we are concerned with the costs of computation in human and mechanical resources. Since mechanical resource costs are easier to estimate, most work in pragmatics has been concentrated on this aspect.

Two basic methods of evaluating the costs of computation are:

(1) instruction mixes—estimates of the running time of programs based on the speed of execution of a standard set of instructions;

(2) benchmark—a standard problem used to measure the speed of a computer system.

Often some combination of both methods is used to compare different systems.

Theoretical approaches to pragmatics include analysis of the fastest algorithms to solve problems, and development of compilers that can optimize the object program for a given source program.

5.2   Syntax

Overview

The earliest electronic computers were programmed using what, in retrospect, can be seen to be very primitive methods. Programs were difficult to write and analyze. Programs written for one computer had to be rewritten in order to be used on a different computer. It was soon realized that with the expanded use of computers, there was a need for machine-independent programming. The solution was to be found in the use of a language for describing algorithms that could then be used on many different computers.

Indeed, today there are many such algorithmic, or procedure-oriented, languages—FORTRAN, COBOL, ALGOL, PL/I, to mention only a few.

The evolution of machine-independent programming led directly to a concern with their precise specification. In order to use the language as a common medium, different users must know exactly what the language is. Further, it is also important that the machine-independent algorithmic language be mechanically translated into the language of each machine on which it will be used. Here, again, a detailed description of the language is needed.

The techniques for language description have, therefore, received a great deal of attention from computer scientists. Quite naturally, computer scientists often find themselves preoccupied with descriptions of the objects they design and use. The descriptive technique becomes a goal in itself, capturing the attention and imagination of the scientist. One of the primary objectives of exploring new descriptive techniques is the establishment of more creative thought patterns. Consider, for instance, the distinction between the Arabic and Roman descriptions of numbers. The Arabic system permits a precise and concise statement of arithmetic problems so that decimal arithmetic is easily mastered by almost everyone. Much of what has baffled laymen as well as scientists about computers has been caused by inadequate descriptive techniques. The novice is often advised to learn computer science by apprenticeship, which is an admission by the trained scientist that he cannot describe what he is doing.

Out of the concern for precise descriptive techniques, grammars for computer languages have developed. The grammar is the set of rules of syntax. These rules of syntax state what constitutes a sentence in the language. The syntax of a computer language is likely to be a very recent development, the product of a conscious design effort, and is comparatively simple. (Some of the design process may be even left to the user of the language in what are known as *extensible languages*.)

Once the need for a grammar was established, computer scientists began to develop a precise and concise descriptive technique for syntax. A committee was formed in the late 1950s to design an algorithmic language for computer scientists. The language proposed in the report of that committee, known as the "ALGOL 60 Report," served to introduce computer scientists to precise syntactic description. The ALGOL 60 committee borrowed and reformulated a descriptive technique used in linguistics. The syntax descriptions of ALGOL 60 became known as the Backus-Naur form (BNF). (John Backus and Peter Naur were both members of the ALGOL 60 committee.)

The rules of syntax in BNF satisfy our intuitive requirements. First, they are precise, while at the same time being concise enough to describe a programming language in several pages. Second, efficient algorithms are known for the syntactic analysis of the programs. This syntactic analysis, which is performed as a prelude to translation (or, as it is more commonly called in computer usage, compiling), determines whether a program is grammatically correct. The program that performs the analysis and translation is called a *compiler*. If the program is not grammatically correct, the compiler often pinpoints the difficulty and suggests possible corrections.

Description of BNF

BNF is a language-describing language. A set of BNF rules provide the specification of a programming language. The programming language specified is called the object language (not to be confused with object program in chapter 3), while the BNF is called the *metalanguage*. A metalanguage is a language used to describe another language.

The sentences of the object language, *L,* are constructed from a finite set of symbols, called the alphabet of the object language, $A(L)$. $A(L)$ depends on the characters available in type fonts and is often restricted to forty-eight or sixty symbols, probably resulting from an accident in printer design. In addition to the set of symbols, $A(L)$, syntactic category names can be defined in BNF. The syntactic category names are called *metalinguistic variables* and they, together with $A(L)$ and a few special symbols in the metalanguage (metasymbols), form the alphabet from which sentences in BNF are constructed.

Each rule of the BNF metalanguage is composed of three parts:

(1) The grammatical class being defined.

(2) A set of one or more definitions.

(3) The metasymbol : : = (reads "is defined as"), which separates the class being defined from the definition.

The grammatical class being defined is a metalinguistic variable name enclosed between two metasymbols ⟨ ⟩, called pointed brackets, such as; ⟨mailing address⟩. The pointed brackets signify that in the metalanguage ⟨mailing address⟩ is a single symbol. Such a metalinguistic variable is often called a *grammatical class name,* and a typical BNF specification of a programming language will have on the order of one hundred such class names; for example, ⟨arithmetic expression⟩, ⟨arithmetic term⟩, ⟨label⟩.

The definition may assume a variety of forms combining metalinguistic variables, metasymbols, and symbols from $A(L)$, the object language alphabet. The only operations that can be used to form definitions are concatenation (linking), and choice of alternatives. The concatenation of metalinguistic variables is shown in the following BNF rule:

$$\langle \text{mailing address} \rangle ::= \langle \text{line 1} \rangle \langle \text{line 2} \rangle \langle \text{line 3} \rangle$$

This rule says that a syntactic element of type ⟨mailing address⟩ may be formed by concatenating an element of type ⟨line 1⟩, an element of type ⟨line 2⟩, and an element of type ⟨line 3⟩. Similarly, we could have another rule:

$$\langle \text{line 3} \rangle ::= \langle \text{city} \rangle \langle \text{state} \rangle \langle \text{zip code} \rangle$$

which is read, informally, "line 3 is defined as a city followed by a state followed by a zip code." (You may note the similarity of these constructs to the grammatical rule for simple declarative sentences—a simple declarative sentence consists of a noun phrase and a verb phrase, of which an example is:

The blue boy,   runs quickly.

noun phrase   verb phrase

Since valid sentences in L are formed only from linking atomic symbols of $A(L)$, all syntactic types must eventually be defined in terms of these atomic symbols. This requirement is met by allowing the definition to incorporate object language symbols at any point. The object language symbols are *not* enclosed in pointed brackets, and the absence of pointed brackets means that they are to be taken as object language symbols. Thus, if the set of rules includes

$$\langle \text{state} \rangle ::= \text{DELAWARE}$$

then the above rule for $\langle \text{line 3} \rangle$ might be rewritten as

$$\langle \text{line 3} \rangle ::= \langle \text{city} \rangle \text{ DELAWARE } \langle \text{zip code} \rangle$$

Of course, if the syntactic type $\langle \text{state} \rangle$ contains only one element, it might as well be omitted, since whenever it is needed the object language form could be used. We know, in fact, that state could contain as many as 50 elements (or 51 if 'D.C.' is put into the syntactic class $\langle \text{state} \rangle$). The metalanguage provides for definitions that allow any one of an unlimited number of alternative options. The metasymbol | (read "or") is used for this purpose. For example,

$$\langle \text{state} \rangle ::= \text{NEW YORK} \mid \text{DELAWARE} \mid \text{VIRGINIA} \mid \ldots$$

This rule says that each of the object forms NEW YORK, DELAWARE, etc. is an element of the class state. Note that in writing alternatives in a BNF grammar, the order of the alternatives does not affect what is being specified.

A powerful feature of BNF is its use of recursive definitions. It allows a grammar of fixed size to specify a language in which there is no maximum limit on sentence size. We know that this possibility of unbounded sentence size is a feature of natural language where additional modifiers or clauses may be added to increase sentence size. It is also reasonable to expect this feature in programming languages where there is no limit to the possible size of arithmetic expressions.

A *recursive rule* is one in which the grammatical class being defined appears as a part of the definition. Such a recursive rule must always provide an "escape" if the rule is not to be circular and yield no object language string. For example, $\langle \text{binary number} \rangle ::= \langle \text{binary number} \rangle \, 0 \mid \langle \text{binary number} \rangle \, 1 \mid 1$. The escape is that alternative which allows us to select the object character as a $\langle \text{binary number} \rangle$.

Returning to our BNF description of ⟨mailing address⟩ we can add the following rule:

⟨directory⟩ : : = ⟨mailing address⟩ | ⟨mailing address⟩, ⟨directory⟩

According to this rule a ⟨directory⟩ is 1 or more mailing addresses, separated by commas.

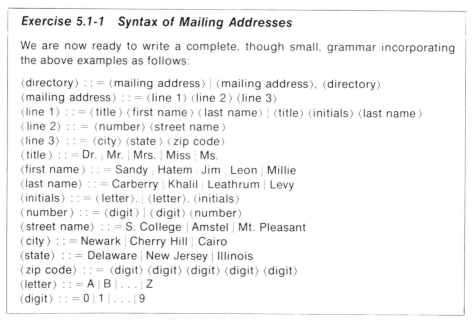

Exercise 5.1-1   *Syntax of Mailing Addresses*

We are now ready to write a complete, though small, grammar incorporating the above examples as follows:

⟨directory⟩ : : = ⟨mailing address⟩ | ⟨mailing address⟩, ⟨directory⟩
⟨mailing address⟩ : : = ⟨line 1⟩ ⟨line 2⟩ ⟨line 3⟩
⟨line 1⟩ : : = ⟨title⟩ ⟨first name⟩ ⟨last name⟩ | ⟨title⟩ ⟨initials⟩ ⟨last name⟩
⟨line 2⟩ : : = ⟨number⟩ ⟨street name⟩
⟨line 3⟩ : : = ⟨city⟩ ⟨state⟩ ⟨zip code⟩
⟨title⟩ : : = Dr. | Mr. | Mrs. | Miss | Ms.
⟨first name⟩ : : = Sandy | Hatem | Jim | Leon | Millie
⟨last name⟩ : : = Carberry | Khalil | Leathrum | Levy
⟨initials⟩ : : = ⟨letter⟩. | ⟨letter⟩. ⟨initials⟩
⟨number⟩ : : = ⟨digit⟩ | ⟨digit⟩ ⟨number⟩
⟨street name⟩ : : = S. College | Amstel | Mt. Pleasant
⟨city⟩ : : = Newark | Cherry Hill | Cairo
⟨state⟩ : : = Delaware | New Jersey | Illinois
⟨zip code⟩ : : = ⟨digit⟩ ⟨digit⟩ ⟨digit⟩ ⟨digit⟩ ⟨digit⟩
⟨letter⟩ : : = A | B | . . . | Z
⟨digit⟩ : : = 0 | 1 | . . . | 9

Although a more elaborate BNF description of a mailing directory could easily be written, we can already generate arbitrarily long mailing lists with this grammar. Notice that only the syntactive structure of the string is described so that the address:

Ms. Jim Khalil
123246325849 Amstel
Cairo, New Jersey 00000

is a perfectly valid ⟨mailing address⟩ syntactically even though it contains obvious semantic errors. For instance, it is structurally correct to select any first name to follow the title Mr., although semantically the choice of Mr. predetermines that the first name to follow must be male. (Chomsky has used the sentence "Colorless green ideas sleep furiously." as an example of a grammatically correct, but meaningless, sentence; i.e., one which is syntactically correct but semantically meaningless.)

Later we describe in detail how to generate and diagram sentences in a methodical manner from a given BNF specification.

In addition to the special notation of BNF used in Exercise 5.1-1, we may also identify the following major parts of such a description:

(1) A set of rules.

(2) A set of metalinguistic variables or nonterminal symbols, denoting grammatical classes.

(3) A distinguished grammatical class called the *root.* In our example ⟨directory⟩ is the root. In a programming language specification it might be a variable called ⟨program⟩ that would serve as the root.

(4) A set of *terminal symbols.* The terminal symbols are the object language alphabet $A(L)$.

The four items above provide an elementary notion of what is meant by syntax, or grammar, G. According to such a syntax description, certain strings of object language symbols will be grammatically correct. The set of such strings is often called the language, $L(G)$, defined by the grammar, when syntactic considerations are foremost.

It is sometimes convenient to add some notations to BNF to facilitate writing grammars, and we shall use the following:

(1) A pair of metalinguistic brackets {,}.

(2) $\{⟨x⟩\}j/i$ to mean not less than i, nor more than j occurrences of ⟨x⟩.

Example: $\{a|b\}3/2 =$ aa, ab, ba, bb, aaa, aab, aba, abb, baa, bab, bba, bbb

(3) $\{⟨x⟩\}^*$ to mean any finite number (including possibly 0) occurrences of x.

Generative process

In this section we consider the use of a BNF grammar, G, in generating grammatical sentences in its language, $L(G)$. In the next section, the dual problem of checking a sentence to see if it is in $L(G)$ will be taken up.

The *generative process* consists of the formation of a finite sequence of metalinguistic sentences leading to a sentence in the object language. This sequence is called a *derivation sequence.* The first sentence in the sequence consists solely of the root. The next sentence is an alternative in the definition of a rule whose lefthand part is the root. For example, if the root is ⟨x⟩ and there is a rule

$$⟨x⟩ ::= ⟨y⟩ \ ⟨z⟩ \ | \ a \ ⟨x⟩ \ b \ | \ c$$

then there are three possible beginnings of derivation sequences:

$$⟨x⟩, ⟨y⟩ \ ⟨z⟩$$
$$⟨x⟩, a \ ⟨x⟩ \ b$$
$$⟨x⟩, c$$

where the last of these is a complete derivation.

Assuming that we have the beginning of a derivation sequence, the sequence may be extended as follows. Select any metalinguistic variables in the last sentence of the partial derivation, and insert in its place any alternative of a definition of a rule whose lefthand part is the variable being replaced. Add the newly formed sentence to the partial derivation sequence. This generative process is repeated until the most recently formed member of the sequence contains only terminal symbols and constitutes a valid string in the language. Of course, if the grammar is incomplete it may never be possible to obtain a terminal sentence, but it is always possible to find a new BNF grammar giving the same language as the original BNF grammar without ever leading to blocked derivation sequences.

As an example, consider the following sample grammar:

$$\langle expr \rangle ::= \langle term \rangle \mid \langle expr \rangle + \langle term \rangle$$
$$\langle term \rangle ::= \langle primary \rangle \mid \langle term \rangle \times \langle primary \rangle$$
$$\langle primary \rangle ::= u \mid v \mid w$$

The root of this grammar is $\langle expr \rangle$. Its nonterminal symbols are: $\langle expr \rangle$, $\langle term \rangle$ and, $\langle primary \rangle$. Its terminal symbols are $u, v, w, +,$ and $\times$.

Here are two derivation sequences using this grammar:

(a) $\langle expr \rangle$
  $\langle term \rangle$
  $\langle term \rangle \times \langle primary \rangle$
  $\langle primary \rangle \times \langle primary \rangle$
  $u \times \langle primary \rangle$
  $u \times v$

(b) $\langle expr \rangle$
  $\langle expr \rangle + \langle term \rangle$
  $\langle expr \rangle + \langle term \rangle \times \langle primary \rangle$
  $\langle expr \rangle + \langle term \rangle \times w$
  $\langle term \rangle + \langle term \rangle \times w$
  $\langle term \rangle \times \langle primary \rangle + \langle term \rangle \times w$
  $\langle primary \rangle \times \langle primary \rangle + \langle term \rangle \times w$
  $u \times \langle primary \rangle + \langle term \rangle \times w$
  $u \times v + \langle term \rangle \times w$
  $u \times v + \langle primary \rangle \times w$
  $u \times v + w \times w$

This method of describing derivation sequences has the advantage of simplicity in that exactly one metalinguistic variable is replaced in each new sentence in the derivation. The disadvantage is that it requires a great deal of writing. An improved system is obtained by simultaneously replacing all variables in each rewriting, each variable being replaced by an appropriate alternative of some definition.

We can diagram this process in what is known as a *derivation tree*. In Figure 5.2 we show the derivation trees of the two derivations given above.

Each tree is a structural description of a generated sentence. Each node in the tree is directly connected to the string of symbols that replace it in the

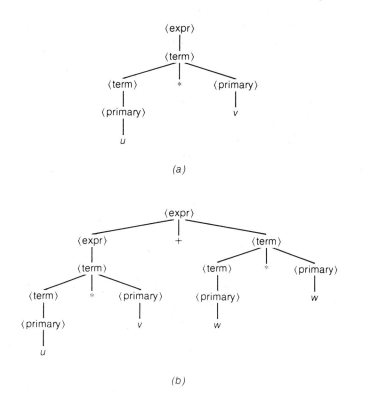

(a)

(b)

Figure 5.2: Derivation Trees

derivation. The topmost node is called the *root* of the tree, and the object language symbols +, ×, *u, v, w* are the *leaves* of the tree. This structural description in tree form is known as a *parse tree,* or derivation tree. When a sentence is being constructed, or derived, the tree is usually called a derivation tree. When a given sentence is being analyzed, or parsed, it is a parse tree. However, the terms are synonymous. A similar linguistic parse tree is shown in Figure 5.3.

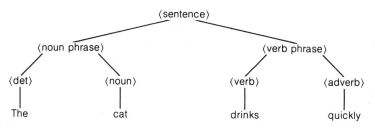

Figure 5.3: A Parse Tree

The notion of parsing and the parse tree of a legal string leads naturally to the notion of *ambiguity.* Grammatical, or syntactic, ambiguity arises when there is a legal string in language that has more than one parse tree in the grammar. Ambiguity can lead to possible alternative meanings, as demonstrated by Chomsky's well-known example:

Time flies like an arrow.

which can mean either
(a) You should time the (fruit?) flies as you would time an arrow.
or
(b) Time passes very quickly.
or
(c) A new breed of flies, time flies, like the taste of an arrow.

5.3 *The Recognition Process*

A. Syntax—Directed Analysis

A *syntax-directed analyzer* is a procedure that can construct the parse tree (or set of parse trees in the case of an ambiguous grammar) for a sentence. The inputs to the syntax-directed analyzer are the sentence to be parsed and a description of the grammar. The analyzer starts with the root of the grammar and attempts to derive the given sentence, keeping a record of what steps it has taken. When the sentence has been successfully derived, the record of steps used is a description of the derivation tree.

There are a variety of procedures that can be used for syntax-directed analysis. Some are more efficient but impose restrictions on the grammar. We describe a simple type of analyzer, of the type known as *top-down*. Top here refers to the root of the tree, and the process may be visualized as an attempt to construct the tree from top to bottom, and left to right.

Starting with the root, generate a sequence of metalinguistic sentences. We attempt at each step to replace the first variable in the current metalinguistic sentence with the first alternative in its definition. If the string of object symbols preceding the first variable in the newly formed sentence is a prefix of the sentence we are trying to parse, we continue. (One string of symbols is A is a prefix of B if A matches the initial part of B symbol-by-symbol, and A is no longer than B.) If the leading string of object symbols is not a prefix of the sentence to be parsed, try to replace the variable with the next alternative. As long as there are more alternatives to be tried, we move to the next alternative. If we run out of alternatives for the current variable, then we must back up to the previous metalinguistic sentence and try the next alternative in replacing its first variable. It may be necessary to back up many sentences, and for a poorly behaved grammar this top-down procedure is not efficient, even when it works.

As an example, using the following simple grammar:

$$\langle z \rangle ::= \langle c \rangle \times \langle c \rangle$$
$$\langle c \rangle ::= a \mid b$$

Let $a \times b$ be the sentence to be parsed. The initial sentence is the nonterminal $\langle z \rangle$, the root of the grammar. We replace $\langle z \rangle$ with $\langle c \rangle \times \langle c \rangle$ and this, in turn, by $a \times \langle c \rangle$. $a \times \langle c \rangle$ is then replaced by $a \times a$, but since $a \times a$ is not a prefix of $a \times b$, we try the second alternative for $\langle c \rangle$ and obtain $a \times b$. This matches the input string so we have succeeded.

We can summarize in table form the sequence of computations used by this top-down syntax directed analyzer. In the left hand column we show the current metalinguistic sentence. In the right hand column, the list of alternatives

most recent sentence	alternatives list
$\langle z \rangle$	1
$\langle c \rangle \times \langle c \rangle$	11
$a \times \langle c \rangle$	111
$a \times a$	112
$a \times b$	

chosen, the alternatives being numbered from left-to-right. Thus, in the third row, 111 indicates that in each possible alternative the first was chosen in each case. In the fourth row, 112 indicates that, in the first two cases, the first alternative was chosen, while in the third case, the second alternative was chosen. Using the final list of alternatives that successfully parse the sentence it is easy to construct the parse tree top-down since we know that the root must be $\langle z \rangle$.

Using the tabular form of description, we can illustrate the computation of the top-down parse of $w + u \times u$ using the grammar:

$$\langle expr \rangle ::= \langle term \rangle \mid \langle term \rangle + \langle expr \rangle$$
$$\langle term \rangle ::= \langle primary \rangle \mid \langle primary \rangle \times \langle term \rangle$$
$$\langle primary \rangle ::= u \mid v \mid w$$

most recent sentence	alternatives list
$\langle expr \rangle$	1
$\langle term \rangle$	11
$\langle primary \rangle$	111
u	112
v	113
w	12
$\langle primary \rangle \times \langle term \rangle$	121
$u \times \langle term \rangle$	122
$v \times \langle term \rangle$	123
$w \times \langle term \rangle$	2
$\langle term \rangle + \langle expr \rangle$	21
$\langle primary \rangle + \langle expr \rangle$	211
$u + \langle expr \rangle$	212

most recent sentence	alternatives list
$v + \langle expr \rangle$	213
$w + \langle expr \rangle$	2131
$w + \langle term \rangle$	21311
$w + \langle primary \rangle$	213111
$w + u$	213112
$w + v$	213113
$w + w$	21312
$w + \langle primary \rangle \times \langle term \rangle$	213121
$w + u \times \langle term \rangle$	2131211
$w + + u \times \langle primary \rangle$	21312111
$w + u \times u$	

This systematic exploration process used to generate a top-down parse is a special case of *backtrack programming.* Backtrack programming is a way of making a set of sequential choices systematically to satisfy the constraint of a problem. Whenever a constraint is violated, the process tries other alternatives. If no new alternative removes the violation of the constraint, then previous choices are revised, starting with the most recently made choice.

B. Recognizers and Parsers

Imagine that the syntax of a language has been described using a BNF grammar. In processing the language, the syntax provides the basis for determining whether a sentence is legal or not. Two questions about any candidate string are:

(1) Recognition—Is the string of symbols grammatically correct?

(2) Parsing—Given that the string is grammatically correct, what is its syntactic structure, or set of possible structures?

Since a successful parse implies a recognition of the string, it can be seen that parsing cannot be easier than recognition. In fact, recognition is often much easier if you do not need the grammatical structure.

Consider the grammar:

$$\langle x \rangle ::= a \langle x \rangle \mid \langle x \rangle b \mid a \langle x \rangle b \mid b$$

Recognition of sentences in the language generated by this grammar is easy if you observe that every sentence in this language consists of 0 or more a's, followed by 1 or more b's, and that every sentence of this form is in the language. A recognizer is flowcharted in Figure 5.4.

The role of the BNF description of the syntax of a language and its recognition or parsing varies from designer to designer. A few of the possibilities are:

(1) The BNF may not be used except as a documentation and instructional device.

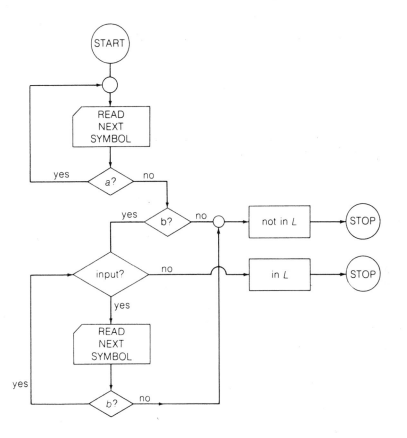

Figure 5.4: A simple recognizer

(2) The BNF may be used as a syntax directed recognizer as described in the previous section.

(3) The BNF may be used as a guide to the systematic design of the recognizer or parser.

(4) The BNF description may be viewed as a description of the recognition parsing algorithm where the following analogies are employed:

BNF	Programming Control Mechanism
$\langle\ \rangle$	Procedure call
end of rule	Return from a procedure
|	Parallel control
$::=$	Procedure definition

We can use this programming interpretation of BNF together with the following symbolic conventions:

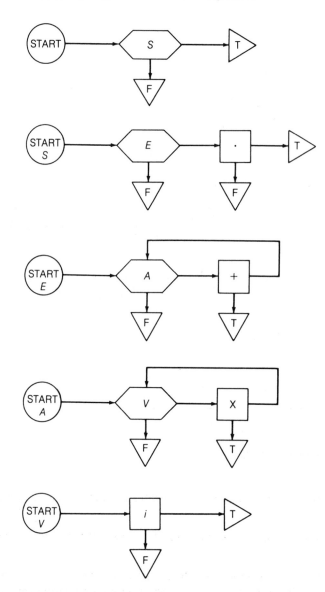

Figure 5.5: *A recognizer for* ⟨S⟩

(1) *Prediction:*   Pass control to the EXPRESSION algorithm. Upon returning, take the T or F branch depending on whether
the value returned is T or F, i.e., if the expression algorithm succeeds or fails.

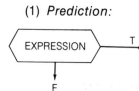

(2) *Scan:*   Compare the next symbol with the terminal symbol *A*. If it matches, take the branch marked T; otherwise take the branch marked F.

(3) *Complete:*   Return to the place where this part of the algorithm was initiated. Let *X* be the value returned.

(4) START: Begin the algorithmic recognition of a syntactic class.

Consider a recognizer for the following grammar:

$$\langle S \rangle ::= \langle E \rangle .$$
$$\langle E \rangle ::= \langle A \rangle \mid \langle A \rangle + \langle E \rangle$$
$$\langle A \rangle ::= \langle V \rangle \mid \langle V \rangle \times \langle A \rangle$$
$$\langle V \rangle ::= i$$

In showing the program we have reduced the complexity of the flowchart

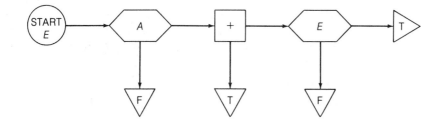

Figure 5.6: A recursive recognizer for $\langle E \rangle$

by replacing the procedure shown in Figure 5.6 by the more concise representation of Figure 5.5. However, a straightforward flowchart can always be drawn directly from the BNF form, since each alternative appears as a row consisting of a sequence of predictions and scans.

5.4   Semantics

A. Introduction

Semantics is the study of meaning. The meaning of a program is the relationship between the input data and the output data. So we can say that to define the semantics of a programming language, we must establish the relationship between input and output.

The semantic problem presents itself on several levels, just as the syntactic problem does. The user of the language must have a precise understanding of the effects of the programs to insure that the programs faithfully represent his intended computation. If the programming language is machine independent, then an algorithmic description of semantics may assure that the same program has the same meaning on different machines.

We start our discussion of semantics with several examples of semantic problems. Then, in the next section, we introduce some concepts that are important in understanding the semantics of computers. Finally, we conclude with a brief introduction to formal semantics and its relation to the correctness of programs.

B. Some Semantic Problems

(1) Transferability—The same program, when run on different machines with the same input data, should produce the same results. If the meaning of constructs in the language is not clear, then different designers will not produce compilers having the same effect.

An example of this was the IF . . . THEN . . . ELSE . . . statement in ALGOL 60. The meaning of "IF p THEN q ELSE R" is q* if p is true and R if p is false. The meaning of "IF p THEN q" is q if p is true, and "do-nothing" if p is false. The meaning of "IF p_1 THEN IF p_2 THEN q ELSE R" is either as the meaning of

$$\text{"IF } p_1 \text{ THEN (IF } p_2 \text{ THEN } q \text{) ELSE } R \text{"}$$

or the same as the meaning of

$$\text{"IF } p_1 \text{ THEN (IF } p_2 \text{ THEN } q \text{ ELSE } R \text{)"}$$

These two possible interpretations can be seen to be different when p_1 is false and p_2 is true. In the first interpretation, the value will be R, while the second interpretation will have a *null* value and no resulting action will occur. A similar difference in interpretations occurs when both p_1 and p_2 are false.

The difficulty that arises here is actually due to syntactic ambiguity. There are two parse trees for the statement! In implementing ALGOL 60, the syntactic ambiguity must be resolved in favor of one or the other forms. An arbitrary choice of meaning (i.e., semantics) is used to resolve the ambiguity. In transferring programs from one computer to another it is essential to know how this is accomplished.

(2) Understanding arithmetic expressions—There are many differences in the possible interpretation of arithmetic expressions, but we shall

---

*More precisely: the meaning of q.

choose only to compare the method of FORTRAN with that of APL. FORTRAN uses "normal" arithmetic conventions, so the value of $3 \times 4 + 5$ is 17. APL does all arithmetic strictly from right to left: $4 + 5$ is 9 and then 3×9 is 27.

(3) Contextual—In some languages the meaning of a symbol depends on on its location. In PL/I, an "$=$" immediately following a variable name at the beginning of a statement means "assign." Thus $X = 3$ means assign the value 3 to X. An "$=$" elsewhere in a statement is taken to be a logical comparison operator and is given the value 1 if the items compared are equal and the value 0 otherwise. Hence, the statement $X = Y = Z$ is interpreted; assign to X the value of $Y = Z$, 1 if the value of Y is the same as the value of Z, *and* 0 if their values are different.

(4) Interlingual—The same symbol in different languages has different meanings, while the same operation in different languages is often conveyed by different symbols. Again, the "$=$" sign in FORTRAN is an assignment operator only, in APL it is an equality comparison operator only, while in PL/I it is an assignment or a comparison operator depending on the context.

The assignment operator in FORTRAN is designated by "$=$". In APL the symbol for assignment is "$\leftarrow$". In ALGOL, assignment is denoted "$:=$".

(5) Storage mapping—Values of variables in a program being run are kept in locations in storage. The value, or meaning, of a variable is partly the quantity retained in memory. Depending on the size of memory storage location, the number of significant digits retained in different machines may not be the same. This will result in different answers being computed, particularly in cases where accuracy is critical, and rounding errors may have an effect.

When sets of variables are treated as a block, the arrangement of the data in memory is important. For example, in FORTRAN you may use a 2×2 array A, consisting of the four elements $A(1, 1)$, $A(2, 1)$, $A(1, 2)$, $A(2, 2)$. These four elements will be stored consecutively in memory. Suppose the two following statements appear as the only common statements in two different FORTRAN subroutines

COMMON A
COMMON B, C, D, E

They will cause B, C, D, E to have the values corresponding to consecutive elements of A. If different arrangements of the elements of A in storage are allowed, (e.g. $A(1, 1)$, $A(1, 2)$, $A(2, 1)$ and $A(2, 2)$ in one computer and $A(1, 1)$, $A(2, 1)$, $A(1, 2)$ and $A(2, 2)$ in another) the different implementations may not be assigning the same values.

(6) Storage initialization—On some computers, the convention is adopted that if a variable is used before being explicitly given a value, then its initial value is 0. This is not universally so, and in other compilers the

programmer must assign a value of "0." Otherwise, whatever happens to be in storage at the time memory locations are assigned will be the value of the variable. Clearly, a program assuming automatic initialization may give quite different answers if the program is used on a computer where initialization must be explicitly done.

(7) Type conversion—The value of a variable includes, among other things, its type. Two common types are REAL and INTEGER. Generally, a larger amount of storage is provided for REAL than for INTEGER so that the number of significant digits retained is larger in the case of REAL variables than it is for INTEGER variables. Now suppose that W and X are real variables and that Y and Z are integer variables. If we make the following sequence of assignments:

$$Y \leftarrow W$$
$$X \leftarrow Y$$
$$Z \leftarrow X$$

we may expect Z to have *approximately* the numerical value of W but we cannot safely assume *equality* of Y and Z or *equality* of W and X. In fact, in addition to the errors introduced by truncating or rounding fractional parts of numbers in type conversions, the maximum allowed size may differ. If so, the real numerical value of W may be larger than the maximum allowed integer value, and in that case we cannot even expect approximate numerical equality of W and Z after the given sequence of type conversion assignments.

(8) Scope—Particularly in long programs, it is desirable to be able to use a variable name without checking the entire program to see if the same name has been used elsewhere. The use of scopes provides the ability to use a name in a part of the program without affecting other uses of the same variable name. For example, in PL/I:

BEGIN;	1
DECLARE X, Y REAL;	2
$X = 10.0$;	3
$Y = 2 \times X$;	4
BEGIN;	5
DECLARE X INTEGER;	6
$X = 2 \times Y$;	7
END;	8
$Y = 3 \times X$;	9
END;	10

The occurrences of X in lines 2, 3, 4, 9 refer to the X that is declared to be a real variable in line 2. The occurrences of X in lines 6, 7 refer to the in-

teger variable declared in line 6. Y in line 7 refers to the variable Y declared in line 2 because there is no intervening declaration in the inner
block, lines 5-8. We say that the scope of real X is the outer block lines
1-4 and 9-10, while the scope of integer X is the inner block, lines 5-8.
Of course, the inner block could contain within it a block in which X
could again be declared real. This new declaration of X would create a
third variable, in addition to the two we now have.

(9) DO LOOP range—The iterative programming construct has been discussed in chapter 2. Consider the FORTRAN form of the iterative statement:

$$\text{DO } L \qquad I = J, K$$

L is a statement label showing the end of the loop, I is the loop variable,
J is to be its initial value on entering the loop (the increment has a default
value of 1 since it is unspecified here), and K is to be the final value. Consider the following program segment:

$$K = 0$$
$$\text{DO 10} \qquad I = 5, 8$$
$$K = K + I$$
$$\text{10 CONTINUE}$$
$$\text{11 } \ldots$$

What are the values of K and I when line 11 is reached via the DO LOOP?
In particular, suppose we replace the DO statement with DO 10 $I = 5, 5$,
what will happen?

We can describe the sentences of the statement precisely by showing the
equivalent flowchart for DO L $I = J, K$. Using the flowchart, we can see
that with the DO statement DO 10 $I = 5, 8$, the values of I and K at line 11
will be 9 and 26, respectively. With the DO statement DO 10 $I = 5, 5$, the
values of I, K will be 6 and 5, respectively.

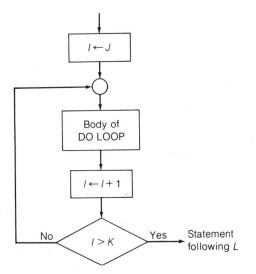

Figure 5.7: **Semantics of the FORTRAN DO LOOP**

In our brief introduction to semantic problems, we have emphasized the types of problems that even the novice programmer is likely to encounter. In the area of semantics it is well to keep in mind the following corollary to Murphy's Law: If a programming construct can be misunderstood, it will be.

C. Semantic Concepts.

Ultimately, in the study of any language, you must understand the subtleties of meaning or semantics of the language. Computer languages are no exception in this regard. The meaning associated with a computer language is closely related to the structure of the underlying computing machine and the nature of the translation from the user language to machine language.

In discussing semantics, we will first define a few very basic ideas and then use these ideas in describing more subtle semantic features of programming languages.

Consider the following definitions:

Environment: The totality of information available to an algorithm.

Reference: Given a symbol and an environment, find the value of the symbol in the context of the environment.

Assign: Associate a new value with a symbol in an environment.

Symbol: A visible sign of something invisible.

Value: That which a symbol "hides."

These very primitive ideas have been defined independently of computers. To make these concepts more concrete, the following examples show some possible realizations:

Environment: Computer Memory
                 Arrays
                 Library of Programs

Reference: The mention of a variable name or identifier such as X or $A1$

   Assign: FORTRAN $=$
             ALGOL $:=$
             APL $\leftarrow$

  Symbol: Identifier of ALGOL
             Variable of FORTRAN
             Representation of number, e.g., 50.

   Value: Real numbers*
             Integers

---

*Note that 13 and XIII are two different representations of the same abstract number. In common usage we tend to confuse the symbol and what it designates. If we want to emphasize the difference we might write: "13" is the decimal representation of 13, just as "1101" is the binary representation of 13. The quotation marks indicate that we are talking about the symbol.

In most computer languages we can identify certain grammatical types as being declarative and others as being active or imperative. There are a great variety of possible uses of declarations in languages, including storage allocation, subprogram definition and data-type definition. One semantic interpretation of declarations is:

> Extend the current environment to include a given symbol with either a given value or a default value.

Thus, we see that what is a declarative statement in the user language is interpreted as an imperative statement by the program that translates from the user language to the machine language. Declarations are thus used to control storage allocation, scope of symbols, and attributes of values:

Storage Allocation: This is the process by which memory is dedicated to a value.

Scope of a Symbol: This is that part of a computer program over which the declared symbol may be used. Some possibilities are local scope (i.e., parameters of a FORTRAN subroutine, block head declarations of ALGOL, etc.) or global scope (i.e., variables of APL, COMMON variables of FORTRAN, etc.).

Attributes of Values: In most programming languages, symbols carry with them some of the characteristics of the values which they hide. Some common attributes of values include Real, Integer, Boolean, and String.

Among the most primitive concepts used in the imperative or active part of a computer program are the ideas of *reference* and *assign*. (Assignment is also referred to as *replacement*.) Reference is achieved in most programming languages by simply mentioning a symbol. That is, by writing X in a program, the programmer is saying "*reference X* of the environment." The most important exception to such a view is when a symbol appears to the left of an *assignment* operator, i.e., $X \leftarrow 5$.

In this case the programmer is saying,* "change the value of X in the environment to be the integer, 5." It is usually implied that reference does not change the value associated with a symbol (i.e., reference is *nondestructive*), while assign is destructive of the starting value.

Thus, the semantics of the statement $x \leftarrow y + 5$ is: assign to x the value of y plus the value of 5. If we wanted to assign the expression $y + 5$ to x, we could say in some programming languages: $x \leftarrow$ "$y + 5$", providing that x is a variable that can have an expression as its value. If we also have the primitive operator, value, which causes an expression to be evaluated, the statements

$$x \leftarrow \text{"}y + 5\text{"}$$
$$z \leftarrow \text{value } x$$

have the effect on z of

$$z \leftarrow y + 5$$

---

*Thus we say that numbers are self-referencing, meaning that we utilize the confusion of symbol and what it designates to achieve a conciseness of language.

Another very important and primitive semantic consideration in the imperative part of a computer program is the implied sequential control of the program. The imperative statements of a program are carried out in their order in the program unless an explicit instruction to the contrary is given. We would expect to have sequential control between lines of FORTRAN program or between statements separated by a semicolon in ALGOL.

In Chapters 6 and 7 we extend these very basic semantic concepts to include composite data structures and control structures. You should not proceed, however, without a thorough understanding of the concepts of symbol, value, reference, assign, and sequential control.

D. Formal Specification of Semantics

Let us summarize what we have said thus far about semantics.

First, the concern with semantics is motivated by problems that have arisen in understanding the effects of programs and programming languages. On the basis of this experience, we can assert that one person's "natural" semantics will not be another's interpretation. If you write a program thinking that the instructions do one thing when, in fact, they do something quite different, you will probably get a program whose effect is very different from what you intended.

Second, the concern with semantics has led us to introduce some semantic concepts that can be seen to depend on the implementation. In effect, what we are saying is that if you want to know exactly how the program works, you had better know its implementation environment. Now, understanding a program in terms of its implementation environment is not really satisfactory because the quantity of information contained in the implementation environment is generally beyond the capacity of any individual. Among other things, the implementation environment includes: compiler, operating system, machine plus all engineering changes, and operator procedures. The experienced programmer can generally cite examples in which each of these items has affected the results of one program or another. Clearly, this is an unsatisfactory situation.

We do not yet have a widely accepted means of specifying semantics, comparable to the use of BNF in describing syntax. Two of the main approaches being used are the following:

(1) *PseudoMachine*—A simplified computer is described and each of its machine instructions are defined in detail. Each higher level instruction is then described in terms of a program on the simplified computer.

(2) *Algorithmic*—A computational rule is associated with each instruction. The rule is an algorithm, stated in mathematical form, allowing a computation of the effect of the instruction.

Note that either of these methods of specifying semantics has the following advantages: the methods are completely formal, and no subjective interpretation is called for. It is thus easily transferred from one person to another. Further, the formal specification is a standard that can be used either for the development of translating programs from user level to machine language or for the proof that such translation programs are semantically correct.

5.5   Pragmatics

A.   General Discussion

Recall that pragmatics is concerned with the practical and psychological aspect of language. Our concern here will primarily be with the practical aspects of programming languages, since very little is known of the psychological aspect.

In general, there are two theoretical measures of the cost of computation. The first is the running time of the program, and the second is the amount of storage it requires. It is sometimes possible to trade one for the other. For example, extensive use of tables in the program may reduce running time while increasing storage. Thus, a combination of the two measures in some appropriate form should be a better approximation of real costs.

However, the actual situation is not quite so simple. Many different resources are usually involved in the computational process, including input devices, main computer, auxiliary memory devices, and output units. Each of these is used a different amount of time. Similarly, there is a hierarchy of memories that is involved in most computations, including possibly several types of memory in the main computers, tapes, discs, and possibly other bulk devices. In practice, the approach to pragmatics has generally been quite ad hoc. For large programs, where the costs of running are significant, an assemblage of performance measuring devices and techniques have been used. [Two of the well-known performance measurement techniques are standardized instruction mixes and benchmark programs. A standardized instruction mix is generally obtained by taking a set of sample programs and collecting statistics about how many times each instruction type occurs. In machine languages where there is not much standardization of instructions, there may be many incomparable instructions. A benchmark program is a program that is chosen to be representative of a particular type of application (e.g. business, scientific, or academic) and is then used to compare costs of different installations.] These performance measurements allow you to compare one implementation with another —on the same or different computers—but does not provide a reliable guide to the programmer.

A further problem in obtaining a good estimate of costs is that the costs are often very much dependent on the implementation environment—in particular, the operating system and the other programs you are sharing the resources with.

In the next section we will sketch briefly two theoretical approaches to pragmatics. However, the entire field of pragmatics is still mostly unexplored.

B. Approaches to Pragmatics

In this section we describe two approaches to pragmatics in which there is active research and development. The first of these is concerned with the compilers that translate from user language to machine language in attempts to improve their performance. The second is an attempt to calculate theoretically what is the best way to solve certain problems.

In improving the compilers, the basic idea is to modify the machine language program so it will be more efficient. There are many ways in which this is possible, but we will provide only one illustrative example. Consider the following program:

$$PI \leftarrow 3.14159$$
$$C \leftarrow 2 \times PI \times R$$
$$A \leftarrow PI \times R \uparrow 2$$
$$V \leftarrow PI \times R \uparrow 2 \times H$$

This program calculates the circumference, base area, and volume of a cylinder of radius R and length H. Essentially, an optimizing compiler would generate code corresponding to the following:

$$C \leftarrow 6.28318 \times R$$
$$A \leftarrow 3.14159 \times R \uparrow 2$$
$$V \leftarrow A \times H$$

The first change made is that since PI is a constant, assigned a value once and never changed, we need not write an assignment statement or keep it as a variable name. Secondly, $2 \times PI$ is also a constant that can be computed only at compile time rather than each time the program is run for different values of R and H. Third, since the part of the computation of V duplicates the computation of A, it need not be repeated. In fact, savings can be effected even in the computation of expressions having common subexpressions, as for example:

$$X + Y \times Z \quad \text{and} \quad W + Y \times Z$$

Since $Y \times Z$ is a common subexpression, the multiplication need only be performed once.

There are many more complex optimizing transformations used in optimizing compilers than we have sketched here. The important property these transformations must have is that they must not change the semantics of the program. In the example above of the computation of the area and volume of a cylinder, one requirement is that the semantics of $3.14159 \times R \uparrow 2 \times H$ be the same as $(3.14159 \times R \uparrow 2) \times H$.

If the first expression is evaluated from right to left as $3.4159 \times ((R \uparrow 2) \times H)$, then under certain roundoff conditions there might be a difference in the least significant digits of the result. In that case, the optimizing transformation would not be justified.

The second approach to pragmatics is generally referred to as the study of complexity of computation. One of the earliest results in this area is that the time required by a computer program to sort a list of n items presented in random unsorted order is proportional to $n \log n$, with the constant of proportionality varying with the sorting technique. General parsing techniques for languages generated by BNF grammars are known to take time proportional to n^2 where n is the length of the program to be parsed, but here a lower bound is not known. Consequently, there is great interest in restricted types of BNF grammar, which can be parsed in time proportional to the length of the input string.

There is also a class of problems for which the best known solution is backtracking. This class of problems includes many that are important in operations research and optimization problems. Since backtracking is generally a lengthy procedure, there is considerable interest in determining if better procedures are available to solve these problems. The answer seems to be that if you insist on getting the guaranteed best solution, then backtracking is about the best you can do.* If, on the other hand, you are content with an almost optimal solution, then there are much improved programming techniques.

Both approaches to pragmatics are the subject of active research.

Summary

Semiotics, the study of symbolic processes, is divided into syntax, semantics, and pragmatics.

Syntax is the study of grammatical forms of language. The form of grammar that has received most universal acceptance for computer languages is BNF. A BNF grammar consists of a finite set of rules, which, through use of recursive rules, can specify arbitrarily long programs. The generative process, which can be diagrammed as a tree, yields objects in the language as well as their structural description.

The recognition process starts with a grammar and a proposed object in the language and determines if the object is indeed in the language. If the recognizer provides as output a description of the grammatical structure of the object, it is known as a *parser*.

Semantics is the study of meaning. The meaning of a computer program is what it computes; and semantic problems arise when what the program com-

---

*No proof of this is available at the current writing.

putes does not agree with our prior expectation. Discussion of computer semantics must refer to the features of the implementations that influence meaning, such as environments, storage allocation strategies, control mechanisms, and implicit data organization. Formal specifications of semantics attempt to restrict the features of the implementation that must be considered in predicting the results of a program.

Pragmatics is concerned with the practical and psychological aspects of semiotics. We have emphasized those costs of computations that seem most accessible—program running time and storage space. Many results in the area of pragmatics do not have a firm theoretical foundation. However, in the area of computational complexity and pragmatic compiler improvements, there has been some theoretical basis established.

The computer scientist is concerned with the whole symbolic process involved with the algorithmic technique. All areas of semiotics are under continual study, with our technical knowledge strongest in syntax and weakest in pragmatics.

References and Suggested Additional Reading

(1) Aho, A.V. and Ullman, J.D.. *The Theory of Parsing, Translation, and Compiling.* Englewood Cliffs, N.J.: Prentice-Hall, 1973.
(2) Bush, R. and Galanter, E. and Luce, D., eds.. *Handbook of Math Psychology.* New York: John Wiley & Sons, 1963.
(3) Elson, M.. *Concepts of Programming Languages.* Chicago: Science Research Associates, 1973.
(4) Gries, D.. *Compiler Construction for Digital Computers.* New York: Wiley & Sons, 1971.

Problems

1. Use BNF to describe the syntax of telephone numbers. Show the parse tree of your telephone number.
2. Extend the syntactic description of expression given in the text to include strings of the form:

$$u \leftarrow w$$
$$w \leftarrow u + v$$
$$v \leftarrow w + u$$
etc.

Suggest a possible semantic interpretation of "$\leftarrow$".
3. In what way does the syntactic description of expression suggest a meaning of expression? Rearrange the description of expression in the text to suggest a different meaning.

4. Develop a BNF-like description of the BNF syntax description language. (Hint: Introduce any new notation that may be necessary.)

5. $\langle expr \rangle ::= \langle term \rangle \mid \langle expr \rangle + \langle term \rangle$
$\langle term \rangle ::= \langle factor \rangle \mid \langle term \rangle \times \langle factor \rangle$
$\langle factor \rangle ::= \langle variable \rangle \mid (\langle expr \rangle)$
$\langle variable \rangle ::= u \mid v \mid w$
Write a program to generate ten legal expressions.

6. If you were given a legal expression, based on the grammar of exercise 5, could you recognize that expression? Give your reasons.

7. (a) Consider the following BNF specification:
$\langle letter \rangle \quad ::= a \mid b \mid c$
$\langle number \rangle ::= 0 \mid 1 \mid 2$
$\langle tag \rangle \qquad ::= \langle letter \rangle \langle number \rangle \mid \langle tag \rangle \langle tag \rangle$
Which of the following is a tag?
(a) *1a1*
(b) *a1b*
(c) *a1*
(d) *ab12*
(e) *b1c1*

   (b) Give a flowchart of a program that will accept only $\langle tag \rangle$s and say "yes", and will reject non-$\langle tag \rangle$'s saying "no."

   (c) Give a BNF specification of $\langle newtag \rangle$, where $\langle newtag \rangle$ is any string of 1 or more $\langle letter \rangle$s followed by 0 or more $\langle number \rangle$s. $\langle letter \rangle$ and $\langle number \rangle$ are as specified above.

8. Describe a recognizer for telephone numbers. Indicate where in the algorithm the parse tree may be built.

9. Flowchart a recognizer for the language defined by the following grammar:
$\langle N \rangle ::= \langle D \rangle \mid \langle D \rangle \langle N \rangle$
$\langle D \rangle ::= 0 \mid 1$

10. Suppose you have a recognizer that requires that the BNF description of the syntax be such that all grammatical rules be one of the following forms:
(a) $\langle A \rangle ::= \langle B \rangle \langle C \rangle$
(b) $\langle A \rangle ::= t$
(i.e. the right hand side of each alternate of each definition must be composed of two grammatical classes or else be composed of single symbol of the language.) Transform the grammar for $\langle EXPRESSION \rangle$ in the previous section to such a form without changing the language. Discuss the possibility of mechanizing your transformation.

11. $\langle expr \rangle ::= \langle term \rangle \mid \langle term \rangle + \langle expr \rangle$
$\langle term \rangle ::= \langle primary \rangle \mid \langle primary \rangle \times \langle term \rangle$
$\langle primary \rangle ::= u \mid v \mid w$
Using a top-down analysis generate a parse of $w \times v + u$.

12. Indicate where references and assignments have occurred in the following statements.
$$Y \leftarrow X + Z$$
$$Y \leftarrow X + Y \times 2$$

13. What is the value associated with the symbol, X, at the end of the following sequence of statements:

$$X \leftarrow 5$$
$$Y \leftarrow X + X$$
$$Z \leftarrow Y + X$$
$$X \leftarrow X \times Z$$

14. Suggest possible semantics to be associated with the following declarations.
    (a) CHARACTER X
    (b) INTEGER Y
    (c) PROCEDURE S

15. Suggest possible interpretations of the concepts of "environment", "symbol", and "value" in terms of computer memory structure.

16. How might sequential control be achieved in a computing machine using a clock and an adder?

Chapter 6

Control Structures

The study and understanding of control of machines and computation was overlooked for many years as computer scientists concentrated on languages and data structures. Most early machines and languages presented very little challenge to control. So long as there was one computing machine with one program in its memory, the problem of control was particularly easy. Such computing systems could be expected to proceed step-by-step through a program, branch to some part of a program based on some well-defined condition, or simply jump to someplace in a program. These early computer systems were not expected to deal with such things as power failures, other computers, other programs, or composite data structures. Economic pressures led to a realization that computer systems must deal effectively with such problems; consider, for instance, the economic effect of running a computer for several hours only to lose all the work due to a power failure.

In order to understand the role of control in a computation, one should understand the fundamental ideas.

Control is the act of determining what to do next in a computation.

A control *structure* is the means of reaching the next part of a computation.

In these definitions the word, *computation,* may be taken to refer to a computer program, an algorithm, or a flowchart.

We shall concern ourselves with the type of control flow within each programmatic unit and the features available for transfer of control between units.

6.1   Sequential Control Flow

In previous chapters, the most primitive manifestations of control have already been discussed. In fact, one can hardly talk about machines and algorithms without introducing *sequential control* and *conditional control.* Sequential control is so much a part of human reasoning that it is seldomly stated explicitly. It is implicitly understood that in a computation the steps are to be performed:

One at a time in the order given

one statement at a time in the order written

one machine instruction after another in the order they are

stored

step *i* then step *j* in the following flowchart

This predisposition toward sequential control which seems to characterize most computer scientists may not be a natural human predisposition. In fact, the human being is quite capable of doing more than one thing at once. Thus we must look at the traditions of computer science to discover the reason for the predisposition toward sequential control. Upon examining the history of computer science, one finds that the earliest models of computation and the earliest machines relied heavily upon sequential control. Thus it is by tradition that sequential control has become the natural, implicit, unstated form of control for a computation.

6.2   Conditional Control

Conditional control, like sequential control, is also an ingredient of most primitive models of computation and machines. Conditional control is the decision making feature of a computation. It is by means of conditional control that computers become aids in human decision making. Unlike sequential control, conditional control is usually expressed very explicitly in a computation. Most computing machines and programming languages have features which explicitly invoke conditional control. Some examples of conditional control statements are:

:If ⟨contents of a specified register of the computer satisifes a given condition⟩
THEN ⟨start taking instructions sequentially starting at location Z⟩.

:If ⟨Boolean Expr⟩ THEN ⟨$STAT_1$⟩ ELSE ⟨$STAT_2$⟩

The logic of the above statement is explained below:

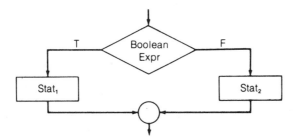

The Boolean expression is a logical construct which, when evaluated using the current values of variables, has a value of TRUE or FALSE. These two primitive controls, sequential and conditional, provide the basis for models of computation such as the Turing machine and for extensive developments in the theory of computation. One could reasonably argue that no other controls are necessary, and in fact the remaining controls are introduced for convenience and conciseness only.

In certain programming languages, this conditional capability is also available at the expression level. For example, in Algol we can have statements of the form:

:⟨variable⟩ ::= IF ⟨Boolean Expr⟩ THEN ⟨Expr⟩ ELSE ⟨Expr⟩;

:GO TO IF ⟨Boolean Expr⟩ THEN ⟨Expr⟩ ELSE ⟨Expr⟩;

Boolean Expressions

A Boolean expression is a combination of logical quantities which can be evaluated via the laws of Boolean Algebra to yield a value of TRUE or FALSE. The individual logical quantities may be simple Boolean variables, relational expressions such as $A < B$, $A = C + D$, $C/E > 4 + E$, or Boolean expressions, all of which have a current truth value of TRUE or FALSE. These are combined into more complex Boolean expressions by using the Boolean operators NOT, AND, OR.

NOT is a unary operator and precedes its operand; the result is a Boolean expression whose value is the opposite of the operand's value. AND and OR are binary operators and appear between their two operands. The result of combining two logical quantities via AND is a Boolean expression whose value is TRUE only if *both* logical quantities have a TRUE value whereas OR yields a Boolean expression whose value is TRUE if *either or both* logical quantities has a TRUE value. These results are summarized in the following tables for two logical quantities A,B; such tables are called truth tables.

A	NOT A
T	F
F	T

A	B	A AND B
T	T	T
T	F	F
F	T	F
F	F	F

A	B	A OR B
T	T	T
T	F	T
F	T	T
F	F	F

More complex Boolean expressions can be formulated; the order of precedence for evaluating operators is NOT, AND, OR, but parentheses may be used to override this. Several examples with their associated truth tables will illustrate the evaluations; the encircled line presents the evaluation for the given variable values.

Example: /

Draw a truth table for the Boolean expression C OR NOT A AND B and evaluate it for A = TRUE, B = FALSE, C = FALSE.

A	B	C	NOT A	NOT A AND B	C OR NOT A AND B
T	T	T	F	F	T
T	F	T	F	F	T
T	T	F	F	F	F
T	F	F	F	F	F
F	T	T	T	T	T
F	F	T	T	F	T
F	T	F	T	T	T
F	F	F	T	F	F

Example: 2

Draw a truth table for the Boolean expression $A < 6$ AND $(B$ OR $C + 2 \neq A)$ and evaluate it for $A = 7$, $B =$ FALSE, $C = 1$.

$A < 6$	B	$C + 2 \neq A$	$(B$ OR $C + 2 \neq A)$	$A < 6$ AND $(B$ OR $C + 2 \neq A)$
T	T	T	T	T
T	F	T	T	T
T	T	F	T	T
T	F	F	F	F
F	T	T	T	F
F	F	T	T	F
F	T	F	T	F
F	F	F	F	F

Example: 3

Draw a truth table for the Boolean expression $A < 6$ AND B OR $C + 2 \neq A$ and evaluate it for $A = 7$, $B =$ FALSE, $C = 1$.

$A < 6$	B	$C+2 \neq A$	$A < 6$ AND B	$A < 6$ AND B OR $C+2 \neq A$
T	T	T	T	T
T	F	T	F	T
T	T	F	T	T
T	F	F	F	F
F	T	T	F	T
F	F	T	F	T
F	T	F	F	F
F	F	F	F	F

6.3   Unconditional Transfer

Among the most controversial of all control structures in use today is the Unconditional Transfer of Control. It provides a means of jumping unconditionally to another part of a program. It may be realized by combining data assignment, sequential control, and conditional control as follows:

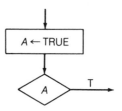

Figure 6.3-1:   Use of Data Assignment for Unconditional Transfer

It usually takes the form: :GO TO ⟨label⟩ where ⟨label⟩ is the name of a programmatic unit. The convenience of GO TO is that most machines have an efficient similar machine instruction. Problems arise, however, in excessive use of the GO TO in that it may be very difficult to prove that a computer program is correct when the GO TO control structure is present.

A prominent school of thought contends that the use of the GO TO statement is harmful and makes programs difficult to read. Furthermore, algorithms described in languages that do not permit the use of the GO TO construct make the logic easier to follow since one can read the program sequentially, rather than going forward and backward through the program. Naturally the elimination of GO TO constructs at the programming level will lead to the elimination of labels which will make the task of translation easier. The contention is that GO TO-Less programming will force the programmer to discipline his thoughts.

The GO TO capability is often found in languages in a more disciplined form. One common construct is

:CASE ⟨expr⟩ OF ⟨STATEMENT LIST⟩

which selects one statement from the ⟨STATEMENT LIST⟩ to be executed and control is returned to the statement following the CASE construct. This return of control is an unconditional transfer in the same spirit as GO TO. The subroutine control structure to be discussed later is a highly disciplined form of GO TO control.

6.4   Iterative Control

One of the most useful and powerful of the control structures to be composed from the very primitive sequential and conditional control is the iterative control structure. Sometimes called loop control, it provides a means of repeating part of a computation without re-writing that part of the computation. Some of the realizations of iterative control include:

:The DO loop of Fortran
:The FOR loop of Algol
:The WHILE DO of Algol

In the development of iterative control structures for programming languages, it was recognized that they provided a mechanism for accessing elements of the array data structure (see chapter 7). Thus much of the style features of early versions reflect such use. It is interesting to note that a relatively new language, APL, has no iterative control structure. Most of the primitive operations of APL apply directly to arrays thus eliminating iterative control.

The user of iterative control must face the question "Once in a loop, how do I get out?". Iterative control structures have two distinct parts: a condition and a body. The condition is tested each time around the loop and provides a way of getting out. Some of the important forms of conditions are:

Count until the loop has been traversed a specified number of times.
Continue looping until some expression becomes false.

There are also two distinctly different arrangements of the condition and body in a iterative control structure. Consider the following two flow-charts of iterative control.

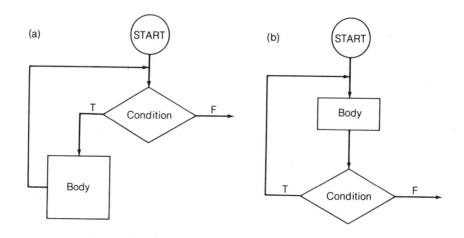

In case (a) the body of the loop may be avoided altogether, whereas in case (b) the body must be traversed at least once. Some common examples of these two types of iterative control are:

<table>
<tr><td>(a)</td><td>(b)</td></tr>
<tr><td>FOR loop of Algol</td><td>DO Loop of Fortran</td></tr>
<tr><td>WHILE DO of Algol</td><td>DO WHILE of Algol</td></tr>
</table>

To make our ideas clear, let us consider the following Algol and Fortran constructs respectively:

a) FOR $V := A$ STEP B UNTIL C DO $S;T$;

where A, B and C are arithmetic expressions while S and T are subcomputation units.

The semantics of this statement is best illustrated by the following sequence of Algol-like statements.

$V \leftarrow A$;
TEST: IF $(V - C) \times$ SIGN$(B) > 0$ THEN GO TO EXIT;
S;
$V \leftarrow V + B$;
GO TO TEST;

EXIT: T;

In a similar manner one can express the semantics of the WHILE DO construct. Thus

WHILE B DO $S;T$;

where A is an arithmetic expression, B is a boolean expression, and S and T are program segments.

TEST: IF NOT *B* THEN GO TO EXIT;
 S;
 GO TO TEST;

EXIT: *T*;

 Also for the DO loop of Fortran
  DO 5 *I* = *L*1, *L*2, *L*3
  S
  5 CONTINUE

The above construct implies:

 I ← *L*1;
 REPEAT: *S*
   I ← *L*1 + *L*3
   IF *I* > *L*2 THEN GO TO EXIT ELSE GO TO REPEAT;
  EXIT: - - - -

We shall now turn our attention to the flow of control between various programmatic units. The main program structures normally found in programming languages are blocks and subprograms or procedures. A block is a set of computational units typically separated from the rest of the program by bracketing these units, i.e., the use of BEGIN and END. On the other hand, a subprogram is a set of statements or a block separated from the program by a procedure declaration. This declaration consists of the type, name, and variables that will be used in the procedure body as formal parameters (see below). Programming languages usually allow procedures to be compiled separately and stored in machine-language code on a back-up storage medium for general use.

Blocks and procedures play a very important role in programming languages. They permit, among other advantages, dynamic storage allocation. In dynamic storage allocation, the amount of storage available to a subprogram is determined at the time the subprogram is used. Different usages of one subprogram within the same program may vary substantially in the amount of storage they use because storage allocation is determined by the parameters of the subprogram. For example, a sorting procedure may allocate as much storage as needed to store the set of elements to be sorted. Variables declared in a block head are local to that block. During the execution of a program, memory is allocated to the variables declared in the head of the block and released on exiting from the block. A variable that is used in a block and not declared in the head of that block is called a global variable.

6.5 Subroutine Control

No control structure has had as significant an impact on the art of computer programming as the subroutine control structure. It is through subroutine control that a good programmer realizes a working algorithm and keeps his work organized in manageable tasks. Subroutine control is a realization of what might be thought of as round-trip control. Through subroutine control, a jump may be made in a computation with the expectation that control will be returned to immediately beyond (in a sequential sense) where the jump was made. In addition, the subroutine can be performed for different sets of parameter values. Thus the instructions for a task can be written once in the form of a subroutine and called into execution from many different points in the main program.

Structure

In achieving subroutine control, the programmer must specify:

1. Subroutine definition
2. The points of jump to the subroutine (i.e. CALL).

The first of these specifications establishes a static entity known as a *routine* while the latter creates a dynamic entity known as a *process*.

The routine created at the time of subroutine definition is typically composed of

1. Subroutine Head: Name of subroutine along with the formal parameter set.
2. Body
3. Global environment

The body specifies the computation to be carried out in the subroutine.

The formal parameter set is a set of symbols that will have different values associated with them each time the subroutine is executed. The formal parameters may appear in the statements comprising the subroutine body. The global environment is the totality of information available at the beginning of the computation, specified by the body, exclusive of the formal parameters and their values. The global environment may be realized as follows:

1. Lexical Global Environment: The environment at the point of subroutine definition (e.g. Fortran and Algol).
2. Dynamic Global Environment: The environment at the point of call on a subroutine (e.g. APL and LISP).

The subroutine jump or CALL specifies the name of the subroutine to be executed along with a set of actual parameters. This set and the set of formal parameters listed in the subroutine head must agree in number, order, and type; that is, the ith actual parameter is associated with the ith formal parameter and both must be of the same type (variable, array, etc.). At the time of execution, the actual parameters designate the values to be used for the associated formal parameters during the subroutine computation.

Main Program

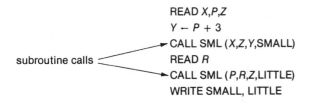

subroutine calls

```
READ X,P,Z
Y ← P + 3
CALL SML (X,Z,Y,SMALL)
READ R
CALL SML (P,R,Z,LITTLE)
WRITE SMALL, LITTLE
```

Subroutine

subroutine head

SUBROUTINE SML(*A,B,C*,ANSWER)

subroutine body

```
IF A < B AND A < C THEN ANSWER ← A
  ELSE IF B < C THEN ANSWER ← B
      ELSE ANSWER ← C
RETURN
END
```

The subroutine SML has four formal parameters: *A,B,C*,ANSWER. The first three represent values to be examined and the fourth represents the result of finding the smallest of these three values. The subroutine is called into execution twice from the main program. The first call associates the actual parameter *X* with the formal parameter *A*, and so forth; similarly the second call associates *P,R,Z*,LITTLE with the formal parameters *A,B,C*,ANSWER respectively. The two calls cause SMALL and LITTLE to assume the smallest of the values of *X,Z,Y* and *P,R,Z* respectively.

Once the jump or call is made to a routine, a process is established consisting of:

1. A New Environment: The global environment of the routine extended to include the formal parameters and their associated values.
2. The Caller Process: This is the process to which control is returned when the computation is complete.
3. State of Computation within the Body.

This new process then becomes the controlling process. Notice that there is sufficient information in the process to carry out the return to the caller process. At the point of return the current process disappears and the caller process takes control.

In the above discussion of subroutine call and return it was stated that values were to be associated with the formal parameters. This association of value with formal parameters is known as parameter passing. At the point of call, these values, known as actual parameters, must be computed. Some of the forms of values which may be passed include:

1. References: A pointer to the value in the caller's environment.
2. Code: A computation which if invoked later will produce the value.
3. Value: This is the fully comptuted actual parameters.

In the case of value parameters, the actual parameter values to be used in place of the formal parameters are determined at the point the subroutine is called into execution. In the case of reference and code parameters, the evaluation is made each time a formal parameter is encountered during execution of the statements in the subroutine body. This can cause different results depending on the method of parameter passing in effect. The following example, using the concept of arrays (ch. 7) illustrates this phenomenon.

EXAMPLE: Subroutine CHNG(A,B) sets B to 8 and A to 0 if $A < B$.

```
SUBROUTINE CHNG (A,B)
IF A < B THEN DO
            B ← 8
            A ← 0
            END
RETURN
END
```

The calling statement in the main program is

CALL CHNG (ARR$_I$, I)

where ARR$_I$ is an element of an array. Suppose that immediately prior to execution of the CALL statement, $I = 5$, ARR$_5 = 3$, ARR$_8 = 12$.

1. If VALUE parameters are used, A and B are assigned the initial values 3 and 5 respectively at the time the subroutine is called. When the computation is completed, A and B have values 0 and 8 respectively; the controlling process must copy these values into ARR$_5$ and I respectively before returning control to the main program.

2. If REFERENCE parameters are used, then pointers to the memory locations containing the values ARR$_5$ and I are associated with A and B respectively. The evaluation of $A < B$ in the subroutine body yields a TRUE value and, using the pointers associated with B and A, I is assigned the value 8 and ARR$_5$ the value 0. Note that the determination of *which* array element to associate with formal parameter A is made at the time the subroutine is called; only the parameter's actual value is calculated later.

3. If CODE parameters are used, then computations to determine the values of ARR_1 and I are associated with A and B respectively; in the case of parameter A, the current value of I will be used to select the appropriate array element. The evaluation of $A < B$ in the subroutine body yields a TRUE value and, using the computation associated with formal parameter B, I is again assigned the value 8. However, the computation associated with formal parameter A now selects element ARR_8, which is then set to 0. Note that the determination of *which* array element to associate with formal parameter A is made anew each time A is encountered in a statement.

The reference parameters were among the first to be implemented in Fortran. The combination of reference and code parameters is known as *call by name* parameters in Algol, and value parameters are known as *call by value* parameters in Algol. Since reference and code parameters may be evaluated an unknown number of times in the body, it is usually safer to employ value parameters in programming. The most important justification of reference parameters arises in passing composite data structures back to the caller's environment, because a reference parameter allows an arbitrary quantity of data to be accessed.

Recursion

In the discussion of routines and processes, no constraint was placed upon the number of processes which could be created from a single routine. In programming systems which permit more than one process per routine, the possibility of recursion arises. That is, a call of a routine is permitted from within its own body. Recursion often provides an expeditious route to implementation of an algorithm. Some well known mathematical functions with recursive definitions include: the factorial function, binomial coefficients, greatest common divisor, and orthogonal polynomials.

Each call upon a subroutine, whether issued from the main program, from another subroutine, or from the body of the subroutine being called, creates a "caller process" and associates a set of actual parameters with the formal subroutine parameters. In the case of recursion, these processes and parameters will essentially be stacked upon one another, and saved, as the subroutine issues a call upon itself before returning control to the preceding calling process. When execution of the subroutine statements is completed, the calling process last placed on the stack is removed and resumes control; this may in effect return control to a statement in the subroutine body.

The Fibonacci series is an example of a simple recursive algorithm. The series is 0,1,1,2,3,5,8,13,21,... where the first and second elements are 0 and 1 respectively and each succeeding element is the sum of its two immediate predecessors; that is, $F_i = F_{i-1} + F_{i-2}$.

Subroutine FIBNAC(K,ANS) calculates the kth element of the Fibonacci series and returns it thru parameter ANS

```
SUBROUTINE FIBNAC (K,ANS)
    IF K = 1 THEN ANS ← 0
    ELSE IF K = 2 THEN ANS ← 1
        ELSE DO
            FIBNAC (K − 1, A1)
            FIBNAC (K − 2,A2)
            ANS ← A1 + A2
        END
    RETURN
    END
```

Suppose the main program contains the statement CALL FIBNAC (4,C). The intent is that subroutine FIBNAC will calculate the fourth element of the Fibonacci series and store it in variable C. When the jump is made to the subroutine, K assumes the value 4 and the point of return upon completion is to the main program. Since the value of K exceeds 2, the statements FIBNAC (K − 1, A1) and FIBNAC (K − 2, A2) are executed. Each is a call upon subroutine FIBNAC; the first calculates the K − 1rst or third element of the series and stores it in A1; similarly the second call calculates the K − 2nd or second element and stores it in A2. Thus upon completion of both statements, the values of A1 and A2 are both 1 and the value of ANS becomes 2. This is returned to the main program as the value of variable C. Compare the two calls issued from the subroutine body. The first, FIBNAC (K − 1, A1) with K = 4, eventually results in two additional calls upon subroutine FIBNAC, whereas the second, FIBNAC (K − 2, A2) with K = 4, returns to its calling process without further recursion. Every recursive subroutine must have conditional statements that limit the depth of recursion; otherwise the subroutine would stack up calls upon itself indefinitely.

Another example of recursion is the calculation of N! where

$$N! = 1 \text{ if } N = 1$$
$$= N \times (N − 1)! \text{ if } N > 1$$

Subroutine FACT (N, TERM) calculates N! and returns it thru parameter TERM.

```
SUBROUTINE FACT (N, TERM)
    IF N = 1 THEN TERM ← 1
        ELSE DO
            FACT (N − 1, INT)
            TERM ← N × INT
        END
    RETURN
    END
```

6.6   Other Control Structures

Parallel Control

The remaining discussion of control structures will be a look into the near future of programming. Many control structures, such as parallel control, have been described and implemented on an experimental basis, but they are still not widely available to programmers. Parallel control permits the user to invoke more than one computation simultaneously. Such a control structure has obvious utility when more than one machine is available. Parallel control is also an important device in describing some algorithms, regardless of how many machines are available. You recall the use of parallel control.

Semaphore Control

Whenever more than one computation is being performed simultaneously as in parallel control, the possibility of conflict in the use of data or other resources arises. The *semaphore* is a recently proposed control structure which is intended to resolve such conflicts. Its name comes from the analogous use of semaphores to resolve conflicts in the use of railroad tracks. Some interesting problems arise in realizing semaphore control, including the possibility of two computations attempting to set a semaphore at the same instant. What may happen is an

"after you, after you, after you, ..."

situation in which nobody proceeds. Implementations of semaphore control have been proposed which prevent such things from happening.

Monitor Control

Modern computer systems are now expected to respond to unexpected and unpredictable events arising either internally or externally. The most familiar example is one of responding to a voltage drop in the power supply in time to save memory before the lights go out. Machines and languages are now being provided with *monitor* control structures to handle responses to such events. Monitor control is typically composed from parallel control with the imposition of a priority relationship between the simultaneous computations. Thus the power failure handler may be "running" in parallel to all other computations but at a very low priority. When the voltage drops, the priority of the power failure handler would be raised above all other computations.

PROBLEMS

1. Describe algorithms for each of the following:
   (a) Computing the factorial of an integer.

(b) Finding the first N prime numbers.

(c) Finding the quotient of two real numbers without division.

(d) Computing the balance in a savings account after each of N years with an interest of 6% compounded quarterly. The starting balance should be a variable in the algorithm.

(e) Determine the size of a population after each of N years when the birth rate has been 5.5 per thousand per year and the death rate has been 4 per thousand per year.

Indicate the control structures employed in each case.

2. Implement and test two of the algorithms in Problem 1.

3. Discuss the control structures employed in the discussion of Recognizers and Parsers in Chapter 4.

4. Develop and discuss control structure analogies in some area of human endeavor (e.g., economics, politics, group behavior, etc.).

5. Develop an algorithm for the realization of the CASE statement.

6. Describe the syntax and semantics of the control structures in BASIC or APL.

7. Pascal's triangle is a representation of the binomial coefficients.

```
1
1  1
1  2  1
1  3  3  1
1  4  6  4  1
1  5 10 10  5  1
       . . .
```

where $P_{ij} = 1$ if $i = 1$ or $j = 1$

$\qquad = P_{i-1, J-1} + P_{i-1, j}$ otherwise

Develop a recursive subroutine for calculating an element of Pascal's triangle.

Chapter 7

Data Structures

7.1   Fundamentals of Data Structures

One of the strongest motivating forces in the development of procedure-oriented languages for computers has been the need for easily manipulated data. In the earliest computer languages the user was forced to refer to data one item at a time, perhaps as a machine word. The user often found that the realities of addressing and storage allocation were irrelevant to the logical structure of the data that was being handled. The most important advantage of the so-called "higher level languages" remains the ease of manipulating data. Many other features have been implemented in such languages, including sophisticated control structures and extension facilities, but data structures remain the most important to the greatest number of users.

A *data structure* is an abstraction of a memory facility for storing data. The data may consist of many component items. How these components relate to one another determines the innate structure of the data itself. There is no best data structure for all problems; the appropriate data structure in each case is dependent on the nature of the data and the computations performed on it.

The fundamental features of data structures are most easily visualized in terms of more familiar notions of structure:

(1) *Building Blocks*: These are the indivisible data items (also called *Atomic Data*). The set of building blocks varies from language to language but a few familiar ones are: memory word, byte, integer, real number, etc.

(2) *Adhesion*: That feature of the data structure that holds it together is also called *data links*. Data structures may have clearly identifiable links or, as in many, the linkage mechanism may be implicit. A few examples include: consecutive memory positions (implicit), pointer vectors (explicit), and tail linkage of LISP 1.5 (explicit).

(3) *Construction Procedure*: In order to refer to a data structure in a program, one must first build it. In most familiar programming languages the construction procedure is declarative in form such as DIMENSION, array, string, etc. The CONS operator of LISP is a familiar imperative construction operator.

In the familiar operations of bricklaying, the bricks are the building blocks, the mortar is the adhesion, and the bricklayer personifies the constructor.

In dealing with data structures in programming languages, you are usually forced into associating type or mode attributes with the data. The attributes provide checks on the operations employed on the structure. Thus, if a data item is a character, we might be prohibited from performing arithmetic on it.

It is convenient to think of these attributes as providing a hierarchy of classification of data structures. Consider first the broadest classification attribute, *kind*.

KINDS OF DATA OBJECTS

(1) *Atomic*: An indivisible object.

(2) *Composite*: An object with parts.

(3) *Link*: An object that points to another object, the link may include a selector that permits the choosing of a particular link from a composite data kind.

Within each data kind we may expect to find a variety of data types.

TYPES OF DATA OBJECTS

(1) Atomic Types	(2) Composite Types	(3) Link Types
(a) Integer	(a) Array	(a) Implicit
(b) Real	(b) String	(b) Explicit
(c) Symbol	(c) List	

In addition to this classification of the objects, we may also classify the operations on the objects. The following classification is often useful:

(a) Constructors: These are operations which build composite data objects.

(b) Reference Operators: The parts of a composite object are obtained through reference operators.

(c) Assignment Operators: These operators provide a means to change to parts of an object.

(d) Predicates: As the name indicates, the operations provide answers to the "Is ....?" question. For instance, an ATOM operator would be true if the object in question is an atom.

(e) Structural Analysis Operators: These operators provide shape and size information about a data object.

Of these operators, only the constructors and reference operators are essential. The other operations are provided for convenience.

In fundamental terms a data structure may be thought of as a set of starting objects and a set of operations allowed upon the objects and their descendants. This view will be developed and illustrated in the case of trees. The starting objects will be empty tree nodes. Constructors would attach the nodes to each other. Tree traversal will be considered as a typical operation on a tree.

7.2   Trees as Data Structures

Consider the representation of a company organization chart, such as shown in Figure 7.1. The structure of such data resembles an inverted tree in which the data is stored at the tree nodes, which emit branches leading to other nodes. Such data occur often and the concept of a tree structure has been formalized.

A *directed graph* is a data structure consisting of nodes and branches; a *node* is a data element, and a *branch* is a pointer from one node to a second node. The first node is called a *predecessor* of the *second node* and the second node is called a *successor of the first*. A *path* is a sequence of nodes $a_1, a_2, \ldots, a_n$ such that a_{j+1} is a successor of a_j. A *tree* is a directed graph in which there is a unique node called the *root* that has no predecessors and in which every node other than the root has precisely one predecessor. A node with no successors is called a *terminal node*. A *subtree* consists of a node of a tree and that portion of the tree that can be reached by paths from the node.

The organization chart of Figure 7.1 is a tree. PRESIDENT is the root and has three successors: V.P. MARKETING & SALES, V.P. RESEARCH & DEVELOPMENT, and V.P. PRODUCTION. There are ten·terminal nodes, including DIRECTOR OF MARKETING, SALESMAN #1, SALESMAN #2, and PLANT TECHNICAL DIRECTOR. One path through the tree leads from PRESIDENT TO V.P. RESEARCH & DEVELOPMENT to RESEARCH DIRECTOR to PHYSCIST. Figure 7.2 illustrates three subtrees of this tree.

Tree structures are useful when the line of succession of data elements is not linear; that is, each data element may have more than one successor or each data element may choose from several possible successors. Figure 7.4 shows a game tree for the tic-tac-toe board of Figure 7.3. Player *O*'s moves are noted in circular nodes and player *X*'s in square nodes. Currently it is player *O*'s turn to move and he has a choice of positions 2, 6, 8, or 9; the game tree has four branches leading from the root, one to each of these four nodes. At each of these Level 1 nodes, the possible moves remaining for player *X* are explored and branches leading to nodes representing these moves are drawn. The same is done for player *O*'s moves from Level 2 positions. Thus, you can trace through any line of play by following the branches from the root; for example, the moves 8 by player *O*, 2 by player *X*, 9 by player *O* lead to point *A* and a win for player *O*.

Although trees are used extensively in game-playing programs, they have many other uses. Consider the problem "A father and two sons are on the left side of a river and want to cross. The father weighs 300 lb and each son weighs 150 lb. There is one boat with a capacity of 300 lb. Assuming that each person can operate the boat and the boat cannot operate itself, how do these people manage to cross the river." We define six operations:

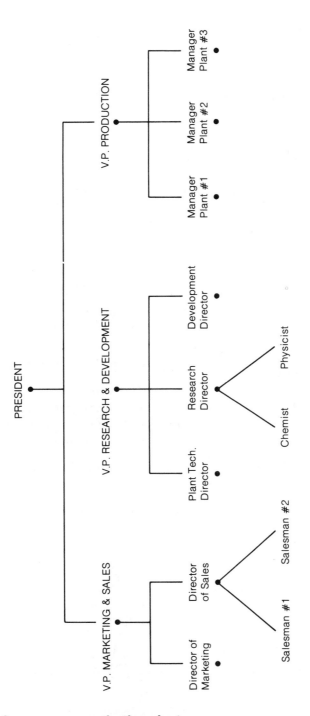

Figure 7.1:   A company organization chart

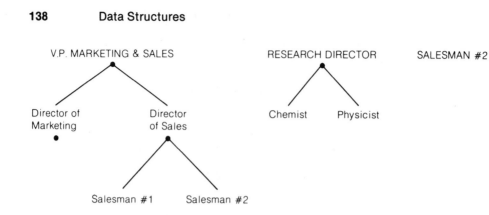

Figure 7.2:   **Three subtrees of the tree of figure 7.1**

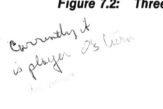

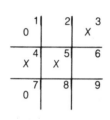

Figure 7.3:   **A tic-tac-toe board**

IR   Boat and one son cross from left to right.
IL   Boat and one son cross from right to left.
FR   Boat and father cross from left to right.
FL   Boat and father cross from right to left.
BR   Boat and both sons cross from left to right.
BL   Boat and both sons cross from right to left.

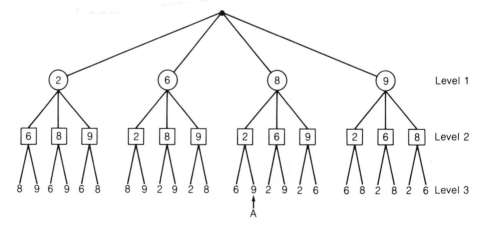

Figure 7.4:   **A game tree for tic-tac-toe**

The decision tree of Figure 7.5 illustrates the many series of operations that might be undertaken. At the root, we have a choice of one son crossing, the father crossing, or both sons crossing from left to right. Moving to node BR (both sons cross from left to right), we can choose between one son or both sons crossing from right to left. Choosing node IL (one son crosses from right to left), we now have a choice of either the father or the son crossing to the right side. The path BR-IL-FR-IL-BR leads to a successful solution.

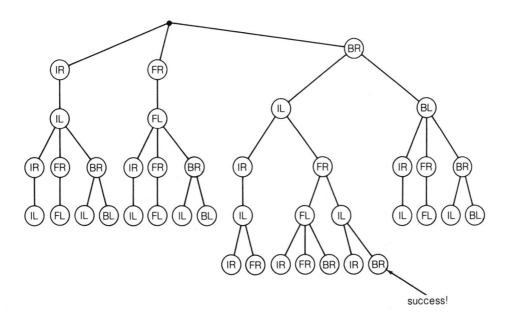

Figure 7.5: *Decision tree for father and sons problem*

An *ordered tree* is one in which the successors of each node are ordered. If the ordered tree is a binary tree, then each node has at most two successors, designated LEFT and RIGHT successor respectively.

Figure 7.6 illustrates the infix representation of an arithmetic expression as an ordered binary tree structure. *Infix representation* is the form with which we are all familiar; each operator is immediately preceded by its left operand and immediately followed by its right operand, determined according to the usual rules concerning operator hierarchy and parentheses. In the infix binary tree structure, each nonterminal node contains an operator; the left and right subtrees of the node are the left and right operands, again represented as binary trees. Thus, the arithmetic expression represented by the binary tree of Figure 7.6 is $(A + B \times C) - D$.

We shall discuss only binary trees in the remainder of this chapter. Binary tree algorithms can be generalized to ordered trees and ordered trees can

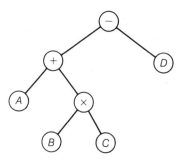

Figure 7.6:   *The infix binary tree structure for the arithmetic expression* $(A + B \times C) - D$

be represented in binary tree form, but both of these topics belong to an advanced text in data structures.

A. Tree Traversal

Many algorithms require tracing through the elements of a data structure such that each element is visited exactly once. This is called a *traversal*. In the case of sequential arrays and link lists, implementation of a traversal was relatively simple. However, in a binary tree structure, you have a choice at each nonterminal node of one of two branches to traverse first. This leads to many alternative methods of traversal, three of which have received much attention. These traversal methods can be defined recursively as:

Preorder Traversal

    A. Visit the root of the tree.
    B. Apply preorder traversal to the left subtree.
    C. Apply preorder traversal to the right subtree.

In the tree of Figure 7.6 preorder traversal proceeds in the following manner:

A. The root $\ominus$ is visited.
B. The left subtree 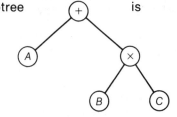 is

traversed in preorder.
    1. The root $\oplus$ is visited.
    2. The left subtree (A) is traversed in preorder.
      a. The root (A) is visited.

b. There is no left subtree.
c. There is no right subtree.
3. The right subtree  is traversed in

preorder.
a. The root ⓧ is visited.
b. The left subtree Ⓑ is traversed in preorder.
  1. The root Ⓑ is visited.
  2. There is no left subtree.
  3. There is no right subtree.
c. The right subtree Ⓒ is traversed in preorder.
  1. The root Ⓒ is visited.
  2. There is no left subtree.
  3. There is no right subtree.
C. The right subtree Ⓓ is traversed in preorder.
  1. The root Ⓓ is visited.
  2. There is no left subtree.
  3. There is no right subtree.

Thus the nodes of this tree are visited in the order:

The other traversal methods are similar:

Postorder Traversal
  (1) Apply postorder traversal to the left subtree.
  (2) Visit the root.
  (3) Apply postorder traversal to the right subtree.

Endorder Traversal
  (1) Apply endorder traversal to the left subtree.
  (2) Apply endorder traversal to the right subtree.
  (3) Visit the root.

B. Applications

Trees have found many applications in computer science, from structures for language syntax (chapter 5) and operations in compilers (chapter 12) to representations of game trees and decision-making alternatives in artificial intelligence (chapter 11). They are of such importance that programming languages such as PL/I and COBOL have special facilities for their construction.

Exercise 7.2-1   Traversing A Tree

Suppose a binary tree is constructed from linked list elements as shown. (Note that in this example each node contains only links.)

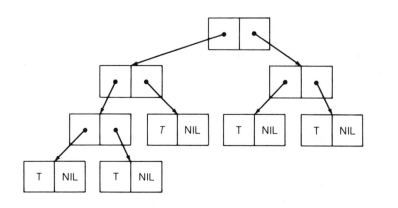

Develop the flowchart for determining the sum of the number of nodes and the number of terminal elements.

Solution: Figure 7.7

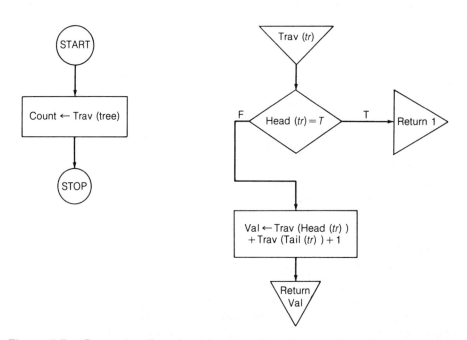

Figure 7.7:   Recursive flowchart for counting the number of nodes and terminal elements in a binary tree

7.3   Data Structures in Programs

A. Static Data Sequences

1) One-Dimensional Arrays

The *data sequence* is the simplest, and earliest to be implemented data structure. It is a collection of data items in which an order is preserved as a part of the structure. It is clearly distinguished from the mathematical notion of a set by this order property. Data sequences are commonly realized as *arrays* and *strings* (implicitly linked, static sequences) and *lists* (explicitly linked, dynamic sequences). The term *array* usually refers to a sequence composed of memory words, while the term *string* is usually a sequence of characters. Static data sequences maintain their size and shape throughout a computation.

Consider a program to find the median of a student's test grades. To accomplish this, the test grades may be read into memory, sorted, and the middle or median test grade extracted. It would be very cumbersome to store and refer to each of these test grades as a different atom with variable names such as X or K. (You might try the following problem: Given variables A, $B, \ldots I, J$, each containing a different number, write a program to store the smallest of these numbers in A, the next smallest in B, and so forth.) An appropriate data structure for this problem would be a single array containing the individual grades, with each individual grade referenced according to its position in the array as a_1, a_2, etc. Because of the linear nature of this array, it is called a *one-dimensional array*.

The precise syntax for using arrays depends on the programming language. As a minimum, the programming language would provide an array constructor and an array referencing mechanism. In most familiar programming languages, the *constructor* is declarative in nature and specifies

(1) the name by which the array is to be referenced,

(2) the type of data (REAL, INTEGER) contained in the array,

(3) the number of component items in the array,

(4) the range of consecutive subscript values for referencing elements stored in positions of the array.

The declarative ALGOL statement INTEGER ARRAY TEST [1:10] causes an array called TEST to be allocated ten contiguous memory locations, which will be used to store the ten component items of TEST. Each of these items is an integer number and is referenced according to its position, numbered 1 through 10, in array TEST.

Once an array has been constructed, its elements may be used in the same way as a simple variable. A particular component of an array is usually referenced by appending a subscript to the array name. Such a subscript may be an integer number as in $TEST_3$, specifying the item in position 3 of array TEST, or it may be another data element as in $TEST_x$, specifying the item in position x of array TEST—in the last case the precise item referenced varies depending upon the value of x at the time the statement including $TEST_x$ is encountered. Such an expression, consisting of an array name followed by a subscript, is called an *array reference*. At the time an array reference is encountered in a statement, the value of the subscript must lie within the range of allowable subscript values specified when the array was constructed.

Exercise 7.3-1   *Printing Negative Numbers*

Draw a flowchart to read a set of twenty numbers and then print the negative ones in reverse order (i.e., the last negative number read is the first one printed). The appropriate data structure for storing the numbers is a one-dimensional array. Construct array NUMB consisting of twenty elements, with positions numbered 1 through 20. Then the flowchart of Figure 7.8 reads the twenty numbers into elements $NUMB_1$ through $NUMB_{20}$ and then outputs each negative number stored in $NUMB_{20}$ through $NUMB_1$.

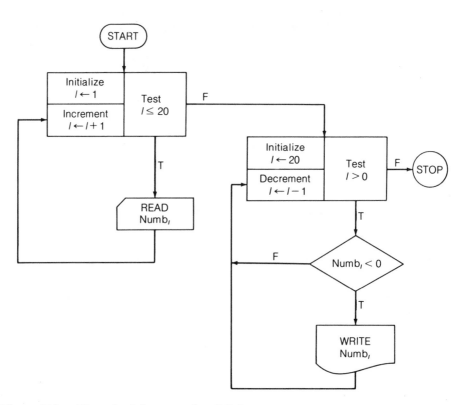

Figure 7.8:   Flowchart for exercise 7.3-1.

Exercise 7.3-2   Finding Highest Test Grade and its Location

Suppose we have an array TEST containing *N* test grades. Draw a flowchart to find the highest grade and its location (i.e., subscript position) in the array.

Initially we assume that the highest grade is the grade in $TEST_1$; we store this grade in variable LARG and its position, namely 1, in variable POS. Then we compare each grade in $TEST_2$ through $TEST_N$ with the current value of LARG; whenever the array element is greater in value than LARG, the value of that element and its position become the new values of LARG and POS respectively.

Thus, LARG and POS always contain the value and position of the highest grade of all those examined so far in array TEST. Figure 7.9 shows the flowchart for this procedure.

Exercise 7.3-3   Finding Median Test Grade with Exchange Sort

Assume we have an array GRADE containing 9 test grades. Draw a flowchart to determine the median grade.

First, we must sort the nine test grades into order, storing the lowest in $GRADE_1$, the second lowest in $GRADE_2$, and so forth with the highest grade in $GRADE_9$. The median grade will then be the grade stored in $GRADE_5$. To sort the grades into order, we shall use the exchange sorting method; more efficient sorting procedures are discussed in chapter 9. First, we find the largest grade and its position among the nine array elements; then we exchange the grade in this position with the grade in $GRADE_9$, so that $GRADE_9$ now contains the highest grade. Next, we find the largest grade and its position among the first eight array elements; then we change the grade in this position with the grade in $GRADE_8$, so that $GRADE_8$ now contains the second highest grade. The process is continued until finally all of the grades are in order. Figure 7.8 shows the flowchart for this procedure.   *10*

---

2) Two-Dimensional Arrays

Consider a program to determine which employees in a company are within one standard deviation of the average employee age. To accomplish this, the employee's names and ages must be read into memory, the average age and standard deviation calculated, and the names of those employees whose ages fall within the standard deviation determined.

It would be very cumbersome to store each employee-age pair in a different array. An appropriate data structure for this data is a *two*-dimensional array, consisting of rows and columns. Each row contains an employee-age pair, with the employee name in the first column and the employee age in the second column. Each individual component is then referenced according to its row-column position in the list, such as $LIST_{1,2}$ or $LIST_{4,1}$ for the age of the first employee or the name of the fourth employee respectively. Such a structure is called a *two-dimensional array*.

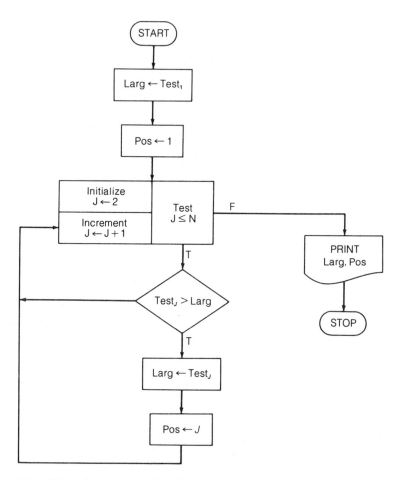

Figure 7.9: Flowchart for finding highest test grade and its location

Once again, the array must be constructed in memory before being used in a program. The declarative ALGOL statement: INTEGER ARRAY EMPLOY [1:20, 1:2] causes an array called EMPLOY to be constructed with twenty rows numbered consecutively as 1 through 20 and with two columns numbered 1, 2. Since the forty elements (20 rows × 2 columns per row) are specified as INTEGER, we are assuming that the names have an integer representation. Figure 7.11 shows an array EMPLOY containing names and ages of employees.

When referencing an element of a two-dimensional array, two subscripts are appended to the array name, indicating the row-column position of the specified element. $EMPLOY_{2,1}$ indicates the element in row 2 and column 1, i.e., the name of the second employee. $EMPLOY_{x,z}$ indicates the element in row X and column Z. As in the case of one-dimensional arrays, the precise element referenced depends on the values of X and Z at the time the state-

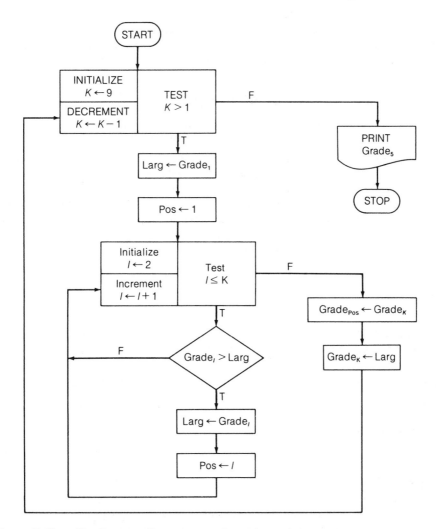

Figure 7.10:   Finding median test grade with exchange sort

Array employ

	Column 1	Column 2
Row 1	Name of first employee	Age
Row 2	Name of second employee	Age
	"	"
	"	"
	"	"
Row 20	Name of twentieth employee	Age

Figure 7.11:   Two-dimensional Array

ment including EMPLOY$_{x,z}$ is encountered. However, the values of the subscript for each dimension must lie within the range of allowable subscript values specified for that dimension when the array was constructed.

Exercise 7.3-4   Calculating Test Averages

Develop a flowchart for computing the average of 5 test scores for each of 25 students. Print the name of each student that is above the class average.

The appropriate data structure is an array, NAME, of 25 student names, TEST consisting of 25 rows (one row per student) and 5 columns (one column for each test score), and an array, STAVG, of one average for each student. Figure 7.12 shows a flowchart for reading the student's names and test grades into the arrays, computing each student's average and storing it in STAVG, while at the same time computing the class average and printing the name of each student whose average is above the class average.

B. Dynamic Data Sequences

Dynamic data sequences differ from static data sequences in that their size and shape may vary during the lifetime of a computation. These variations may be viewed as being the result of several construction or destruction operations, rather than the single declarative construction encountered in the previous section.

1) Stacks and Queues

Stacks and queues are two special types of dynamic data sequences with many applications. A *stack* is a sequence in which all insertions and deletions are made at one end of the sequence called the TOP. Such a structure resembles a stack of trays in a cafeteria—employees return trays and patrons remove trays from the top of the stack so that the last tray returned to the stack is always the first tray removed from it.

A *queue* is a sequence in which all insertions are made at one end of the sequence, called REAR, and all deletions are made at the opposite end, called FRONT. Such a structure resembles a queue of cars at a highway toll booth—cars enter the queue at the REAR of the queue and are removed from the FRONT one at a time as their toll is paid.

Stacks and queues are often referred to as LIFO (Last In—First Out) and FIFO (First In—First Out) structures respectively. An example of the application of stacks and queues is illustrated by the handling of deposits and withdrawals to savings accounts. Suppose you have a savings account that pays 4% per year or 1% per quarter and the interest is compounded quarterly. Interest is paid only on deposits left at the end of each quarter. You make the following set of transactions:

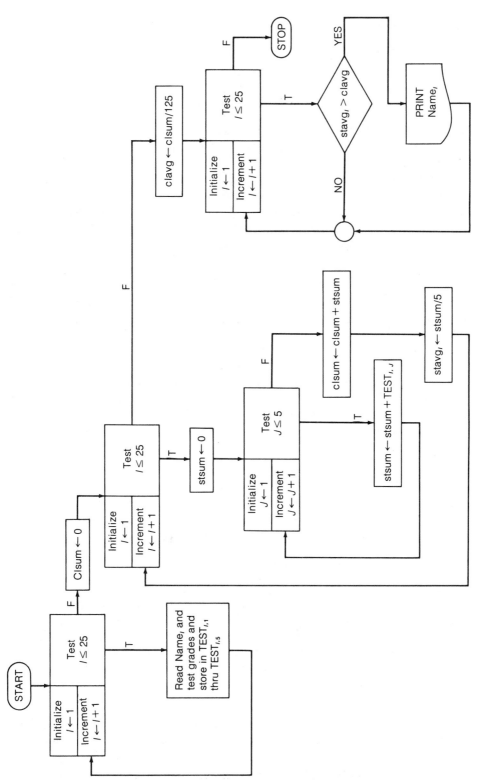

Figure 7.12:   Flowchart For Calculating Test Averages

149

Jan. 1	Deposit	$300
Feb. 1	Deposit	$300
Mar. 1	Withdrawal	$300
Apr. 1	Interest calculated	

If the money in the account is placed in a FIFO data structure, then the March 1 withdrawal removes the money deposited on January 1, resulting in only the February 1 deposit remaining in the account. Thus, the interest paid on April 1 will be $300 \times (1\% \times 2/3) = \$2.00$ (since the rate is 1% per quarter and the Feb. 1 money was in the account for 2/3 of a quarter).

On the other hand, if the money in the account is placed in a LIFO data structure, then the March 1 withdrawal removes the money deposited on February 1, resulting in the January 1 deposit remaining in the account. Then the interest paid on April 1 is very different; namely, $300 \times (1\% \times 3/3) = \$3.00$. (Recent laws now require banks to use a LIFO system.)

Stacks and queues occur frequently in computer science. *Stacks* are used for storing parameters passed to recursive programs and by compilers for translating programming languages. *Queues* are used in many discrete simulation programs and in operating systems for handling requests for machine facilities. An important application of queues is in the buffering of input/output data. The input/output facilities are the slowest part of a machine. Overall machine speed is increased if output can be placed in a queue and transferred independently, although slowly, by the I/O unit to the external medium while the central processing unit continues with other tasks.

2) Linked Lists

In all of the data structures discussed thus far, the adhesion of the individual elements has been implied. For example, it is understood that the elements physically preceding and following element $TEST_I$ in array TEST are elements $TEST_{I-1}$ and $TEST_{I+1}$ respectively. Thus, to search through a list of this type, you visit the array locations consecutively.

However, if a dynamic data sequence is subjected to many additions or deletions, then the structure becomes difficult to work with. Suppose a company has a sequence of employees stored in alphabetical order in an array; if a new employee is added to this sequence, then all names following this new employee name in alphabetical order must be moved down one position to free the required array location. Similarly, if an employee quits the company, all names following this deleted name must be moved up one position to fill the vacant location.

Another difficulty is that each array must be large enough to handle the maximum number of entires that will occur at any one time. If the programmer is working with many arrays in a program, each array is usually only partially filled and not all arrays become full at the same time. With so much of the arrays empty, there is wasted space. You can only allocate the available memory to the various arrays according to their estimated requirements— but in actual usage, one array may become full while there is still unused space in the other arrays. Unfortunately, the overflowing array cannot access this empty space.

Linked lists overcome these two difficulties. A *linked list* is a sequence in which each element contains a link or pointer to the location of the next element in the list. The last element of the list contains a predefined link value, *Nil*. Figure 7.13 illustrates a linked list structure.

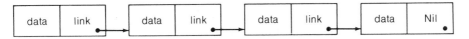

Figure 7.13:   Linked List Structure

C.   Operations on Linked Lists

As in preceding discussions of data structures, the basic operations on linked lists include referencing and constructing operations. In this case the operations are particularly simple, yet quite powerful when all the possible compositions of operations are considered. Two referencing operations, HEAD and TAIL, will be employed. These operations produce the first element of a linked list, and the remaining list with the first element eliminated, respectively. They play the same role as subscripting for arrays in that they allow referencing into the substructure. The constructor, CONS, takes a list element and an already built list and builds a new list with the list element as the head and the previous list as the tail. The starting point for the construction of a list is the special NIL list.*

Consider the following three lists representing lists of students in each of three subjects:

PHYSICS ← CONS("BOB", CONS("ANN", CONS("AL", NIL)))

MUSIC ← CONS("MARY", CONS("JOE", NIL))

COMPSCI ← CONS("CAROL", CONS("JOHN", CONS("LOUIS", CONS ("JEAN", NIL))))

or utilizing the representation in Figure 7.13.

(1) PHYSICS

*Those of you familiar with LISP will recognize HEAD and TAIL operations as CAR and CDR respectively.

(2) MUSIC

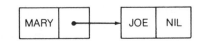

(3) COMPSCI

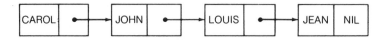

A new element may be added to a list by linking it to the previous elements

MUSIC ← CONS ("JIM", MUSIC)

which changes the MUSIC list to

An element may be removed from a list by delinking it. For example, to remove JOHN from the COMPSCI list:

COMPSCI ← CONS(HEAD(COMPSCI), TAIL(TAIL(COMPSCI)))

which produces the following structure

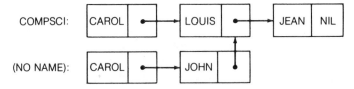

Notice that the previous instances of CAROL and JOHN are still present. They may be inaccessible because no name is given to the old list. The space allocated by the old elements, CAROL and JOHN, may be recovered and used for something else if it is inaccessible. No assumption is made that the elements of a list are physically next to each other in a memory. The links may be arbitrarily long.

A new element may be inserted into a list by a similar reorientation of the links. Suppose the name CARL is to become the second element of the PHYSICS list:

PHYSICS ← CONS(HEAD(PHYSICS), CONS("CARL", TAIL(PHYSICS))))

The resulting structure is:

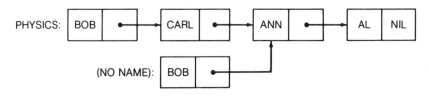

Once again, an old element, BOB, is left in a potentially inaccessible condition by the operation.

The operation HEAD, TAIL, and CONS, may be used with control operations such as condition and iteration to perform searching through a list structure.

Exercise 7.3-5

Draw a flowchart to remove the last element from a linked list.

Solution: Suppose the name of the list is STUDNT. The flowchart of Figure 7.14 first searches for NIL, then removes the last element.

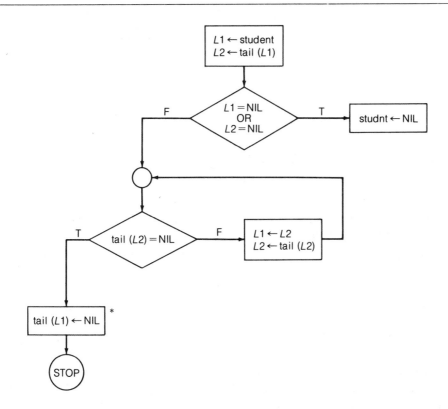

*This computation indicates the destructive assignment of NIL to the link subelement of $L1$.

Figure 7.14:   Removing the last element from a linked list

Exercise 7.3-6   Adding an Element to a Link List

Draw a flowchart to search a linked list called PEOPLE for the name MARY and add a new name CARL following MARY.

Solution: The flowchart, Figure 7.15 first searches for MARY, then restructures links to include the element, CARL.

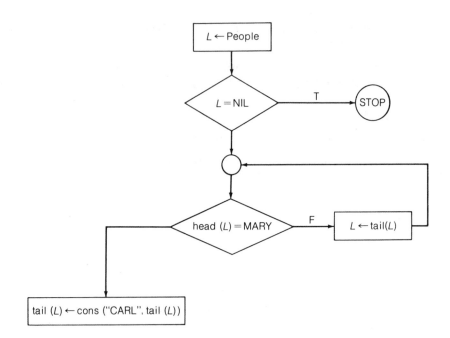

Figure 7.15: **Adding an element to a linked list**

Exercise 7.3-7   Constructing a Linked List

Draw a flowchart to construct a linked list called CHILD and obtain five names from input to place on this list.

Solution: The recursive algorithm described by the flowchart of Figure 7.16 builds the list, CHILD.

The lists described in this section are often called *one-way linked lists* since the links point in only one direction, from an element of the list to its successor. Other linked list structures have been designed for special applications. These include *circular lists* (the last element's link points back to the head element instead of being set to NIL). *two-way lists* (each element contains two links, one pointing to its successor and one to its predecessor in the list), and *threaded lists* (each element may contain several links, each related to a different list of which the element is a member).

Advantages and disadvantages

Linked list structures have advantages and disadvantages compared with arrays. Addition and deletion of elements in linked lists is very easy since only two links need to be altered—the link of the element being entered or removed and the link of the preceding element in the list. This distinct advantage gives linked lists many applications, such as computer text editing. In addition, several linked lists can share one large memory; the only restric-

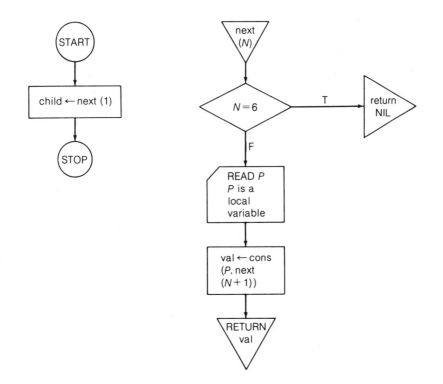

Figure 7.16: Recursive construction of a linked list

tions to be placed on the size of any individual list is that the total memory used by all the lists must not exhaust the available memory.

However, linked lists require two entries per element: data and link. Thus, linked lists require twice as much memory as sequential lists, although many times both data and link can be packed into one memory word. In addition, references to random parts of the list, such as retrieval of the Ith element, are much more difficult. Many algorithms, such as interval halving to search a sequence, are applicable to arrays but not to linked lists.

Again, the choice of a data structure depends upon both the innate structure of the data itself and upon the computations to be performed.

7.4   Realization of Data Structures

A. Storage of Arrays in Memory

Array elements are usually stored consecutively in contiguous memory locations. In the case of a one-dimensional array, TEST, of ten elements, TEST, through $TEST_{10}$ are stored consecutively in a designated 10-word block of memory. However, in the case of two-dimensional arrays, two alternative memory schemes are possible.

The first stores the array elements by rows, allocating consecutive memory locations first to all elements of the first row, then to all elements of the second row, and so forth. This is called *row-major form* and is implemented when an array is constructed in PL/I or ALGOL. The second scheme stores array elements by columns and is called *column-major form*; it is implemented when an array is constructed in FORTRAN. Figures 7.17 and 7.18 show an array PAYMT of 3 rows and 2 columns stored in row-major and column-major form respectively.

In order to access element $LIST_{I,J}$ of an M row $\times$ N column array stored in row-major form, the machine must count down $(I - 1) \times N + J - 1$ locations past the first location A assigned to this array; this causes the machine to pass over the $(I - 1) \times N$ locations assigned to the elements of the first $I - 1$ rows and then pass over the $J - 1$ locations assigned to the first $J - 1$ elements in row I, finally reaching the location assigned to element $LIST_{I,J}$. Thus, the address of the location assigned to element $LIST_{I,J}$ is $A + (I - 1) \times N + J - 1$. A similar formula is used to calculate the address of an array element stored in column-major form.

Location A	$PAYMT_{1,1}$		Location A	$PAYMT_{1,1}$
$A+1$	$PAYMT_{1,2}$		$A+1$	$PAYMT_{2,1}$
$A+2$	$PAYMT_{2,1}$		$A+2$	$PAYMT_{3,1}$
$A+3$	$PAYMT_{2,2}$		$A+3$	$PAYMT_{1,2}$
$A+4$	$PAYMT_{3,1}$		$A+4$	$PAYMT_{2,2}$
$A+5$	$PAYMT_{3,2}$		$A+5$	$PAYMT_{3,2}$

Figure 7.17   Array PAYMT (3 rows $\times$ 2 columns) stored in row-major form.

Figure 7.18   Array PAYMT (3 rows $\times$ 2 columns) stored in column-major form.

Exercise 7.4-1

Develop an addressing formula for 3-dimensional arrays. Generalize your result to N-dimensional arrays.

Most programming languages do not test whether the subscripts of a subscripted variable are within the range of allowable subscripts specified when the array was constructed. They test only whether the subscripts cause the address of the location for that element to fall outside the block of memory allocated to that array. Consider the case of the 3 row $\times$ 2 column array PAYMT stored in row-major form (Figure 7.17). A reference to $PAYMT_{2,2}$ causes a reference to memory location $A + 3$ which is within the block of memory allocated to this array. A reference to $PAYMT_{5,2}$ causes a reference to memory location $A + (5 - 1) \times 2 + 2 - 1$ or location $A + 9$, which is outside this block, and the machine responds with an error message. However, a reference to $PAYMT_{1,4}$, although illegal in that the second subscript is outside the specified range, which is 1 through 2, causes a reference to memory location $A + (1 - 1) \times 2 + 4 - 1$ or location $A + 3$. Although the machine interprets this as a valid reference, it is really an error and has the effect of using array element $PAYMT_{2,2}$. Thus, the programmer should be aware of how arrays are constructed and stored in memory.

B. Implementation of Stacks and Queues

The programmer can easily construct stacks and queues. Let STAK be a one-dimensional array of N elements; the array elements form the consecutive potential elements of the stack. If the stack is not empty, then $STAK_1$ is always the bottom element of the stack; a variable TOP is used as a pointer to the location of the top element of the stack. Figure 7.19 shows a stack that currently contains three entries.

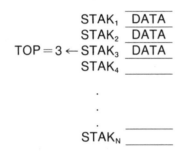

Figure 7.19:   A Stack Containing Three Entries

Initially TOP ← 0 since the stack is empty. To add an element DATA to the stack, pointer TOP is incremented by one, effectively placing a new array element on top of the stack, and DATA is stored in this new element. The flowchart in Figure 7.20 illustrates this process.

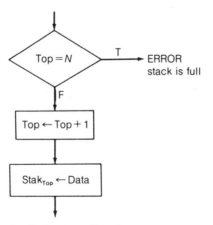

Figure 7.20:   Adding An Entry to a Stack

To remove an element from a stack and place its contents in ITEM, the contents of the stack entry to which TOP points is stored in ITEM and TOP is decremented by one, effectively removing this element from the stack. The flowchart of Figure 7.21 illustrates this process.

The process of adding an element to a stack is often called a *push-down* since the other stack elements are pushed one position further down from the stack top; similarly the process of deleting an element from a stack is called a *pop-up*.

In constructing a queue, pointers must be maintained to both the front and rear locations. Let QUE be a one-dimensional array of N elements. The array elements form the consecutive potential elements of the queue. Variable FRNT points to the array location preceding the first element of the queue and variable RER points to the location of the last element of the queue. Figure 7.22 shows a queue that currently contains three entries.

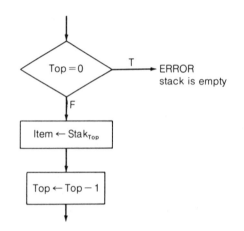

Figure 7.21: Removing an Entry from a Stack

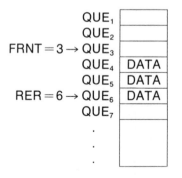

Figure 7.22:   A Queue Containing Three Entries

Initially FRNT ← 0 and RER ← 0 since the queue is empty. To add an element DATA to the queue, RER is incremented by one, effectively appending a new array element to the end of the queue, and DATA is stored in this new element. The flowchart of Figure 7.23 illustrates this process.

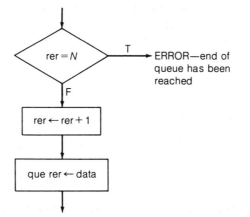

Figure 7.23:   Adding an Entry to a Queue

To remove an element from a queue and place its contents in ITEM, pointer FRNT is incremented by one, effectively removing the front entry from the queue, and the contents of this array element to which FRNT points are stored in ITEM. The flowchart of Figure 7.24 illustrates this process.

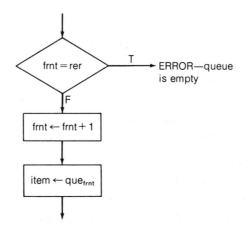

Figure 7.24:   Removing an Entry from a Queue

One difficulty with the above construction is that, on reaching the physical end of the array allocated to the queue, you have no mechanism for utilizing memory that may have been freed by removing elements from the front of the queue. Problem 9 at the end of this chapter suggests construction of a circular queue to overcome this limitation.

Summary

Data structures take many forms, from simple variables and sequential arrays to one-way linked lists, binary trees, and more complex structures not discussed in this chapter. There is no best data structure for all problems; the choice of data structure depends on the innate structure of the data itself and the operations to be performed on that data. In some cases, no formalized data structure is appropriate, and the programmer must construct his own method of representation.

References and Suggested Additional Readings

(1) Bell, C.G. and Newell, A. *Computer Structures: Readings and Examples.* New York: McGraw Hill, 1971.

(2) Berztiss, A. T. *Data Structures—Theory and Practice.* New York: Academic Press, 1971.

(3) Elson, Mark. *Data Structures.* Palo Alto: Science Research Associates, 1975.

(4) Knuth, D. E. *The Art of Computer Programming, Vol. 1, Fundamental Algorithms.* Reading, Mass.: Addison-Wesley, 1958.

(5) Stone, H.S. *Introduction to Computer Organization and Data Structures.* New York: McGraw Hill, 1972.

Problems

Assume you have an array STT containing *N* elements. Draw flowcharts to accomplish each of the following:

1. Find the element of array STT whose absolute value is largest.
2. Sort the elements of array STT into order according to absolute value.
3. Output the average of each group of three successive elements of array STT.
4. Reverse the order of the elements of array STT.

Assume you have a two-dimensional array PEOPLE consisting of 25 rows (one row per person) and 3 columns (name in column 1, age in column 2, salary in column 3). Draw flowcharts to accomplish each of the following. (Problems 5–7).

5. Sort the elements of array PEOPLE into order according to each person's age.
6. Sort the elements of array PEOPLE into order according to each person's age— but if two people are the same age, then the person with the lower salary is to occur first in the sorted array.
7. Compute the average salary of all people whose age is between 25 and 35 inclusive.
8. Determine the formula used to calculate the memory address of a two-dimensional array element stored in column major form.

9. Alter the queue algorithms of Section 7.2 so that on reaching the physical end of the array allocated to the queue, the front and rear pointers loop around to reuse memory at the physical beginning of the array—provided that particular memory has been freed and is no longer part of the queue.

Assume you have a linked list called CLASS. Draw flowcharts to accomplish each of the following:

10. Remove the first five elements from CLASS.
11. Append the elements of a second list called STUDENT to the end of linked list CLASS.
12. Search linked list CLASS for the name JOHN; remove all elements after JOHN from linked list CLASS and place them on a new linked list call GRAD.

In a two-way linked list, each element contains two links, one pointing to its successor and one to its predecessor in the list.

13. Alter the flowcharts of Section 7.3 so that they operate upon two-way linked lists.
14. Draw a flowchart to remove the *last* five elements from a two-way linked list.
15. The Missionaries and Cannibals Problem: Three missionaries and three cannibals are on one side of a wide river. The only means of crossing the river is via a small boat that can carry at most two people. If at any time there are more cannibals than missionaries on one side of the river, the cannibals will eat the missionaries. Assuming that each person can operate the boat, draw the decision tree illustrating the series of operations that might be undertaken to move the missionaries and cannibals to the other side of the river and find the path leading to a successful solution.
16. Draw a flowchart to visit the nodes of a tree using postorder traversal.
17. Draw a flowchart to visit the nodes of a tree using endorder traversal.

Chapter 8

Numerical Applications

As noted in chapter 1, the early development of computer science was closely tied to the demands of science and technology. In particular, nuclear science and aerospace science could not have reached their present states of development without the aid of the digital computer in its role as a numerical computer. The demands for accuracy and speed that evolved in such applications gave impetus to the advancement of computer technology.

The purpose of this chapter is to examine carefully the foundations of numerical computation, the scope of numerical applications, and those features that distinguish numerical from non-numerical computations. In keeping this discussion free of mathematical arguments, it may seem that the entire subject of numerical computation is rather pedestrian. In fact, the specialist in numerical computation usually finds it necessary to draw on the insights of mathematics, statistics, and physics, as well as a sizeable bag of tricks.

8.1   Examples of Numerical Computation

In this section, a few problems that require numerical computation will be cited and discussed. In many cases, a detailed discussion of the solutions of each of these problems would require a volume in itself. These applications may be partitioned into strategic and tactical problems on the basis of whether computation time is a major consideration in the solution of the problem.

Some strategic numerical computations

(1) *Design of Nuclear Reactors:* You may wish to determine the geometry and thickness of shielding required to make a nuclear reactor safe. This problem requires a mathematical model of the motion of subatomic particles and radiation. Computation based on such a model is used to predict the intensity of nuclear particles and radiation outside the reactor. Since nuclear phenomena tend to be random in nature, statistical notions play an important part in such computations.

(2) *Choice of Site for a Deep-water Oil Terminal:* This problem will require the computation of the motion of oil spills from a proposed site for an oil terminal. The motion may be described by nonlinear partial differential equations. Random affects of wind and current may once again impose a statistical element in the computations.

(3) *Design of Transportation Systems:* This problem involves the optimal choice of routes and terminal locations in a transportation network. The optimization procedure itself may involve iteration and, in some cases, recursion during the search for the best solution to the problem.

Some tactical numerical computations

In the preceeding examples, the required computations may need an amount of time that approaches the life-time of the application. The importance of such computations is further emphasized by the following examples.

(1) *Air Traffic Control:* The volume of domestic air traffic has led to computer-aided air traffic control. The position, heading, and variability for each aircraft are computed. Diversions are commanded whenever any aircraft presents an unacceptable risk of collision.

(2) *Weather Prediction:* Atmospheric data form the basis of prediction of future weather conditions and trends. The motion of the atmosphere may be modelled with nonlinear partial differential equations. The results of such computations may be graphical (i.e., weather maps). This problem is probably the most difficult of all the tactical applications that have been attempted.

(3) *Automatic Aircraft Pilots:* Computer systems have been designed to handle some flight problems that leave human pilots helpless. In addition to the usual take-off, cruise, and landing problems, computers play an important role in pathological situations such as landing on a very short runway, flying an aircraft when major components may be missing, and emergency diversions to avoid collisions.

8.2   Important Features of Numerical Computations

Numerical computations are distinguished by their reliance on real numbers (i.e., floating point numbers). This use of real numbers is founded in tradition and historical accident, but is well justified in terms of programming convenience and precision of computation. Physical quantities do arise with unpredictable magnitude and would be very difficult to scale to a fixed point domain.

The great majority of programs written for numerical computation are written in FORTRAN. The connection between numerical computation and FORTRAN is another historical accident. FORTRAN was one of the earliest high-level programming languages and numerical computations dominated the early applications of computers. In spite of nearly universal agreement that FORTRAN needs major improvement for numerical computation, it continues to survive in a form very close to the original.

8.3   Error Analysis

In this section, we are concerned with the behavior of errors in numerical computation. The modern digital computers, in spite of all the powers attributed to them, do commit errors when dealing with real numbers. In fact, it is reasonable to assume that ERRORS ARE INEVITABLE in numerical computation. Because of this unfortunate omnipresence of errors, our concern in the analysis of error is not the elimination of errors but the control and prediction of the magnitude of errors. A computation's value is greatly enhanced if, in addition to the result, you are able to obtain information about the accuracy of the result.

In spite of the inevitability of errors, it is reasonable to assume that errors occur as very small numbers. This property, often called the *infinitesimal* property, of errors is of considerable value in the analyses that follow. Whenever it is convenient to do so, products of two or more infinitesimal numbers may be taken to be zero. Thus, multiplying an error by itself may produce a product that can be completely ignored.

Review of representations of real numbers

Since most numerical applications employ the real number as the fundamental atomic data type, we are justified in discussing error analysis in terms of real numbers. Remember that real numbers are typically represented in the memory of a digital computer by a bit format as shown in Figure 8.1. The number is represented at a finite precision determined by the width of the mantissa, t. Regardless of how many bits are required to represent a number, the actual representation may be limited to t bits of precision.

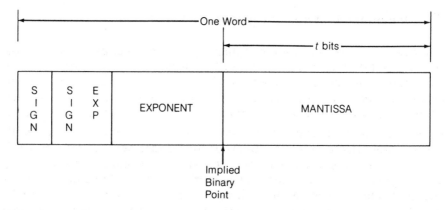

Figure 8.1:   A typical real number format

Just as some numbers do not have finite decimal representations (e.g. $1/3$, π), some real numbers do not have a finite binary representation. Thus, in the process of storing such a number, an error is incurred.

Exercise 8.3-1

Convert the decimal number, 0.37, to its binary equivalent. Does it have a finite binary representation? Can it be proven?

Sources of Error

The errors incurred in a computation are from numerous sources and are carried throughout a computation into the final result.

The sources of error may be classified into:

Initial error
Round-off error
Truncation error

The purpose of this section is to discuss the possibilities of analyzing the magnitude of each of these sources of error.

The term, *initial error,* refers to that error that is present in the data to be used in a computation. This error occurs prior to any thought of the use of a computer. Estimation of the magnitude of the initial error requires considerations of sensor accuracy and efficiency of data transmission. If a computer is to be used in an application such as weather prediction, you must recognize that the data used in the computation may be of limited accuracy.

Round-off errors arise when real numbers are stored in a finite precision format, such as Figure 8.1. Assuming the base of the exponent of such a number is two, you can show by examination of the round-off process that the round-off error, e_r, is limited by

$$|e_r| < 2^{EXP-t-1} \qquad \text{8.3-1}$$

If the mantissa of the real number is normalized in such a way that the left-most bit of a positive mantissa is one, then the magnitude of a number, x, is bounded by

$$|x| \geq 2^{EXP-1} \qquad \text{8.3-2}$$

Combining these two inequalities leads to

$$|e_r| \leq |x| \times 2^{-t} \qquad \text{8.3-3}$$

Although somewhat conservative, the bound (upper limit) given in Equation 8.3-3 is quite useful in error analysis. It is reasonable to assume that such an error is incurred whenever a number is stored in a computer memory.

Truncation error is caused by neglecting terms when an infinite process is approximated by a finite one. For example, such errors appear when an infinite series is summed by an approximate method or when we replace a differential equation with its discrete difference analogue.

As an example, consider the evaluation of

$$\sin x = x - \frac{x^3}{3!} + \frac{x^5}{5!} - \frac{x^7}{7!} + \frac{x^9}{9!} - \frac{x^{11}}{11!} + \frac{x^{13}}{13!} + \cdots$$

The value of the sine function computed by the use of these first seven terms has eight significant digits. The sums of the terms not used, i.e., $x^{15}/15!, \ldots,$ presents the truncation error in using this approximation.

Propagation of error

In this section, we consider the mechanism by which the errors considered in the previous section appear in the result of a computation. The initial, round-off, and truncation errors all *propagate* through a computation by processes illustrated by the following analyses.

Let us represent the error in a quantity a by e_a. The true value written, $\bar{a}$, is then $a - e_a$. Similarly, we may write $b = \bar{b} + e_b$. If we add a and b, we get (neglecting rounding error for the moment),

$$\bar{c} + e_c = \bar{a} + e_a + \bar{b} + e_b \qquad \text{8.3-4}$$

Since the true value of the sum, $\bar{c}$, is $\bar{a} + \bar{b}$, the error in the value $a + b$ which we obtained is just $e_a + e_b$. The relative error in the sum is therefore:

$$\frac{e_c}{c} \qquad \text{8.3-5}$$

which we can write:

$$\frac{e_c}{c} = \left(\frac{a}{a+b}\right)\left(\frac{e_a}{a}\right) + \left(\frac{b}{a+b}\right)\left(\frac{e_b}{b}\right) \qquad \text{8.3-6}$$

Thus, the relative error in a sum $a + b$ is obtained by multiplying the relative error in a by $a/(a + b)$ and the relative error in b by $b/a + b$ and adding the results. We may symbolize this result in graphical form

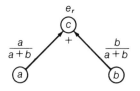

to indicate that when two operands a and b enter the $+$ operation, their relative errors are multiplied by the factors on the corresponding arrows and added to determine the relative error they contribute to the sum. In addition, we place an e_r by the node symbol $\bigcirc$ to remind us that in addition to the error in the sum that comes from the operands, there is rounding error in the addition operation itself.

Similarly, when the operation is subtraction, we have:

$$\frac{e_c}{c} = \left(\frac{a}{a-b}\right)\left(\frac{e_a}{a}\right) - \left(\frac{b}{a-b}\right)\left(\frac{e_b}{b}\right) \qquad \text{8.3-7}$$

which can be expressed graphically:

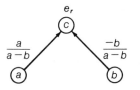

A curious phenomenon develops in subtraction, when the magnitude of the error in the result may approach the magnitude of the difference:

$$|e_c| \approx |a - b|$$

The effect is known as *cancellation*. It arises particularly when two very large numbers of nearly the same magnitude are subtracted.

In the case of multiplication, we can write:

$$\bar{c} + e_c = (\bar{a} + e_a)(\bar{b} + e_b) = \bar{a}\bar{b} + \bar{a}e_b + \bar{b}e_a + e_a e_b \qquad \text{8.3-8}$$

Therefore

$$e_c = \bar{a}e_b + \bar{b}e_a + e_a e_b \qquad \text{8.3-9}$$

Utilizing the infinitesimal property of the errors e_a and e_b, we can neglect the term $e_a e_b$; also, since a is close to $\bar{a}$ and b close to $\bar{b}$, we can write approximately

$$e_c = be_a + ae_b \qquad \text{8.3-10}$$

so that

$$\frac{e_c}{c} = \frac{e_a}{a} + \frac{e_b}{b} \qquad \text{8.3-11}$$

For multiplication, the relative errors add, and this is symbolized by the process graph

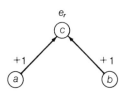

Exercise 8.3-1

Develop an algorithm for computing the roots of a quadratic polynomial. Be sure to avoid unnecessary subtractions that may lead to cancellation.

For division we have

$$c + e_c = \frac{\bar{a} + e_a}{\bar{b} + e_b} = \frac{\bar{a} + e_a}{\bar{b}\left(1 + \dfrac{e_b}{\bar{b}}\right)} \qquad \text{8.3-12}$$

Now

$$\frac{1}{1 + x} = 1 - x + x^2 - x^3 + \dots \qquad \text{8.3-13}$$

provided $|x| < 1$. Since $e_b / \bar{b}$ will usually satisfy the condition that $|e_b / \bar{b}| < 1$, we can write:

$$c + e_c = \frac{\bar{a} + e_a}{\bar{b}}\left(1 - \frac{e_b}{\bar{b}} + \left(\frac{e_b}{\bar{b}}\right)^2 - \dots\right) \qquad \text{8.3-14}$$

Multiplying out, and neglecting all terms containing products of errors, we have approximately

$$c + e_c = \frac{\bar{a}}{\bar{b}} + \frac{e_a}{\bar{b}} - \frac{\bar{a}e_b}{(\bar{b})^2} \qquad \text{8.3-15}$$

so that the error in c is

$$e_c = \frac{e_a}{\bar{b}} - \frac{\bar{a}e_b}{(\bar{b})^2} \qquad \text{8.3-16}$$

or, replacing $\bar{a}$ by a and $\bar{b}$ by b,

$$e_c = \frac{e_a}{b} - \frac{ae_b}{b^2} \qquad \text{8.3-17}$$

Equation 8.3-17 illustrates the possibility that the error e_c may be extremely sensitive to the errors e_a and e_b when the denominator b is very small. Such a computation is referred to as *ill-conditioned.* This property of a computation is particularly important in some highly involved computations. No matter what is done to control truncation and rounding errors, the computation may be extremely sensitive to the initial error, in which case the result cannot be used.

The relative error in c is given by

$$\frac{e_c}{c} = \frac{e_a}{a} - \frac{e_b}{b} \qquad \text{8.3-18}$$

which is expressed in the process graph

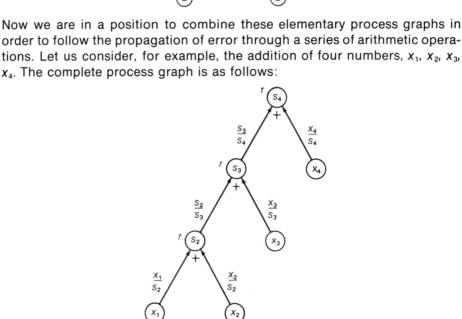

Now we are in a position to combine these elementary process graphs in order to follow the propagation of error through a series of arithmetic operations. Let us consider, for example, the addition of four numbers, x_1, x_2, x_3, x_4. The complete process graph is as follows:

where we have written

$$s_2 \text{ for } x_1 + x_2$$
$$s_3 \text{ for } x_1 + x_2 + x_3$$
$$s_4 \text{ for } x_1 + x_2 + x_3 + x_4$$

The relative error in s_2 is found by adding the appropriate multiples (shown on the arrows in the graph) of the relative errors in x_1 and x_2, then adding the rounding error r generated in the first addition. Thus,

$$\frac{e_{s_2}}{s_2} = \frac{x_1}{s_2}\left(\frac{e_{x_1}}{x_1}\right) + \frac{x_2}{s_2}\left(\frac{e_{x_2}}{x_2}\right) + (e_r)_2 = \frac{e_{x_1} + e_{x_2}}{s_2} + (e_r)_2 \qquad \textbf{8.3-19}$$

where e_{x_1}/x_1 is the relative error in x_1, and, similarly, for e_{x_2}/x_2 and e_{s_2}/s_2, and $(e_r)_2$ is the rounding error in s_2. The second equation is obtained from the first by cancellation and factoring.

The relative error in s_3 is similarly found to be

$$\frac{e_{s_3}}{s_3} = \frac{s_2}{s_3}\left(\frac{e_{s_2}}{s_2}\right) + \frac{x_3}{s_3}\left(\frac{e_{x_3}}{x_3}\right) + (e_r)_3 = \frac{e_{s_2} + e_{x_3}}{s_3} + (e_r)_3 \qquad \textbf{8.3-20}$$

But from Equation 8:3-19

$$e_{s_2} = e_{x_1} + e_{x_2} + (e_r)_2 \, s_2, \qquad \textbf{8.3-21}$$

obtained from 8.3-19 by cross-multiplying by s_2, and therefore substituting the right-hand side of equation 8.3-21 for e_{s_2} in equation 8.3-20 yields:

$$\frac{e_{s_3}}{s_3} = \frac{e_{x_1} + e_{x_2} + e_{x_3} + (e_r)_2 \, s_2}{s_3} + (e_r)_3 \qquad \textbf{8.3-22}$$

Finally, we have

$$\frac{e_{s_4}}{s_4} = \frac{s_3}{s_4}\left(\frac{e_{s_3}}{s_3}\right) + \frac{x_4}{s_4}\left(\frac{e_{x_4}}{x_4}\right) + (e_r)_4 = \frac{e_{s_3} + e_{x_4}}{s_4} + (e_r)_4 \qquad \textbf{8.3-23}$$

But from Equation 8.3-22, cross-multiplying by s_3 yields:

$$e_{s_3} = e_{x_1} + e_{x_2} + e_{x_3} + (e_{r\cdot2})s_2 + (e_r)_3 s_3 \qquad \textbf{8.3-24}$$

and therefore, substituting the right-hand side of equation 8.3-24 for e_{s_3} in equation 8.3-23 yields:

$$\frac{e_{s_4}}{s_4} = \frac{e_{x_1} + e_{x_2} + e_{x_3} + e_{x_4} + (e_r)_2 \, s_2 + (e_r)_3 \, s_3}{s_4} + (e_r)_4$$

$$= \frac{e_{x_1} + e_{x_2} + e_{x_3} + e_{x_4}}{s_4} + \frac{(e_r)_2 \, s_2 + (e_r)_3 \, s_3 + (e_r)_4 \, s_4}{s_4} \qquad \textbf{8.3-25}$$

or, if we replace s_2, s_3, and s_4 with their values in terms of x_1, x_2, x_3, and x_4,

Recall that $s_2 = x_1 + x_2$
$$s_3 = x_1 + x_2 + x_3$$
$$s_4 = x_1 + x_2 + x_3 + x_4$$

$$\frac{e_{s_4}}{s_4} = \frac{e_{x_1} + e_{x_2} + e_{x_3} + e_{x_4}}{s_4} +$$

$$\frac{x_1\big((e_r)_2 + (e_r)_3 + (e_r)_4\big) + x_2\big((e_r)_2 + (e_r)_3 + (e_r)_4\big) + x_3\big((e_r)_3 + (e_r)_4\big) + x_4\,(e_r)_4}{s_4} \qquad \textbf{8.3-26}$$

The first term in Equation 8.3-26 does not depend on the order in which the numbers are added; it is simply the sum of the errors divided by the sum of the numbers. The second term, however, which represents the contribution of rounding error, does depend on this order. For example, if we add the numbers 10, 3, 7, 2 in that order, the rounding error contribution is (utilizing the inequality equation 8.3-3):

$$\frac{1053 \times 2^{-t}}{22} \qquad \text{8.3-27}$$

However, if we add them in the order 2, 3, 7, 10, the rounding error term is

$$\frac{652 \times 2^{-t}}{22} \qquad \text{8.3-28}$$

This propagation of roundoff errors leads to a phenomenon called *instability*. A numerical algorithm is said to be unstable if the cumulative effect of all roundoff errors grows exponentially with the number of operations involved.

Forward error analysis

The analysis of error illustrated in the previous section is an example of *forward error analysis*. The errors in the result are determined by the errors in the operands. In an extensive, highly involved computation, the errors in each intermediate result would be carried along each step of the way.

This type of analysis is quite useful in computing bounds on the magnitude of errors. By taking absolute values of Equations 8.3-6, 8.3-7, 8.3-11, and 8.3-18, the respective errors may be bounded by

$$\left|\frac{e_c}{c}\right| \leq \left|\frac{a}{a+b}\right| \times \left|\frac{e_a}{a}\right| + \left|\frac{b}{a+b}\right| \times \left|\frac{e_b}{b}\right| \qquad \text{(addition)} \qquad \text{8.3-29}$$

$$\left|\frac{e_c}{c}\right| \leq \left|\frac{a}{a-b}\right| \times \left|\frac{e_a}{a}\right| + \left|\frac{b}{a-b}\right| \times \left|\frac{e_b}{b}\right| \qquad \text{(subtraction)} \qquad \text{8.3-30}$$

$$\left|\frac{e_c}{c}\right| \leq \left|\frac{e_a}{a}\right| + \left|\frac{e_b}{b}\right| \qquad \text{(multiplication)} \qquad \text{8.3-31}$$

$$\left|\frac{e_c}{c}\right| \leq \left|\frac{e_a}{a}\right| + \left|\frac{e_b}{b}\right| \qquad \text{(division)} \qquad \text{8.3-32}$$

Using these bounds, very conservative estimates of the errors may be obtained. Where safety is an overwhelming consideration, as in nuclear reactor design, such error analyses are justified.

As an alternative to bounding the errors in a computation, a less conservative analysis would require viewing errors as random variables. The expected value and variance of the errors would be estimated instead of the bounds.

Backward error analysis

A particularly powerful method of error analysis known as *backward error analysis* leads you to a different view of the problem. Whereas in the previous section we began with initial and rounding errors and attempted to estimate the errors in the result, in backward error analysis we begin with the computed result and ask, "What problem has been solved?" In such an analysis, if the problem solved is not within an acceptable neighborhood of the problem that should have been solved, then the result must be discarded. A new attempt to obtain a result would require smaller initial and rounding errors.

8.4   Examples of Numerical Algorithms

Solution of equations

The manipulation of matrices and the solution of linear systems of equations are among the most frequently encountered tasks in computing. Because linear functions are best understood, problems in computer science, statistics, engineering, mathematics, and optimization tend to be formulated as a sequence of linear equations. For this reason, we choose to illustrate the numerical class of problems by considering the numerical solution of a system of linear equations.

The general case involves n equations and n unknowns. This system of equations can be written as follows:

$$a_{11}x_1 + a_{12}x_2 + \ldots + a_{1n}x_n = f_1$$
$$a_{21}x_1 + a_{22}x_2 + \ldots + a_{2n}x_n = f_2 \qquad \text{8.4-1}$$

$$\cdot$$
$$\cdot$$
$$\cdot$$

$$a_{n1}x_1 + a_{n2}x_2 + \ldots + a_{nn}x_n = f_n$$

or equivalently in the matrix form

$$\mathbf{A} \cdot \mathbf{x} = \mathbf{f} \qquad \text{8.4-2*}$$

where $\mathbf{A}$ is the coefficient matrix $\mathbf{x}$ is the vector of unknowns and $\mathbf{f}$ is the vector of righthand sides. Although there are many algorithms, depending on the properties of the coefficient matrix $\mathbf{A}$, for solving such a system, all of them are variations of the Gaussian elimination. This procedure works as follows:

First Step: Eliminate the term containing x_1 from each equation following the first equation. To do this, assume that $a_{11} \neq 0$; otherwise interchange the first equation with the first equation whose first coefficient is nonzero. Multiply both sides of the first equation by $-a_{ij}/a_{11}(j=2, \ldots, n)$ and add the resultant

---

*A matrix $\mathbf{A}$ is a rectangular array of numbers arranged in rows and columns. The (i, j) entry a_{ij} is located at the intersection of the ith row and j^{th} column of A. A matrix which has the same number of rows and columns is called a *square matrix*. If a matrix has only one column (row), it is called a *column (row) vector*. The multiplication of a matrix by a vector is defined in terms of Equation 8.4-1.

equation to the second, third, . . . , n^{th} equation to reduce the original system to the form:

$$a_{11}x_1 + a_{12}x_2 + \ldots + a_{1n}x_n = f_1$$
$$a_{22}^{(1)}x_2 + \ldots + a_{2n}^{(1)}x_n = f_2^{(1)}$$
$$a_{32}^{(1)}x_2 + \ldots + a_{3n}^{(1)}x_n = f_3^{(1)}$$

8.4-3

$$a_{n2}^{(1)}x_2 + \ldots + a_{nn}^{(1)}x_n = f_n^{(1)}$$

The set of equations shown in equations 8.4-3 is derived from the original set of equations, 8.4-1, as discussed. To distinguish between the constants in the original equations and the constants after the first step, a superscript of (1) is added to those constants which are modified. (Note that only the equations beyond the first are modified in the first step. In general, in the kth step, only the equations beyond the kth are modified, and a superscript (k), is used).

Second Step: In this step we eliminate the term containing x_2 from each equation following the second. Suppose $a_{22}^{(1)} \neq 0$; otherwise rearrange the equations as before. Add the appropriate multiple of this new second equation to the third, fourth, . . . , n^{th} equation, so that the set of equations becomes

$$a_{11}x_1 + a_{12}x_2 + a_{13}x_3 + \ldots + a_{1n}x_n = f_1$$
$$a_{22}^{(1)}x_2 + a_{23}^{(1)}x_3 + \ldots + a_{2n}^{(1)}x_n = f_2^{(1)}$$
$$a_{33}^{(2)}x_3 + \ldots + a_{3n}^{(2)}x_n = f_3^{(2)}$$

$$a_{n3}^{(2)}x_3 + \ldots + a_{nn}^{(2)}x_n = f_n^{(2)} \qquad \textbf{8.4-4}$$

Remaining Steps: This process is continued until we finally obtain a set of equations in the following triangular form:

$$a_{11}x_1 + a_{12}x_2 + a_{13}x_3 + \ldots + a_{1n}x_n = f_1$$
$$a_{22}^{(1)}x_2 + a_{23}^{(1)}x_3 + \ldots + a_{2n}^{(1)}x_n = f_2^{(1)}$$
$$a_{33}^{(2)}x_3 + \ldots + a_{3n}^{(2)}x_n = f_3^{(2)}$$

8.4-5

$$a_{nn}^{(n-1)}x_n = f_n^{(n-1)}$$

The solution of this triangular system is simple. The last equation is solved for x_n. Knowing x_n, we can compute x_{n-1} from the second-to-last equation and so on until the first equation is solved for x_1. The following numeric example should make this procedure clear.

$$2x_1 + 3x_2 - x_3 = 5$$
$$4x_1 + 4x_2 - 3x_3 = 3 \qquad \qquad \textbf{8.4-6}$$
$$2x_1 - 3x_2 + x_3 = -1$$

Multiplying the first equation by -2 and adding it to the second equation yields

$$2x_1 + 3x_2 - x_3 = 5$$
$$-2x_2 - x_3 = -7 \qquad \qquad \textbf{8.4-7}$$
$$2x_1 - 3x_2 + x_3 = -1$$

Multiplying the first equation by 1 and adding it to the third equation, we have

$$2x_1 + 3x_2 - x_3 = 5$$
$$-2x_2 - x_3 = -7 \qquad \qquad \textbf{8.4-8}$$
$$-6x_2 + 2x_3 = -6$$

To eliminate x_2 from the third equation, we subtract from it three times the second. Thus

$$2x_1 + 3x_2 - x_3 = 5$$
$$-2x_2 - x_3 = -7 \qquad \qquad \textbf{8.4-9}$$
$$5x_3 = 15$$

Now, we find that from the last equation $x_3 = 3$. Knowing this value, we solve the second equation for $x_2 = (-7 + 3)/-2 = 2$. The first equation yields $x_1 = (5 - 6 + 3)/2 = 1$.

The numbers a_{11}, $a_{22}^{(1)}$, $a_{33}^{(2)}$, ..., which are used as denominators in the process of elimination, are called *pivots*. We have chosen them so they are not zero. Unless a pivot is exactly zero, the interchange of equations is unnecessary in theory. Nonetheless, roundoff errors in the arithmetic operations may lead to very large errors if the pivots are small. To avoid this problem, it is customary to search a column for the coefficient of maximal absolute value and choose that element as a *pivot* (see exercise 3).

Locating a root of an equation

As an example of using iteration in numerical applications, let us consider the problem of solving the nonlinear equation $f(x) = 0$. The iterative process involves guessing an approximate root and substituting it into the equation to obtain a next approximation that we hope is closer to the root. This approximation in turn is used to get the next approximation. The iteration ceases when it has either converged to the true root with sufficient accuracy or has indicated that it will not converge.

We shall discuss here one simple procedure known as the *Bisection Method*. It is based on the fact that if $f(x)$ changes sign between $x = a$ and $x = b$, say $f(a) < 0$ and $f(b) > 0$, and $f(x)$ is continuous on the closed interval $[a, b]$, then there exists at least one root between a and b. The question is, "How can we locate a root in this interval more accurately?" A procedure that comes directly to mind is to consider the midpoint, c, of the interval $[a, b]$ and evaluate $f(c)$ to determine whether the root lies between a and c or between c and b (see the figure below). Now we repeat the procedure by halving the new interval to get a better approximation of the root. This process is repeated until the desired degree of accuracy, tolerance, is realized.

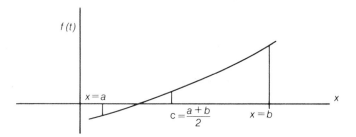

A flowchart of this procedure is on page 173.

In this algorithm we have chosen as a convergence criterion the value of the function at the approximate root.

8.5   The Future of Numerical Applications

Most computer centers have "canned" procedures for the scientific user. Each of these procedures is suited for solving a particular problem, e.g., you may find ten routines for solving a linear system of equations. Each procedure is usually tailored to solving a problem having certain properties and employing a particular approach. If a user is not aware of these limitations, he will usually waste much time until he gets a solution for his problem.

A recent approach is the development of what we call *polyalgorithms*. A polyalgorithm comprises a set of algorithms suitable for solving a certain class of problems, as well as the logic necessary for choosing the best algorithm for the user's problem. The user passes all his requirements to the polyalgorithm, e.g., the problem data, accuracy required, any characteristics of the problem, etc. The polyalgorithm will pick the most appropriate of its components to satisfy the user's requirements. If for some reason this component does not achieve what is required, the polyalgorithm, after taking into consideration the reasons for this unsuccessful trial, will pick another of its components based on this past history. The polyalgorithm will continue doing this until the user's requirements are satisfied or all paths are exhausted. At that point, all the appropriate generated information is passed

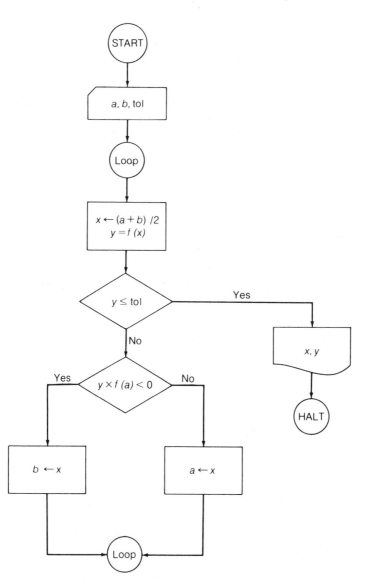

to the user. For examples of polyalgorithms, refer to Khalil's recent work (see references at end of chapter) as well as to Gear's polyalgorithm for solving ordinary differential equations.

Summary

Numerical applications continue to play a very important role in the overall perspective of computing. The mathematical foundations of numerical applications have undergone considerable development, and the algorithms have in many cases been packaged for use with very little user interaction.

Numerical applications still profoundly affect features of programming languages. In particular, data structures in programming language continue to
show the dominant influence of numerical applications.

This chapter has provided a glimpse of the important features of numerical
applications. From the underlying considerations of errors and their behavior
to the illustrations of the structure of numerical algorithms, the intent has
been to stress the basic principles of numerical computations as well as the
pragmatic considerations in obtaining results.

References and Suggested Additional Readings

(1) Acton, F.S.. *Numerical Methods that Work.* New York: Harper & Row, 1970.
(2) Hamming, R.. *Applied Numerical Analysis.* New York: McGraw-Hill, 1971.
(3) Khalil, H.M. and Ulery, D.L.. "LINEAL: A System for Numerical Linear Algebra",
The Computer Journal, 17, (August, 1974): 267–74.
(4) Gear, C.W.. *Numerical Initial Value Problems in Ordinary Differential Equations.*
Englewood Cliffs, N.J.: Prentice-Hall, 1971.

Problems

1. Calculate S_1, S_2, S_3 on a digital computer where

$$S_1 = \sum_{A=1.0}^{10000.} 9./A^3; \qquad S_2 = \sum_{A=10000.}^{1.0} 9./A^3;$$

$$S_3 = 9. \sum_{A=1.0}^{10000.} 1./A^3$$

Print your answers to 11 significant digits. Why do the answers for S_1, S_2, and S_3
differ? If the machine you are working with truncates numbers rather than rounds
them (i.e., if the machine can hold four digits, then 0.3567 6520 would be stored as
0.3567 and not as 0.3568), then which of the above, S_1, S_2, or S_3, is the most accurate? Explain your answer.

2. Give an estimate of the time and space requirements for solving a system of k
equations by Gaussian elimination without pivoting.

3. Develop an algorithm for the Gaussian elimination with pivoting.

4. Find manually the exact solution of:

$$100. \, x + 99. \, y = 199$$
$$99. \, x + 98. \, y = 197$$

Suppose that due to rounding the righthand members become 198.99 and 197.01
respectively. How would the solution be affected? (Hint—hold 8 digits during solution.)

5. State six main objectives to be satisfied by a polyalgorithm designed for solving a numerical problem.
6. Make up a flowchart for evaluation of:

$$y = a_1 + a_2 x^2 + a_3 x^4$$

and find an expression for the relative error in y on the following assumptions:
(a) a_i are known without error;
(b) x has initially a relative error e_x;
(c) there is no rounding error in adding a number to 0 or in multiplying a number by 1.

Chapter 9

Nonnumerical Applications

Although the earliest applications of computers were numerical, the non-numerical applications are by far the most numerous and the most pervasive. From the operation of a modern telephone switchboard to the preparation of bills for a small business, the computer can be found in almost every facet of human activity. No cther area of application commands the same attention of computer scientists, nor offers the same opportunities for service to society.

The purpose of this chapter is to provide a basis for understanding problems associated with nonnumerical applications. The approach will be analytic in the sense that the area will be discussed by considering small well-defined parts. However, the whole is not the sum of its parts. In the synthesis of large scale nonnumerical applications, some very important social, psychological, and legal problems arise. These problems are not evident when the scientist is choosing between algorithms or selecting appropriate data structures. It is while solving these local solutions that such problems arise as:

(1) No one person understands the whole application well enough to verify that it works.

(2) The synthesized application may be rejected by its intended user because it is "inhuman." Even worse, the resulting product may induce abnormal human behavior, (i.e., extremes of fear, frustration, or violence).

(3) The synthesized application may violate basic human rights. The combination of all the parts may constitute a collection of information and a means of transmission of the information that is legally libelous.

In being analytic in discussions of nonnumerical application, there is no intent to minimize the problems mentioned above. Instead, by appreciating the progress made in computer science, the reader will see that science and technology have brought society to the point that these psychological, sociological, and legal problems cannot be ignored.

9.1   Examples of Nonnumerical Applications

Nonnumerical applications may be divided roughly between business (commercial) data processing and noncommercial symbol manipulation projects. In the business area, the element of numerical processing may become significant in fiscal computations. Business data-processing applications include payroll, general accounting, billing, etc. These routine applications have often become the foundations of more sophisticated computer systems intended to provide management with tactical and strategic information for investment risk analysis, market behavior studies, inventory control, and many others. These systems are classified as nonnumerical applications because of the extent to which symbolic information, such as names, addresses, and social security numbers, is manipulated.

Noncommercial applications, in contrast to business applications, rely almost entirely on symbolic computations. A few examples are considered here:

Student Records: At all levels of education, records of progress for each student are often put on computer files. This allows rapid updating and reporting of progress on an individual basis as well as studies of the effectiveness of education.

Health Care Delivery: Large scale data-processing systems have been implemented for diagnosis, emergency care, and treatment for medical patients. The data bases created in such applications are often used for research into spread of diseases, resource utilization, and inferences required for new diagnostic procedures. Computers also play a peripheral role in intensive care monitoring and in prosthesis (i.e., control of artificial limbs, etc.).

Text Editing: Significant progress has been made recently in computer-aided editing. Newspaper publishers in particular utilize the nonnumerical capabilities of computers in line justification and layout of the printed page. The speed and quality of such editing more than justify the use of the computer.

Compilation of Computer Programs: A computer program written in a procedure-oriented language such as FORTRAN or COBOL must be translated to machine language before execution. This translation process includes recognition of valid numbers and identifier names and conversion of statement constructs to an intermediate form from which the machine language instructions are more easily produced.

Heuristic Problem Solving: Game-playing programs, mechanical theorem provers, and question-answering machines are among a few of the results of research into the area of artificial intelligence. (chapter 11)

Document Retrieval: Systems have been implemented to aid in searching for information relevant to a designated topic. Such systems are becoming widely used in libraries, both academic and industrial.

9.2   Features of Nonnumerical Computations

As was the case with numerical computations, historical accidents and scientific realities have each contributed to the important features of nonnumerical applications. The languages used in such work have been predominantly COBOL and PL/I, with SNOBOL, LISP, APL, and several special purpose languages each serving some specialized needs. COBOL (Common Business Oriented Language) was developed specifically for business data processing. It was intended to correct some of the difficulties encountered in the use of FORTRAN in such applications. PL/I was developed later to incorporate the best of COBOL, FORTRAN, and ALGOL in a single language. The major use of PL/I remains in the business data-processing area.

The data structures employed in nonnumerical applications depend on the amount of data, its structure, and the operations to be performed on it. Both sequential and nonsequential memory allocation may be employed; section 9.4 describes the structure of a typical large scale data base. The atomic data are usually treated as symbols rather than numbers, and the most prevalent operation on symbols is the matching test (i.e., are two given symbols the same?). Of the many possible realizations of symbols, the character (usually 8 bits) is the most common.

Operations

In nonnumerical applications, you must be able to analyze the data from many perspectives as well as add new data to, and remove old data from, the data base. A few common operations are listed here and defined in general terms.

Sorting: A set of data is placed in ascending or descending order (for example, alphabetical order for names).

Searching: Given a data element, the memory location of a matching piece of data is found.

Data Elimination: A given data element is removed from the data set.

Addition: A given data element or set of data is added to the data set, with its location often determined by some ordering property.

Extraction: A new data set is formed with those data elements that satisfy a given property. (e.g., you may construct a data set containing only those individuals whose last names begin with "L.")

9.3   Nonnumerical Algorithms

Sorting

One of the most frequent tasks in data processing is ordering a data set. As a matter of fact, it is estimated that over 25% of computing time is spent on ordering lists of items.

Some of the most important applications of ordering are:

(1) It aids searching for a specified item as we shall see later. You can imagine the trouble we would have if the telephone directory were not ordered alphabetically.

(2) If more than one data set has been ordered to the same ordering property, the problem of finding matching entries is easily handled in one pass.

(3) It reduces the effort spent in deleting items, since deletion is composed of two steps: search and removal.

Although there are many sorting algorithms, there is no one technique that is best for every situation. Some are useful for internal sorting, i.e., when the data set to be sorted can be stored in main memory; others are suitable for sorting external tape files. However, when selecting a sorting procedure, you must consider the structure and location of the data set and the particular efficiencies imbedded in the algorithm itself. To illustrate these criteria, we shall discuss and compare several sorting algorithms.

Internal sorting

One straightforward method for ordering an internal list of items into increasing (or decreasing) order is called the *exchange sort*. In this method, the first item is compared in turn with each item suceeding it in the list; whenever the first item is larger, the positions of the two compared items are exchanged. Thus, at the end of the first pass, the smallest item will occupy the first position of the list. This process is then repeated by comparing the second item in the list with each item succeeding it, then the third item, and so on. At the end of the Ith pass or Ith repetition of this process, the first I items will be in ascending order; for a list of N items, $N - 1$ passes are required to achieve an ordered list.

Exercise 9.3-1

Suppose the list of data to be sorted is 8, 5, 9, 3, 4. Determine the number of exchanges that occur during each pass of an exchange sort.

On the first pass 8 occupies the first position and is compared with 5, the element in the second position; an exchange occurs and the resultant list is 5, 8, 9, 3, 4. 5 now occupies the first position and is compared with 9, the element in the third position, and no exchange occurs. 5 is next compared with 3, the element in the fourth position; an exchange occurs and the resultant list is 3, 8, 9, 5, 4. 3 now occupies the first position and is compared with 4, the element in the fifth position, and no exchange occurs. At the end of this first pass, two exchanges have been made and the smallest element, 3, is in the first position of the list. The next three passes proceed in a similar manner; a total of seven exchanges occur in sorting this set of data.

Exercise 9.3-2

Assume we have an array DATA containing N data elements. Draw a flowchart

to sort this data set into ascending order using the exchange sort. (A less efficient variation of this exchange sort was presented in Exercise 6.1-3.)

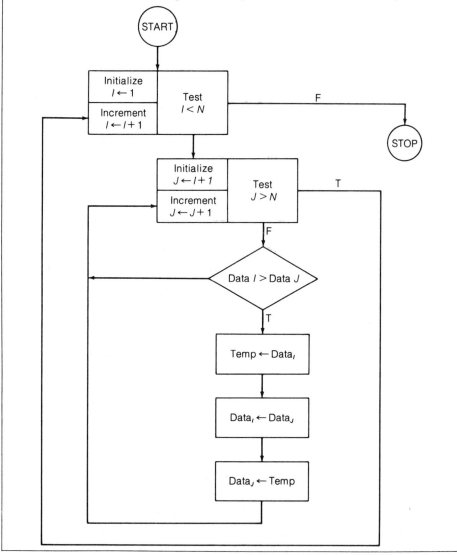

A popular sorting method is called the *bubble sort*. In this method, the first
two items are compared, and their positions are exchanged if the first item
is larger than the second. Then the second and third items are compared,
and their positions are exchanged if the second item is larger than the third.
This process is repeated in turn for each pair of successive items in the list.
At the end of this first pass through the list, the largest item will occupy the
last position of the list. At the end of the Ith pass or I^{th} repetition of this entire procedure, the last I items will be ordered; for a list of N items, $N-1$
passes are required to sort the list.

Exercise 9.3-3

Suppose the list of data to be sorted is 8, 5, 9, 3, 4. Determine the number of exchanges that occur during each pass of a bubble sort.

On the first pass, the first two successive elements, 8 and 5, are compared; an exchange occurs and the resultant list is 5, 8, 9, 3, 4. The next two successive elements, 8 and 9, are compared and no exchange occurs. The next two successive elements, 9 and 3, are compared; an exchange occurs and the resultant list is 5, 8, 3, 9, 4. Finally the last two successive elements, 9 and 4, are compared; an exchange occurs and the resultant list is 5, 8, 3, 4, 9. At the end of this first pass, three exchanges have been made and the largest element, 9, is in the last position of the list. The next three passes proceed in a similar manner; a total of seven exchanges occur in sorting this set of data.

Upon completion of the Ith pass of the bubble sort, the last I positions of the list contain the I largest elements in increasing order; pass $I + 1$ need only compare those items that remain to be ordered, namely the first $N - I$ elements of the list.

A significant efficiency can be added to the bubble sort by noting that if no exchanges occur during a pass through the list, then the list is already sorted—even if the specified $N - 1$ passes have not been completed. (Why does this statement fail to hold for the exchange sort?) Thus, a "flag" or variable can be set to 1 at the beginning of each pass, and zeroed if an exchange occurs; a test of the flag on completion of each pass will indicate whether an exit can be made from the sort procedure or whether the next pass through the list is required.

A comparison of the bubble sort and the exchange sort emphasizes the importance of such efficiencies. We shall compare the two techniques for the worst case, when the data is originally in descending order, and the best case, when the data is originally in desired ascending order. We shall use the number of comparisons and the number of exchanges that occur during each sort process as our criteria of efficiency.

An example of the worst case is the list 9, 8, 6, 5, 2. For such a list, the exchange sort and bubble sort both involve $N - 1$ comparisons and $N - 1$ exchanges on the first pass, $N - 2$ comparisons and $N - 2$ exchanges on the second pass, ... and 1 comparison and 1 exchange on the $N - 1$rst pass. Thus, a total of $1 + 2 + \ldots + (N - 2) + (N - 1) = N(N - 1)/2$ comparisons and exchanges are required, and the exchange and bubble sorts appear to behave similarly.

An example of the best case is the list 2, 5, 6, 8, 9. For such a list, the exchange sort involves the same number of comparisons as in the worst case analysis, but no exchanges. However, the bubble sort flag test produces an exit at the end of the first pass, therefore involving only $N - 1$ comparisons and no exchanges. Thus, in the best case analysis, the bubble sort requires $1 + 2 + \ldots + (N - 2) = (N - 1)(N - 2)/2$ fewer comparisons than the exchange sort.

Exercise 9.3-4

Assume we have an array DATA containing N data elements. Draw a flowchart to sort this data into ascending order using the bubble sort.

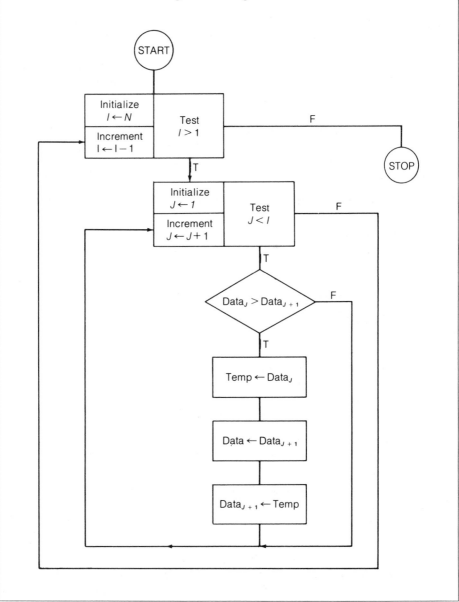

It is unlikely that such sorting procedures will often encounter totally ordered or reverse ordered lists. Most data sets to be sorted will fall some-
where in the middle, in which case they will require more than one pass but
fewer than $N - 1$ passes for ordering. If a list becomes sorted on the Ith pass,
the bubble sort will detect this and exit on the $I + 1$st pass; if the list is long,
this saving of $1 + 2 + \ldots + (N - (I + 3)) + (N - (I + 2))$ comparisons will be
appreciable.

The efficiency of data-processing algorithms is important due to the immense size of the data bases on which they operate.

Often two sorted lists are to be combined into one sorted list. This might
occur, for example, if an ordered list of new employees is to be added to a
company personnel roster. This can be accomplished by merely appending
the new list to the original and applying the bubble sort to the composite list.
However, a more efficient method of accomplishing this task is by a procedure known as *merging*.

To merge two lists A and B, the first item from A is compared with the first
item from B and the smallest placed in the first position of a new list C. Then
the item not placed in list C is compared with the next item of the other list
and the smallest placed in the next position of list C. This process is continued until all elements of either list A or list B have been placed in list C, at
which point the remaining elements of the other list are appended to the end
of list C. List C is now an ordered composite of lists A and B.

Exercise 9.3-5

Suppose the two ordered lists to be merged are 3, 6, 8, 13, 15 and 4, 5, 6, 9. Determine the order in which elements are placed in the composite list.

3 and 4 are compared and 3 is placed in the new list.

6 and 4 are compared and 4 is placed in the new list.

6 and 5 are compared and 5 is placed in the new list.

6 and 6 are compared and both 6 and 6 are placed in the new list.

8 and 9 are compared and 8 is placed in the new list.

13 and 9 are compared and 9 is placed in the new list.

This exhausts the elements of the second list; the remaining elements of the first
list, 13 and 15, are moved to the new list. The resultant composite list is 3, 4, 5, 6,
6, 8, 9, 13, 15.

Exercise 9.3-6

Assume we have two arrays, A and B, containing NA and NB ordered data elements respectively. Draw a flowchart to merge these two ordered lists into a
composite list C of NC ordered elements.

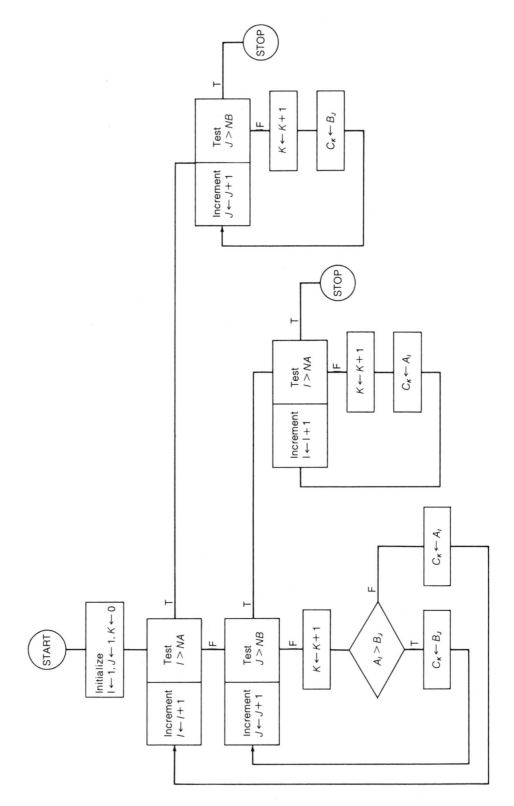

Exercise 9.3-7

Contrast the number of comparisons involved in ordering the composite list 3, 6, 8, 13, 15, 4, 5, 6, 9 via the bubble sort with the number of comparisons occurring in a merge of the two lists 3, 6, 8, 13, 15 and 4, 5, 6, 9.

The bubble sort requires six passes before the composite list is both sorted and its ordered condition is detected; thus a total of $8 + 7 + 6 + 5 + 4 + 3 = 33$ comparisons are involved. The merge of the two individual lists involves 6 comparisons, as shown in Exercise 9.3-5.

Several ordered lists can be merged into one ordered composite list by merging the first two lists A and B into a new list C, copying list C into list A and a new list into list B, and repeating this process. At the end of the Ith repetition of this procedure, list C will be a composite ordered list containing the elements of the first $I + 1$ individual lists. A total of $N - 1$ repetitions is required to merge N ordered lists.

External sorting

A data set may be larger than core memory; such a list must be sorted in bulk memory (in this context bulk file and external file are synonomous). The bubble sort is not efficient for sorting external files because of the large number of transfers between external and internal memory required for comparison and interchange of data items. In addition, the interchange of data on external files may require backspacing a linear memory device (i.e., a tape) which is a time-consuming operation and is usually avoided.

The merge process can be used to formulate a merge-sort, often referred to as a *tape-sort,* for sorting external files. The process works as follows:

(1) Four files—A_1, B_1, and A_2, B_2—are required. The N data items on the file to be sorted are divided into files, A_1 and B_1, each of length $N/2$.

(2) On the first pass, each item from file A_1 is merged with the corresponding item from file B_1 and the ordered pair stored alternately on files A_2 and B_2. At the end of pass 1, files A_2 and B_2 each contain $N/4$ pairs of ordered items.

(3) On the second pass, each pair of ordered items from files A_2 and B_2 are merged and the four ordered elements stored alternately on files A_1 and B_1.

(4) This process continues alternating between files A_1, B_1, and A_2, B_2 as input and output files. On the Ith pass, sets of $2^I - 1$ ordered data items are merged from the current input files and the 2^I ordered items placed alternately on the two current output files.

Example

A_1	B_1		$\begin{bmatrix}\text{END OF}\\\text{PASS 1}\end{bmatrix}$			$\begin{bmatrix}\text{END OF}\\\text{PASS 2}\end{bmatrix}$		$\begin{bmatrix}\text{END OF}\\\text{PASS 3}\end{bmatrix}$	
			A_2	B_2		A_2	B_2	A_2	B_2
3	4	first ordered pair	3	6	second ordered pair	3	1	1	
8	6		4	8		4	1	1	
								2	
2	9	third ordered pair	2	1	fourth ordered pair	6	2	3	
1	1		9	1		8	9	4	
								6	
								8	
								9	

The merge-sort process requires $K = log_2 N$ passes if N, the number of items to be sorted, is a power of 2. The algorithm requires minor modifications otherwise (see Problems), since the files will sometimes contain an unequal number of items.

Note that a list of N elements can be sorted by starting with N lists of length one and merging them into longer and longer lists. That is why many authors claim that the flowchart for merging two files is the flowchart of data processing.

Searching

As we have mentioned, one of the advantages of sorting is to facilitate locating an item. The expected search time for one item in an unordered key file is proportional to N (N is the number of items in the file), whereas in an ordered file, the time is proportional to $[log_2 N] + 1$.

Binary search applies to lists ordered in an ascending manner. To locate the position of an element ITEM, the element located at the midpoint of the list is compared with ITEM. If ITEM has the smaller value, then ITEM must reside in the first half of the list; otherwise it must reside in the latter half. Thus, the area of the list to be searched is halved. The procedure is repeated for this half-list and the area to be searched is again halved. This continues until the item is located or the area of the list to be searched becomes empty. In this latter case, the algorithm halts with the message "FAILURE." This successive *halving* of the search area has resulted in the name *interval halving* for the binary search algorithm.

Compilation

During the compilation process, program statements are translated into an internal form that is then processed to generate the machine language code. The internal form is chosen to remove semantic considerations such as parenthetical groupings and the order of hierarchy of Boolean operators. We shall discuss one internal form, Polish postfix notation, named after the Polish mathematician Jan Lukasewicz, and apply it to the compilation of arithmetic expressions.

Arithmetic expressions are written in "infix" form, in which each operator appears between its two operands. The operands are determined by applying the usual rules involving parenthetical groupings, hierarchy of operators, and left to right evaluation for operators of equal hierarchy. Such an expression can be represented by a binary tree in which:

(1) each node of the tree contains an operator or variable

(2) a node containing an operator has left and right subtrees, representing the operator's left and right operands respectively

(3) a node containing a variable is a terminal node

Example: The arithmetic expression $A + B \times C$ is represented by the binary tree

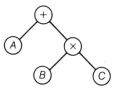

Example: The arithmetic expression $A \times B + C$ is represented by the binary tree

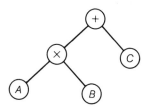

Notice that in both cases the root is $+$; multiplication takes precedence over addition and thus $A \times B$ and C are the operands for $+$. Parentheses must be used if you want to alter this operator order.

Example: The arithmetic expression $(A + B) \times C$ is represented by the binary tree.

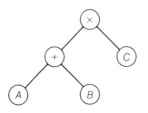

Example: The arithmetic expression

$$(A + B \times C - E) \times B - (C + A)/D$$

is represented by the binary tree

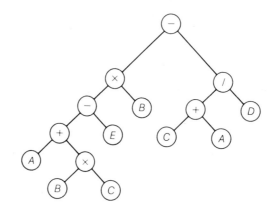

To translate such expressions directly to machine language code, the compiler would need to scan back and forth across the expression, determining operators and operands and generating the appropriate code. However, if the expression is represented in Polish postfix notation, the machine code can be generated with only one simple left-to-right scan.

In postfix form, each operator is immediately preceded by the postfix representation of its left and right operands.

Example:

Infix Representation	Postfix Representation
$A + B$	$AB +$
$A + B \times C$	$ABC \times +$
$A \times B + C$	$AB \times C +$
$(A + B) \times C$	$AB + C \times$
$(A + B \times C - E) \times B - (C + A)/D$	$ABC \times + E - B \times CA + D/ -$

Machine language code can be easily generated from the postfix representation using the following process:

(1) Get the next element of the postfix expression
(2) If a blank, stop
(3) If a variable, push it onto STACK
(4) If an operator, then
   (A) remove the top two variables from STACK
   (B) generate the machine language code to combine these variables via the given operator and store the result in a temporary variable
   (C) push this temporary variable onto STACK
(5) Go to step 1

The only problem that remains is translating the given infix expression into postfix form. Notice that a listing of the nodes of the binary tree for the infix representation, using an end order tranversal, yields the postfix representation. Fortunately, an algorithm exists for generating the postfix form without first obtaining the binary tree representation. A hierarchy is assigned to the operators:

Operator	Hierarchy
* exponentiation	4
$\times$	3
/	3
+	2
–	2
(	1

The infix string INF is scanned from left to right, one symbol at a time, and the Polish postfix string POST is generated as follows:

(1) Get the next symbol of string INF
(2) If a blank, then remove symbols one at a time from STACK and append them to string POST until STACK is empty.
(3) If a variable, then append it to string POST
(4) If a (, then push it onto STACK
(5) If a), then remove symbols one at a time from STACK and append them to string POST until a (is removed from STACK—discard both) and (.
(6) If an operator then remove symbols one at a time from STACK and append them to string POST until STACK is empty or until the top element of STACK has *lower* hierarchy than this new operator, and then push this new operator onto STACK
(7) Go to step 1

Example: $A + B \times C$
(1) Rule 3: *A* is moved to POST (POST is "*A*")
(2) Rule 6: + is pushed onto STACK
(3) Rule 3: *B* is moved to POST (POST is "*AB*")
(4) Rule 6: $\times$ has greater hierarchy than + so $\times$ is pushed onto STACK
(5) Rule 3: *C* is moved to POST (POST is "*ABC*")
(6) Rule 2: POST becomes "*ABC* $\times$ +"

Example: $(A+B) \times C$

(1) Rule 4: (is pushed onto STACK
(2) Rule 3: A is moved to POST (POST is "A")
(3) Rule 6: + has greater hierarchy than (so + is pushed onto STACK
(4) Rule 3: B is moved to POST (POST is "AB")
(5) Rule 5: + and (are removed from STACK and + is moved to POST (POST is "$AB+$")
(6) Rule 6: × is pushed onto STACK
(7) Rule 3: C is moved to POST (POST is "$AB + C$")
(8) Rule 2: POST becomes "$AB + C \times$"

Example: $(A+B \times C-E) \times B$

(1) Rule 4: (is pushed onto STACK
(2) Rule 3: A is moved to POST (POST is "A")
(3) Rule 6: + has greater hierarchy than (so + is pushed onto STACK
(4) Rule 3: B is moved to POST (POST is "AB")
(5) Rule 6: × has greater hierarchy than + so × is pushed onto STACK
(6) Rule 3: C is moved to POST (POST is "ABC")
(7) Rule 6: × and + are removed from STACK and moved to POST; − is pushed onto STACK (POST is "$ABC \times +$")
(8) Rule 3: E is moved to POST (POST is "$ABC \times + E$")
(9) Rule 5: − and (are removed from STACK and − is moved to POST (POST is "$ABC \times + E -$")
(10) Rule 6: × is pushed onto STACK
(11. Rule 3: B is moved to POST (POST is "$ABC \times + E - B$")
(12) Rule 2: POST becomes "$ABC \times + E - B \times$")

9.4   Large Scale Data Bases

Structure[1]

Until the development of large scale data bases, each department of an organization maintained its own data storage and programs to process the data. This resulted in duplication of data (such as storage of student names by both the Deans Office and the Financial Aid Office); the inability of departments to produce certain reports that, although useful, did not justify the expense of maintaining the required data; and other problems such as maintaining the consistency of the data stored in many different locations.

An integrated data base is a collection of data used by many departments of an organization. The data base is supervised by a Data Base Administrator whose tasks include interacting with the individual departments to ascertain their requirements, effecting appropriate storage of the required data, de-

---

[1]Date, C. J., *An Introduction to Database Systems,* Addison Wesley, 1977.

veloping methods of accessing the data, and instituting appropriate security procedures to protect the data from unauthorized retrieval or modification. Such an integrated system eliminates data redundancy and makes a greater amount of information accessible to each department. In addition, the consistency of the data used by different departments is maintained.

The efficient storage and utilization of a large data base is a major priority. The architecture of a data base system consists of three components: the physical database, the general data model, and the user data model. The physical database contains the actual stored data and the procedures for searching and accessing this data. The form in which the data is stored and the required search routines are determined by the Data Base Administrator upon analyzing the requirements of the individual users.

The general data model is a logical overview of the entire database, outlining the type of information available without regard to how it is stored or retrieved by the system. A mapping between the data model and the physical data base is maintained within the overall control system; upon request for an item of information in the general data model, this mapping determines where the desired data occurs in the physical storage structures and the appropriate routines which must be utilized to retrieve it.

The general data model facilitates an increasingly important characteristic called physical data independence. The overall logical view of the data is not dependent upon the physical storage structures or search and retrieval strategies. Thus a change in computer hardware, for example, will not be noticed by the users—only the mapping between the general data model and the physical database will be affected and this is the responsibility of the Data Base Administrator.

The user data model is derived from the general data model. Many different and overlapping user data models may exist, each of which provides a logical view of that data required by a particular application and in a format appropriate for the application. Once again, a mapping exists between the user data model and the general data model; upon request for an item of information in the user data model, this mapping provides the reference to the appropriate item or items in the general data model; the mapping between the general data model and the physical data base then facilitates selection of the actual required stored data items.

The user data model facilitates logical data independence. The individual user's view of the data is not dependent upon the overall general data model. Thus an increase in the type and variety of information stored, or a change in the format in which this data is viewed as a whole, will not be noticed by the individual user—only the mapping between the user data model and the general data model will be affected and this is the responsibility of the Data Base Administrator.

These concepts of data independence are extremely important within an integrated database system and determine the degree to which the individual applications are affected by changes within the database system. Many current systems contain a large degree of physical data independence but logical data independence remains a theoretical goal.

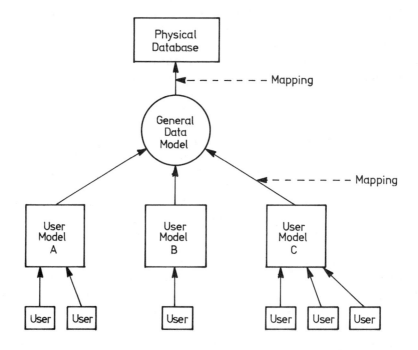

Figure 9.1:   Structure of an integrated database system.

Physical Database

Large scale data-processing applications usually employ a data organization built around the notions of files and records. A file is a collection of records that may or may not be ordered. A record is an ordered collection of data groups. Each data group is one or more primitive data objects such as characters, numbers, bits or links. This organization is illustrated in Figure 9.2; in this university record system, each record consists of the four data groups NAME, RANK, SALARY, and SEX, whose values provide information relative to a given instructor. The set of records for all instructors forms the FILE.

One or more of the groups within the records may be designated a KEY; the KEY in each record can be matched against a specified data value to select a subset of the records in the file. A primary key is a data group whose value is unique in each record; such a key is used to extract or

		GROUP: Name
All the information		GROUP: Rank
RECORD: about DAVID JONES		GROUP: Salary
		GROUP: Sex

		GROUP: Name
All the information		GROUP: Rank
RECORD: about JOHN DOE		GROUP: Salary
		GROUP: Sex

FILE:
All the
information
about every
instructor.

•
•
•

		GROUP: Name
All the information		GROUP: Rank
RECORD: about ANN SMITH		GROUP: Salary
		GROUP: Sex

Figure 9.2: A typical file organization for a university record system.

specify one particular record in a file. Social Security numbers are commonly used as primary keys. A secondary key is a data group whose value may be the same in several records. In the university record system example, the secondary key SEX might be used to extract the set of all male faculty.

A large scale database is built around a master file that contains most of the information being stored. Because of the size of such a file, considerable effort is devoted to avoid moving it or any of its parts.

An added level of indexing, called the primary key file, is usually built around the master file to permit symbolic addressing. Each record of the key file consists of two groups: primary key value and the record number of that particular record in the master file. The records of the key file are generally contiguous whereas those of the master file may be scattered about on a bulk memory device.

The key file contains only the individual key values and the information for accessing each associated record of the master file; thus it is considerably less bulky than the master file and may be easily reordered, copied, etc. The sorting and searching, relative to the key data group, that might be performed on the data base would therefore be done on the key file without disturbing the master file.

Retrieval based upon secondary keys can be implemented with additional key files. A secondary index might list a value along with the record numbers of all records whose secondary key has that value; alternatively, the secondary index might contain one secondary key value—record number entry for each record in the master file. This latter structure is called an inverted file. Note that in the primary key index, the primary key value is unique for each entry whereas in the inverted file index, several entries may have the same secondary key value.

MASTER FILE:

Record Number	Name	Rank	Salary	Sex
1	JONES	Lecturer	10,000	M
2	SMITH	Professor	25,000	F
3	DOE	Asst. Prof.	15,000	M
4	BLOOM	Professor	28,000	M
5	CLARK	Lecturer	15,000	F

PRIMARY KEY FILE

Key Value	Record Number
BLOOM	4
CLARK	5
DOE	3
JONES	1
SMITH	2

SECONDARY KEY FILE
(Inverted File)

Key Value	Record Number
ASST. PROF.	3
LECTURER	1
LECTURER	5
PROFESSOR	2
PROFESSOR	4

Figure 9.3:   Key Files in Large Scale Databases.

Logical Organization

Several methods exist for representing the general user data models. One of the easiest to visualize is the relational approach. Informally, a relation may be viewed as a table consisting of m rows and n columns. Each row represents an element of the relation; thus the relation consists of m distinct elements. Each column represents an attribute or data group whose value must be specified for each element of the relation; thus each element of the relation depicts an association of n attribute values.

Consider the instructor relation of Figure 9.4. Each row of this relation associates a given instructor with particular RANK, SALARY, AGE, and SEX attribute values—that is, it *relates* them to one another.

In addition, a relation may associate items that are attributes of other relations. The relation TEACH of Figure 9.4 describes the instructor and room assignment for each course.

The general data model consists of a set of relations depicting all the information, both data items and their associations with one another, stored within the database. The user data model is a limited view of only that information required by that user. For example, a relation in the user data model may be derived from one in the general data model by omitting certain attribute columns (such as the SALARY attribute column in the INSTRUCTOR relation).

RELATION INSTRUCTOR

NAME	RANK	SALARY	AGE	SEX
BLOOM	Professor	28,000	52	M
CLARK	Lecturer	15,000	27	F
DOE	Asst Prof	15,000	24	M
JONES	Lecturer	10,000	31	M
SMITH	Professor	25,000	54	F

RELATION STUDY

COURSE	DEPARTMENT	CREDIT HOURS
ENGLISH	HUMANITIES	3
MATH	SCIENCE	4
HISTORY	SOCIAL STUDIES	3
PHYSICS	SCIENCE	3
FRENCH	HUMANITIES	4

RELATION TEACH

COURSE	INSTRUCTOR	ROOM
HISTORY	SMITH	STATE 30
MATH	JONES	STATE 24
PHYSICS	CLARK	OLAN 15
ENGLISH	BLOOM	DOD 65
MATH	CLARK	STATE 72

Figure 9.4:   Relational Approach to Data Models.

Note that this logical modelling of the database does not concern itself with the storage or ordering of the data in actual memory.

9.5   Future of Non-numerical Applications

If recent history is any indication of the trends in non-numerical applications, it would appear that progress will be closely tied to progress in the speed and cost of bulk memory devices. We are at a threshold where a significant break-through in memory technology will make it possible to process large amounts of data which may be interrelated in only a very "fuzzy" way. Data processing will become a process of drawing inferences from such collections of data.

Exercise 9.5-1

Given a health care data base containing the medical records for 200 million people, how would you go about determining if two individuals exhibiting the same rare disorder have a common heredity?

The full development of what is already known about non-numerical computations will have a significant impact upon many areas of human activity. In the study of algorithms for symbolic integration in the calculus, it has been discovered that the process can be completely mechanized. Eventually, this discovery will have a considerable impact upon the teaching of mathematics. The viewpoints and techniques employed in automatic theorem proving have been found to be effective in the management of large scale data bases (the data is viewed as a set of axioms, and the information being sought is viewed as a theorem to be proven). Non-numerical techniques are already being employed in the analysis and generation of music. Questions or origin, and cultural influences on literature are being resolved with non-numerical algorithms.

Summary

Although non-numerical applications are very recent developments, and the underlying principles of such applications are not well understood, no other area of activity in computer science has pervaded so far into everyday life. This paradoxical situation is both a great opportunity and a great danger. Few other areas of scientific activity enjoy so much demand and support. Each scientific breakthrough may contribute to the health and quality of life for millions of people. Each poorly understood application may lead to equally wide-spread disillusionment, alienation, and unrest in society.

References and Suggested Additional Readings

(1) Aron, J.D. "Information Systems in Perspective", *ACM Comp. Surveys,* Vol. 1, No. 4, 1969. An elementary survey of information systems and their elements.
(2) Dodd, G.G. "Elements of Data Management Systems", *ACM Comp. Surveys,* Vol. 2, No. 1, 1969. Gives a good description of the basic types of data management techniques.
(3) Knuth, D.E. "The History of Sorting", *Datamation,* Dec. 1972.
(4) Martin, W.A. "Sorting", *ACM Comp. Surveys,* Vol. 3, No. 4, 1970. Surveys most of the known sorting algorithms—it is recommended for the reader who needs to know more about the subject at an elementary level.
(5) Date, C.J. *An Introduction to Database Systems,* Addison Wesley, Reading, Massachusetts, 1977.
(6) Tsichritzis, D., and Lochovsky, F. *Data Base Management Systems,* Academic Press, New York, 1977.

Problems

1. Assume we have an array DATA containing N elements. Draw a flowchart to sort this data set into order, using a bubble sort with an exit test for detecting an ordered list.

2. Another sorting technique consists of starting with the second element of a list and in turn comparing each element of the list with its predecessor. Whenever two elements are out of order, the second is exchanged with successive predecessor elements until it is no longer smaller than its predecessor. The process then continues with the element in the position following the one for which this upward movement was initiated. Draw a flowchart to sort a list using this method.

3. Compare the efficiency of the sorting method of Problem 2 with that of the exchange sort and the bubble sort.

4. One way of sorting records without having to move them is redesigning them so each record contains a specific field, called a *pointer field*. The contents of this field points to the next record. Thus, after sorting a file the position of the first record is known. The pointer in the first record will give the location of the second record. The pointer in the second record will give the location of the third record and so on. Develop an algorithm to perform this task.

5. Draw a flowchart to merge M ordered lists of $N_1, N_2 \ldots, N_M$ elements respectively into a composite ordered list DATA.

6. Develop an algorithm for a merge-sort in which N, the number of items to be sorted, is not necessarily an integral power of 2.

7. One method of sorting external files combines the advantages of both the bubble sort and the merge-sort. Each set of k successive items on the external file are read into core memory, sorted, and stored on a second file. Thus, the merge-sort process begins with a file consisting of N/K sets of K ordered items. Develop an algorithm for such a sorting procedure.

8. Develop a recursive algorithm for binary search.

9. Write an article (1000–2000 words) about the data management system available at your installation.

10. Give the Polish postfix representation for each of the following arithmetic expressions:
$$C - D + E \times (D - F)$$
$$C - (D + E) \times D - F$$
$$(C - (D + E)) \times D - F$$
$$G - F/(((C - D) \times A + F) \times R - E/F)$$

11. (a) What would be the postfix form for an arithmetic assignment statement?
(b) Formulate a procedure for obtaining the postfix representation of an arithmetic assignment statement.

12. Another version of Polish notation is prefix form, in which each operator is immediately followed by the prefix representation of its left and right operands respectively. Give the prefix representation of the arithmetic expressions of problem 10.

13. Formulate a procedure for obtaining the prefix representation of an arithmetic expression.

Chapter 10

Social Issues in Computing

"Whereas the earliest effects of computers have been on the technology, in the end, the most profound effects will be on man himself and on how he thinks about men."

—George E. Forsythe
*Perspectives on the Computer
Revolution*, p. 380

Introduction

Since the development of the first electronic digital computers, it has been apparent that the computer is a technological development that will change much in our society. We will consider some of the effects that computers are having and will be likely to have—including the controversial aspects of computer usage.

No one reading this book has been unaffected by the computer. If the reading is being done as part of a college course, it is likely that the registration and course lists were processed by computer. If the book was purchased, the sales slip may have been processed by computer; the reorder form and inventory updating almost surely were. If the book was borrowed from a library, either the library recorded this loan information by computer—in which case the computer will automatically prepare overdue notices and billing—or the library is probably considering acquisition of a computer.

In much the same way, every facet of our lives is already being affected by computers, and the application of computers can be considered to be still in its infancy. The variety of tasks the computer will be able to perform will be much greater when computers are able to respond to vocal communication–almost surely before the end of the century.

How many jobs will be lost to computers as the price of computation decreases, and the versatility of computers increases? Will automation-induced mass unemployment actually be a major effect of the computer, as foreseen by some early pioneers in cybernetics?

Finally, what will be the effect of the application of this new science to our values? How will our privacy and freedom be affected? How will we adjust in a society in which machines play an increasing role in recordkeeping, in running our lives, and even in formulating future plans?

10.1   Computers in the Social Milieu

An overview

Let *x* be almost any topic you wish to choose; it is likely that an article, or book, has already been written about *computers and x.* Considering only what has already been implemented, the field is too broad for a comprehensive survey. In Table 10.1-1, a sample of computer applications is presented.

Weather Forecasting	Employment Job Banks
Air Traffic Control	Computer-Aided-Instruction
Engineering Design	Supermarkets
Engineering Production and Plant Control	Libraries
Instrumentation and Monitoring Systems	Architecture
Banking	Concordance Preparation
Credit Systems	Archaeology
Reservation Systems	Military Weapons Systems
Police Records	Election Forecasting

Table 10.1-1:   Typical computer applications

Analysis of the types of tasks assigned to the computer within each area also shows a great diversity. Figure 10.1 shows typical application of computers to urban society. As can be seen in Figure 10.1, there are generic categories into which computer usages can be classified. In each class of applications, the specific items can be broken down into those that are state-of-the-art and others that are either in the planning stages or are still speculative.

An example of a well-understood class of applications is the processing of large volumes of data as typified in the banking and insurance fields. Here, costs can be realistically assessed and weighed against the benefits or disadvantages of computerized operations.

A newer application of computers, as yet to be proven on a broad scale, is their extensive use in supermarket retail sales. In this area there is active work on implementation, preliminary standardization of tagging practices, and data entry devices. The projection of the fully automated supermarket is still premature, although you can anticipate continuing experiments in the integration of sales, inventory, planning, and other aspects of the management and operation of retail supermarkets.

Still further in the future and presently in the research stage, are the development of robots, the use of computers for long range planning of society, and more intelligent computer systems.

The computer in social planning

A plan is a design, and the success of the plan will, in general, depend on how well the interaction between components of the plan are understood, and on how carefully the implications of the component actions are predicted.

Consider the planning of the flight of a space probe to land on Mars. The components of the plan are the motions of planets in the solar system, the motion of the space probe under gravitational forces, the behavior of the

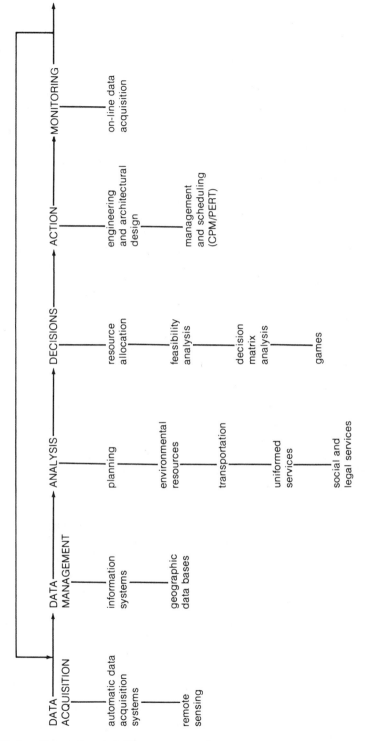

Figure 10.1: **The urban system process loop**

rocket engines, and the functioning of supporting systems. The equations of motion are among the most precisely known physical laws, the behavior of the rocket engines is quantified by extensive engineering tests, and the behavior of other supporting systems is also widely analyzed and tested. Hence, the planetary space probe behavior is generally accurately forecast.

As a second example, consider the construction of a building. The relationship between the time materials are ordered and delivery times can be estimated, as can construction times, allowing for a systematic prediction or scheduling of construction.

In each of these examples, our past experience has been quantified and allows us to estimate future events and plan accordingly. Note that even in these cases where much data is available, there are unpredictable random events that we cannot control, such as poor weather, fires, defective components, accidents, and so forth. Still, it is possible to estimate each of these factors statistically and to formulate contingency plans.

Consider next the planning associated with the introduction of computerized retail sales in the supermarket. In this case, there is considerably less accumulated data on the performance of salespeople and customers in the projected environment. Development of plans would typically involve both experimenting to obtain data on system performance and analysis of data under a variety of hypothetical situations.

The principal tool for analyzing and predicting performance of complicated systems, whose overall performance is not known, is called *simulation*. In simulation, a computer model is hypothesized and its behavor is studied. There are a number of specialized computer languages for simulation, such as SIMSCRIPT, based on FORTRAN, and SIMULA, based on ALGOL. It is also possible to write a simulation directly in any procedure-oriented language.

Since in simulations you study the effects of random variations in the components of the computer model, a source of random events is required. Generally, a random number generator is provided by the procedure-oriented language. Let us suppose that the random number generator provides us with a number n, between 1 and 100, each time we use the variable RAND, so that the program

$$i \leftarrow 1;$$
$$\text{DO WHILE } (i \leq 20);$$
$$\quad a_i \leftarrow \text{RAND};$$
$$\quad i \leftarrow i + 1;$$
$$\text{END};$$

would generate twenty random numbers in locations a_1 to a_{20}. To simulate arrival of customers at the supermarket, at an average rate of one every five minutes, we could program a subroutine to be called every minute of simulated time, and generate a customer entering the market if the value of RAND is between 1 and 20. There are, to be sure, many more complicated statistical distributions, but these can all be approximated by appropriate subroutines using RAND as the basic source of random data.

Figure 10.2 shows a simplified block diagram of a supermarket simulation. In this simulation, we can study the effects of express lines, of the change in the speed of checkout vs. customer time on the checkout queue, the tradeoff of increasing the speed of an individual checkout station vs. increasing the number of checkout stations.

Even if we have no knowledge of the overall supermarket functioning, we can estimate the total system performance *providing we know how the components behave and interact.* In this case, we need to know about the statistics of customer arrival and shopping patterns, and the behavior of checkout counters. Of course, we have simplified the true situation—neglecting many factors such as the effect of special sales, breakdown of registers, etc. You might argue that, in principle, all these factors could be included, provided we knew their effects and we usually do not.

Simulation and planning on a large scale has been studied by Forrester. He has applied the techniques of simulation to the study of urban problems, among other social problems. He says:

> It is my basic theme that the human mind is not adapted to interpreting how social systems behave. Our social systems belong to the class called multi-loop nonlinear feedback systems. In the long history of evolution, it has not been necessary for man to understand these systems until very recent historical time. Evolutionary processes have not given us the mental skill needed to properly interpret the dynamic behavior of the system of which we have now become a part.

> In addition, the social sciences have fallen into some mistaken "scientific" practices that compound man's natural shortcomings. Computers are often being used for what the computer does poorly and the human mind does well. At the same time, the human mind is being used for what the human does poorly and the computer does well. Even worse, impossible tasks are attempted while achievable and important goals are ignored.*

Forrester then discusses system dynamics, and the application of the methods of the physical sciences to the social sciences. He argues that an analytical phase (model building) must precede the implementation of social programs. The analytical model can then simulate the model and calculate the consequences of the explicit assumptions.

On the basis of his simulation studies, Forrester concludes that federal policies for solving urban problems are counterproductive because the social system behaves counterintuitively. This effect (of nonintuitive behavior) is seen as a general characteristic of social systems.

---

*(Reprinted from) Jay W. Forrester, "Counterintuitive Behavior of Social Systems," in *Toward Global Equilibrium: Collected Papers,* ed. D.H. Meadows and D.L. Meadows (Cambridge Mass., Wright-Allen Press, 1973).

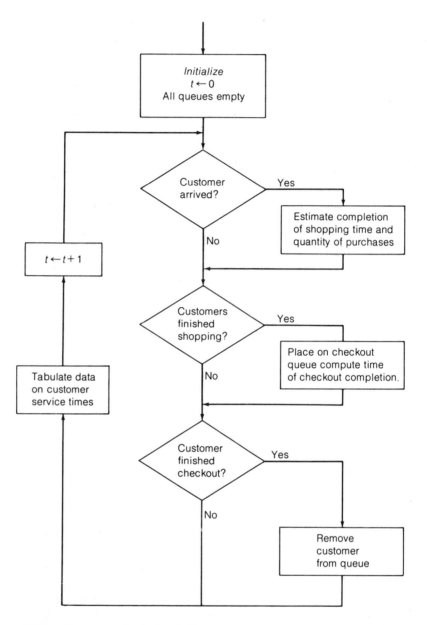

Figure 10.2:   Supermarket simulation

A detailed critique of Forrester's methodology and conclusions has been presented by Kadanoff.* Kadanoff claims that Forrester's conclusions are not counterintuitive but are implicitly built into the simulation. In particular, Kadanoff questions:

*A.P. Kadanoff in *Simulation* vol. 16, no. 6, (1971): 261–68. Reprinted in *Best Computer Papers of 1971.*

(1) The simplicity of the simulation model.
(2) The assumption of controversial goals implicitly, e.g., to make the city less attractive to unskilled labor.
(3) The assumption of specific relations among components of the model where these are not known.
(4) The quantification of value judgments.

10.2   Social Implications of Computers

Values

A precise characterization of values in the context of social behavior is difficult. Let us start with a dictionary definition:

> value (val′ yōō), n . . 10. values, sociol. the ideals, customs, institutions, etc. of a society toward which the people have an effective regard. These values may be positive, as cleanliness, freedom, education, etc., or negative, as cruelty, crime, or blasphemy. 11. *Ethics*. any object or quality desirable as a means or as an end in itself.*

Here we see that values in an ethical context are defined somewhat differently from values described in a sociological context.

Stated in somewhat different terms, the elusiveness of the definition comes from its conceptual nature:

> What makes the subject of values so difficult? For one thing, values— whether seen as conceptions of the desirable, as the underpinning of culture, or as the basis for motivation and behavior—are not easily identified and measured. Because values represent factors that underlie behavior and attitudes and are therefore at a high level of abstraction, it is difficult to construct meaningful indicators with which to measure or study them.**

Compounding the problem of defining values is the changing nature of values. Furthermore, you often have the impression that it is the technology that has a greater effect on values and their changes than values have in determining the directions of technology. Whether this is so, in fact, is not clear since our technology is surely an embodiment of some preconception— an idea precedes an invention. Still, the prevailing conception appears to be one of a dynamic interaction between values, behavior, and technology.

Are computers dehumanizing people? Does the additional management control that the computer provides in its ability to handle very large amounts

---

The Random House Dictionary of the English Language. Jesse Stein, Ed. in Chief, New York: Random House, 1966. By permission.
**"Technology & Values." I. Taviss, Harvard University Program on Technology and Society, Research Review No. 3, (Spring 1969), Cambridge, Mass.

of data facilitate centralized control in a bureaucracy removed far from its constituency? Does the accumulation of large amounts of data on each of us in centralized locations pose a threat to us, particularly when some of the data are in error or subject to misinterpretation?

We will consider two areas where computer impact can be expected to be significant. The first of these is computer-assisted instruction (CAI). The second is the question of privacy. In neither of these areas are there clearly established and universally agreed values.

An example of the study of values in the educational environment is the work of S. Simon.* According to his characterization of values, values must be:

(1) prized and cherished
(2) publicly affirmed
(3) chosen from alternatives
(4) chosen after considering consequences
(5) chosen freely
(6) acted upon
(7) consistently linked to other values

It appears from this characterization that values are a personal set of standards and one purpose of education is the clarification of an individual's values, i.e., his self-identification. We might ask how CAI contributes to this aspect of education.

Similarly, in studying the question of privacy, it appears that privacy is something we expect and cherish, but has not been well-defined.

Perhaps, in the case of privacy, the paradoxical nature of the value problem is most apparent. Privacy seems by its nature to be a personally defined value. Is it conceivable even that A and B might decide for C what is private to C without, by that very act, infringing on C's personal prerogative to define his or her own privacy?

Computer science cannot solve all the ethical, sociological, educational, and legal problems of society, but computer scientists must interact with all of these problems, and be sensitive to them.

Computers in education

A classification of all the areas of education in which computers are being used and can be used would include administrative and personnel data, educational records, payroll, scheduling, research, and computer-assisted instruction (CAI). Many of these applications are well-understood from a technical point of view, although some of them do raise serious privacy issues. It seems, however, that the largest potential application of computers is in the instructional process itself.

---

*J. Goodman, "Sid Simon on Values." *English Teacher's Companion.* (New York: Scholastic Book Services, 1974). pp. 141–48.

In the instructional process, computers have been used for grading multiple-choice and true-false examinations and for other record-keeping functions. Also, computers are used to demonstrate their application in a variety of disciplines, such as data analysis in typical social or behavioral sciences or computation in physical sciences. And, surely, we can expect a broader application as increased accessibility of computer terminals or pocket calculators makes the slide-rule and handbook of tables obsolete.

What is left, then, as a questionable area of computer application, is the role of the computer in programmed instruction. How broad a role, if any, will programmed instruction play in education? To what disciplines, if any, is it applicable?

Further, what will be the role of the instructor in the educational process? In fact, will technology tend to automate much of the classroom and remove the interpersonal learning situations?

Finally, on what basis are programmed learning machines being developed? How can we ensure that what is taught is not only what can be programmed into a machine? Can we provide safeguards to assure the continuance of a diverse set of opinions and viewpoints?

Milhollan and Forisha state that

Teaching is an activity which emerges from some conception about how learning occurs . . . If we value the achievement of a synthesis of a teacher's values and goals with his conception of learning and with his educational practice, this goal may be vastly facilitated by a more integrative orientation to the study of learning theory.*

They consider, in detail, the comparison and contrast between two disparate views of the educational process. On one hand, they choose B. F. Skinner as the representative of the behaviorist school of thought that asserts that all actions are responses to external stimuli and all behavior is conditioned. On the other hand, they select Carl Rogers as an exponent of the phenomenological view of psychology, which is humanistic in outlook, viewing human behavior as a unique phenomenon with a free will.

An analysis and comparison of these contrasting approaches to education is beyond the scope of our text. Suffice to say that programmed instruction and teaching machines have been developed as a direct outgrowth of Skinner's psychology and approach to education. To the extent that this approach is accepted and applied we can expect that machines may supplement or replace human instructors.

The potential danger is that teaching machines and programmed instruction may gain acceptance in schools, not because the method they use is desirable, but because they may provide a more economical alternative, or simply from fascination with the devices. So far, the costs of terminal connect time

---

From Skinner to Rogers—Contrasting Approaches to Education. F.M. Holland and B.E. Forisha. (Lincoln, Neb: Professional Educators Publications, 1972). p. 8.

have precluded any wide-scale use of computers in instruction, although various experimental projects have been undertaken. One of the main objectives of such projects is to provide low cost terminals and computer interaction. (It has been one of the curiosities of the computer development that the only area that has not shown very significant cost/performance improvements is input/output.) Assuming that an order of magnitude change in costs occurs in interactive computer usage, so that the cost of a terminal equipped classroom used for an hour is comparable to the cost of an hour's instruction by a teacher, you can expect a much broader application of CAI, particularly in areas where drill and programmed instruction can be applied.

Computers and Privacy

Of all of the social issues which have arisen from computer technology, privacy remains one of the most poorly defined and intricate in its impact. Highly technologic societies are grappling with new constitutional and legal questions which derive from the fact that it is now possible and economical to gather, store and integrate data about individuals in quantity and detail that was unthinkable a few decades ago. Before this technological development, a person's privacy was protected by the sheer cost of invading it. Computers have significantly reduced the cost and time required to collect personal dossiers. While accuracy and authenticity of personal data remain as problems in computer systems, an irrational trust and faith in computer processed data has developed and has exacerbated the privacy issues.

United States Senator Henry M. Jackson, co-sponsor of the Privacy Act of 1974 summarized the privacy issues as:

> "The issue of the right of privacy is at a crossroads. The policy choices to be made in the next few years will determine whether our nation will leash technology to prevent its stampede over the right to privacy, or whether enormous interconnected data systems carrying information about all of us will grow unchecked."[1]

As noted in Chapter 1 of this book, much of the pressure for automated personal data systems has arisen from the growth of the numbers of people. Governments must serve more and more people. Schools and universities have more students. Hospitals and courts must deal with more cases. An economical way of handling the records had to be found. The computer has been the answer to the problem, but the answer has been almost too good. It is easier to collect irrelevant data than to be discriminating in data collection. It is easier to merge data files than to gather new, pertinent data.

The individual, when faced with obtaining services from an organization using automated personal records, must evaluate the service in terms of potential loss of privacy. The individual needs to have confidence in the accuracy of

---

[1]McClellan, G. S., *The Right to Privacy, The Reference Shelf,* Volume 48, Number 1, p. 213, H. W. Wilson Co., New York, 1976.

the data when it is stored and that the accuracy can be authenticated later. There is also a need to know the uses and disclosures of the data (both according to regulations and actual).

These individual concerns have been given considerable attention particularly within the U.S. Congress. A heightened awareness of new scientific and technical problems has emerged. Computer scientists are realizing the need for new approaches to computer security, user authentication, and the inclusion of data transmission information within data bases.

In the United States, the legislative actions regarding privacy have tended to be limiting rather than extending in nature. The Constitutional protections are not explicit, and, thus, what protections which exist are based upon case law. A new awareness of privacy issues developed during the Watergate crisis, but, prior to Watergate, legislative and regulatory reforms had been under study for several years. A select committee of Congress had a decisive role in quashing the National Data Bank idea in the 1960's. The Department of Health, Education, and Welfare formed an Advisory Committee on Automated Personal Data Systems which drafted a report in 1973 called "Records, Computers, and the Rights of Citizens" which found that:

> "An individual's personal privacy is directly affected by the kind of disclosure and use made of identifiable information about him in a record. A record containing information about an individual in identifiable form must, therefore, be governed by procedures that afford an individual a right to participate in deciding what the content of the record will be, and what disclosure and use will be made of the identifiable information in it."[2]

This report and its findings were important stepping stones to two subsequent legislatives acts: 1) The Family Education Rights and Privacy Act, 2) The Privacy Act of 1974. The Fair Credit Reporting Act (1971) and the Equal Employment Opportunity Act (1972), while addressing other issues, also established a climate and awareness necessary for the privacy acts.

The Privacy Act of 1974 has become a landmark piece of legislation due to the attention that it gives to broad policy issues. The specifics of the Privacy Act of 1974 apply to data gathering and disclosure practices of the federal government. Compliance has led to a flurry of reporting by federal agencies but little in the way of fundamental change in practices. The greatest impact of the Act has been in acknowledging general principles:

"The Congress finds that:

(1) the privacy of an individual is directly affected by the collection, maintenance, use, and dissemination of personal information by Federal agencies;

(2) the increasing use of computers and sophisticated information technology, while essential to the efficient operations of the Government,

---

[2]U.S. Department of Health, Education and Welfare, *Records, Computers, and the Rights of Citizens,* Washington, D.C., 1973.

has greatly magnified the harm to individual privacy that can occur from any collection, maintenance, use, or dissemination of personal information;

(3) the opportunities for an individual to secure employment, insurance, and credit, and his right to due process, and other legal protections are endangered by the misuse of certain information systems;

(4) the right to privacy is a personal and fundamental right protected by the Constitution of the United States; and

(5) in order to protect the privacy of individuals identified in information systems maintained by Federal agencies, it is necessary and proper for the Congress to regulate the collection, maintenance, use, and dissemination of information by such agencies."[3]

The Privacy Act of 1974 established the Privacy Protection Study Commission which has had a broad mandate to study many issues related to privacy and to recommend follow-up legislation.

The Privacy Protection Study Commission has focused upon some very general issues and has suggested some useful definitions and principles which will influence the design of computer systems and data bases very directly. Beginning from the principles as stated in the 1973 HEW report,

1. There must be no personal data record-keeping systems whose very existence is secret.

2. There must be a way for an individual to find out what information about him is in a record and how it is used.

3. There must be a way for an individual to prevent information about him obtained for one purpose from being or made available for other purposes without his consent.

4. There must be a way for an individual to correct or amend a record of identifiable information about him.

5. Any organization creating, maintaining, using, or disseminating records of identifiable personal data must assure the reliability of the data for their intended use and must take reasonable precautions to prevent misuse of the data.[4]

The Privacy Protection Study Commission proceeded to identify systemic features of record keeping systems and public policy objectives.

Systemic Features of Personal Data Record Keeping

First, while an organization makes and keeps records about individuals to facilitate relationships with them, it also makes and keeps records about individuals for other purposes, such as documenting the record-keeping

---

[3]Public Law 93-574, The Privacy Act of 1974, Sec. 2(a).
[4]U.S. Department of Health, Education, and Welfare, op. cit., p. 41.

organization's own actions and making it possible for other organizations-government agencies, for example, to monitor the actions of individuals.

Second, there is an accelerating trend, most obvious in the credit and financial areas, toward the accumulation in records of more and more personal details about an individual.

Third, more and more records about an individual are collected, maintained, and disclosed by organizations with which the individual has no direct relationship but whose records help to shape his life.

Fourth, most record-keeping organizations consult the records of other organizations to verify the information they obtain from an individual and thus pay as much or more attention to what other organizations report about him than they pay to what he reports about himself; and

Fifth, neither law nor technology now gives an individual the tools he needs to protect his legitimate interests in the records organizations keep about him.[5]

Privacy Protection Policy Objectives

- to create a proper balance between what an individual is expected to divulge to a record-keeping organization and what he seeks in return (to minimize intrusiveness);

- to open up record-keeping operations in ways that will minimize the extent to which recorded information about an individual is itself a source of unfairness in any decision about him made on the basis of it (to maximize fairness); and

- to create and define obligations with respect to the uses and disclosures that will be made of recorded information about an individual (to create legitimate, enforceable expectations of confidentiality.[6]

The Commission has applied these principles and objectives to specific recommendations for new legislation and practices for both the public and private sector. For example, the Commission "emphatically rejects" the "generalized government asset" view of the use of data collected by the Internal Revenue Service.[7] The "generalized government asset" policy would allow any disclosure pursuant to government objectives. On the issue of the use of a universal identifier which the Security Number is becoming, the Commission recommends:

That the Federal government not consider taking any action that would foster the development of a standard, universal label for individuals, or a central population register, until such time as significant steps have been taken to implement safeguards and policies regarding permissible uses and

---

[5]The Privacy Protection Study Commission, *Personal Privacy in an Information Society*, p. 8, Washington, D.C., 1977.
[6]ibid, p. 14
[7]The Privacy Protection Study Commission, *Federal Tax Return Confidentiality*, p. 26, Washington, D.C., 1977.

disclosures of records about individuals in the spirit of those recommended by the Commission and those safeguards and policies have been demonstrated to be effective.[8]

Thus, the Privacy Protection Study Commission has begun to make specific recommendations for legislative action in the privacy area. Most of the attention is being given to governmental policies thereby setting standards which may ultimately be applied in the private sector.

Privacy concerns have encountered some direct conflicts with other important public policy issues. Most notably, the move toward "sunshine laws" which require extensive disclosure of public records does ultimately lead to disclosure of individual information. Privacy protection for public officials and public employees remains an area for special consideration. It will probably be some time before legislation in this area stabilizes to a point of proper balance between the public interest and the individual's interest.

The role of computers in privacy policy is a good example of the impact of technology upon public policy. Technological developments can occur so quickly that laws and customs are left useless and ineffective. Before the legislative processes catch-up, there may be serious losses of liberties and human rights. The social impacts raise questions about governmental control of technology and the need to streamline and speed-up the assessment of the impact of technology.

References and Suggested Additional Readings

(1) McClellan, G. S., *The Right to Privacy, The Reference Shelf, Volume 48, Number 1.* H. W. Wilson Company, New York, 1976.

(2) Taviss, I., "Technology and Values." Harvard University Program on Technology and Society, Research Review Number 3, Cambridge, Massachusetts, Spring, 1969.

(3) *Federal Tax Return Confidentiality.* The Privacy Protection Study Commission, Washington, D.C., 1977.

(4) *Personal Privacy in an Information Society.* The Privacy Protection Study Commission, Washington, D.C., 1977.

(5) *Records, Computers, and the Rights of Citizens.* U.S. Department of Health, Education and Welfare, Washington, D.C., 1973.

---

[8]The Privacy Protection Study Commission, *Personal Privacy in an Information Society*, op. cit., p. 617.

Chapter 11

Artificial Intelligence

Conventional programming is the programming of algorithms that detail the step-by-step solution or operation of a problem or process. The composition of music, the invention of scientific devices, and most such intelligent behavior cannot be algorithmically described. Limitations on machine size and speed exclude a large percentage of the remaining areas of consideration. For example, it has been estimated that over 10^{120} move combinations must be examined in a full chess look-ahead procedure. Even if computer size and speed were increased to several times present day standards, construction of a perfect chess player would remain unfeasible.

Research in artificial intelligence has expanded computer applications to include processes requiring intelligent thought and judgment decisions. During the past decade, machines have used mechanical reduction techniques in theorem proving. Problem solvers, patterned after human thought processes, have successfully attacked difficult problems in logic and mathematics. Game-playing programs have defeated above average opponents in chess and checkers. Machines have simulated human thought and decision-making in such areas as concept formation and trust investment. And machines, like people, have modified their behavior by learning from experience.

11.1   Can Machines Think?

A great deal of discussion and argument has surrounded the question of whether a "thinking" or "intelligent" machine exists or can ever exist. One common argument is that machines do only what they are programmed to do. However, the program provides only the basic decision-making processes; these allow the machine to analyze problems, make decisions (often decisions unanticipated by the human programmer), and even learn and alter its structure based on the environment in which it has been performing. Such a machine will produce results that could not be "planned" by its human programmer.

What exactly is meant by an "intelligent" machine? In 1950, years before any working models of machines which might presume to be "intelligent" were developed, the mathematician A.M. Turing* proposed what has become known as the *Turing test* to determine whether a machine can think. This test takes the form of an "imitation game" played by a man, a woman, and an interrogator. Each is separated so that the only communication among the three is the questions posed by the interrogator and the answers produced by one or both of the subjects. Both subjects attempt to convince the interrogator that they are the woman and it is the job of the interrogator to determine the real identities. For example, the interrogator might ask each subject to describe the different brands of lipstick with which the subject is familiar, which brand is preferred, and why. In Turing's article, the example he uses

---

*Turing, A.M. "Computing Machinery and Intelligence." *Mind.* 59 (October 1950):433–460.

is "Will X please tell me the length of his or her hair?" Of course, this question is no longer used because even if the respondent answers truthfully, the answer is not conclusive.

The Turing test assigns the computer the part of the man; its job, therefore, is to "imitate" a woman and thereby cause the interrogator to make the wrong choice. Whether the machine can "think" is then related to how well it can play this imitation game.

Although machines have not yet reached the level of satisfying "Turing's test," remarkable progress has been made. Machines outperform their designers, produce elegant proofs for theorems, and learn from their experience.

11.2   Problem Solving

Machines have been developed that successfully solve problems involving "intelligent" or nonroutine behavior. Such machines include the Logic Theory Machine* for proving theorems in the propositional calculus and the General Problem Solver** for solving problems of a wide variety of different types. To illustrate the concepts embodied in these problem solving programs, we shall consider the following simple problem:

A set of plane flights between cities is shown in Figure 11.1. Given cities *A* and *B*, determine a set of flight connections between *A* and *B*. (Note that an optimum set of connections is not required.)

Problems of this type often lend themselves to trial-and-error search for a solution in a set of possible solutions. Two problem solving methods of this type are the state-set and the problem reduction approaches.***

State-set approach to problem solving

In the state-set approach to problem solving, a set of states is used to represent possible situations or positions of the problem. For example, in the case of the airline flight problem, the state set is the set of all ordered sequences of cities connected successively by direct flight. One state in this set is (Houston, Miami, Philadelphia) since Houston is connected directly to Miami and Miami is connected directly to Philadelphia. The initial state is the sequence consisting of only one element, city *A*. The goal state, the state which we want to reach, is any state represented by a list beginning with city *A* and ending with city *B*.

---

*Newell, A. and Shaw, J.C. and Simon, H.A. "Empirical Explorations of the Logic Theory Machine." Proceedings of the 1957 Western Joint Computer Conference.

**Ernest, G.W. and Newell, A. GPS: *A Case Study in Generality and Problem Solving.* (New York: Academic Press, 1969).

***Nilsson, D.J. *Problem-Solving Methods in Artificial Intelligence.* (New York: McGraw-Hill, 1971)

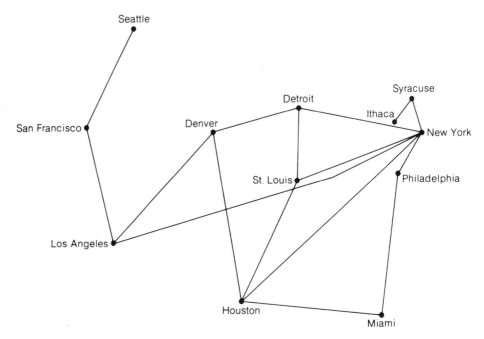

Figure 11.1: Typical flight connections

An operator generates a new state from an old one; i.e., it takes us one step in attempting to solve the problem. In our sample problem, the operators are all two-tuples (k_1, k_2) such that a direct flight exists from city k_1 to city k_2. Not every operator can be applied to every state. The operator (St. Louis, New York) can only be applied to states represented by a sequence of cities ending in St. Louis; it transforms this state into a state represented by adding New York to the sequence. For example, the operator (St. Louis, New York) generates the state (Denver, Detroit, St. Louis, New York) from the state (Denver, Detroit, St. Louis); however, the operator is not applicable to the state (Houston, Miami, Philadelphia). A solution to the airline flight problem is a sequence of operators that generate the goal state $G = (A. . .B)$ from the initial state (A).

Thus, the state-set method of problem solving requires an initial state describing the start of the problem, a set of operators that can be applied to solve the problem, and a goal state designating the end of the problem.

The *search set* consists of all states that can be generated by applying sequences of operators to the initial state. These may be represented by a state tree whose root is the initial state; the successors of a node of this tree are formed by applying each applicable operator to the state represented by the node. A solution to the problem is obtained by searching this tree for the goal state; the solution is then the set of operators or branches leading from the root to this goal state. Figure 11.2 illustrates part of a search space tree for the airline flight problem if city *A* is Los Angeles and city *B* is Miami (we have left out branches that lead back to a preceding state). The solution is shown by heavy lines.

Two methods of searching the search space tree for a solution are depth-first-search and breadth-first-search. The depth-first method applies an operator to the tree node of greatest depth, determines whether the new node is the goal state, and if not, repeats the procedure. It should be obvious that this can lead to an infinite exploration of only one branch of a tree, perhaps a branch which never leads to a solution. Thus, some limit *p* is placed upon the depth to which this search is made. An operator is applied to the node of greatest depth less than *p;* thus, a branch of the tree is explored until it reaches a depth of *p,* at which point another branch is explored.

The breadth-first method applies all operators, one at a time, to the initial state node and examines each new node in succession to determine if it is the goal state. If not, the set of operators is applied to each of these generated nodes to produce a new set of states which are examined in succession and so forth. Thus, all branches are expanded to depth *k* before any branch is expanded to depth *k* + 1.

The breadth-first method will find the shortest set of operators leading to a solution, if a solution exists, and the depth-first method allows us to investigate a few branches more fully before considering other branches or possible solutions.

These search methods are often impractical, however, since in very complex problems the search space tree is extremely large; limits on processing time and available memory prevents expanding the entire tree to any great depth. Thus, the tree must be "pruned," i.e., many of its branches removed, so that the remaining branches may be explored in greater depth. A *heuristic*

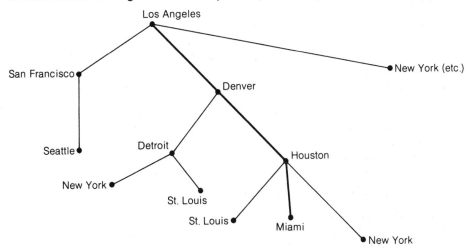

Figure 11.2:   A portion of the search space tree for the airline flight problem

is a rule of thumb, strategy, or method used to reduce the amount of work necessary to solve a problem. In the case of a tree search, heuristics may be used to eliminate branches which are unlikely to lead to a solution, to order the remaining branches so that the most promising ones are investigated first, and to determine the depth to which a given branch is investigated. Heuristics have one very definite disadvantage. They are only "rules of thumb" and are not guaranteed to be correct; thus, they may remove a branch leading to a solution or place it far down the priority list for investigation.

In our airline flight problem, several heuristics might be used to reduce the search; for example,

> "Do not apply operator (k_1, k_2) if city k_2 is further
> from the goal city B than k_1."

Such a heuristic would prevent us from exploring connections that actually have us going backwards; however, in the example it would also prevent us from ever finding a set of flights connecting St. Louis and Denver.

Another heuristic might be

> "The operators (k_1, k_2) will be ordered in terms of
> increasing distance of city k_2 from goal city B."

This heuristic applies the operators in order of how close they bring us to the goal state B. Thus, the most promising branches of the tree are explored first.

The efficiency of a problem solver is directly related to the usefulness and validity of its heuristics.

The problem reduction approach

A second approach to problem solving is that of problem reduction. This approach attempts to reduce the problem to a set of trivial subproblems. The solution of the subproblems then produces the solution of the original problem. Problem reduction is closely related to the principle of programming called "invariant imbedding" which was discussed in chapter 1.

In the case of our airline flight example, the problem of obtaining flight connections from Los Angeles to Ithaca can be reduced to the two subproblems of obtaining connections from Los Angeles to New York and from New York to Ithaca. These two subproblems should each be easier to solve than the original problem. Los Angeles to New York is a trivial subproblem since there is a direct flight; New York to Ithaca requires a connection at Syracuse.

The problem reduction approach again uses states and operators to generate new states; descriptions of subproblems must also be provided. Heuristics are used to reduce the problem into component subproblems, then reduce the component subproblems into component subproblems, and so forth. A given problem can usually be reduced into more than one set of subproblems; thus, a search is still required among the sets of generated sub-problems to find a set that can eventually be solved either trivially or via further subproblem reductions.

In both the state-set and the problem reduction approaches, the data structure used to represent the states, operators, and problem descriptions has a strong influence on the success of the problem solver. Many types of data structure have been used; the choice depends on the type of problem being solved.

11.3   Backtracking

Implicit in the search of a state-set tree or a subproblem tree is the concept of backtracking: if the path searched ends in failure (either actual failure due to inability to generate new states or easier subproblems, or heuristic failure due to estimation that the current path is not leading to a solution), then the search must "backtrack" to a previous node and investigate a different portion of the tree. The following problems will illustrate backtracking and the concepts of the preceding sections.

Magic square problem

The magic square problem consists of a 3×3 square and nine 1×1 tiles containing the digits 1 through 9. The problem is to place the tiles in the square such that the sum of the digits across each row, down each column, and along each diagonal is the same.

Since each digit will appear only once in the 3×3 square, it is easily seen that each row-sum must be $(1 + 2 + \ldots + 8 + 9)/3 = 15$. Thus, an easy (and fool-proof) heuristic for guiding the search for a solution is that the sum along each row, column, and diagonal must never exceed 15 and must be less than 15 if the row, column, or diagonal is not filled.

Our initial state is the empty 3×3 square; operator (K, I, J) will insert digit K in row I and column J of the square (the operator is not applicable if digit K has already been added to the square or if row I, column J position is already occupied). We shall apply applicable operators in order from largest to smallest three-tuple (we shall consider operator (A, B, C) to be larger than operator (D, E, F) if ABC is a larger three-digit number than DEF) and use a depth-first search with the depth limited by our heuristic.

Figure 11.3 illustrates a small portion of the search for a solution. The nodes are numbered according to the order in which they are generated. Back-tracking occurs at node ⑱ when all attempts to place a 6 in the square

	7	
8		
		9

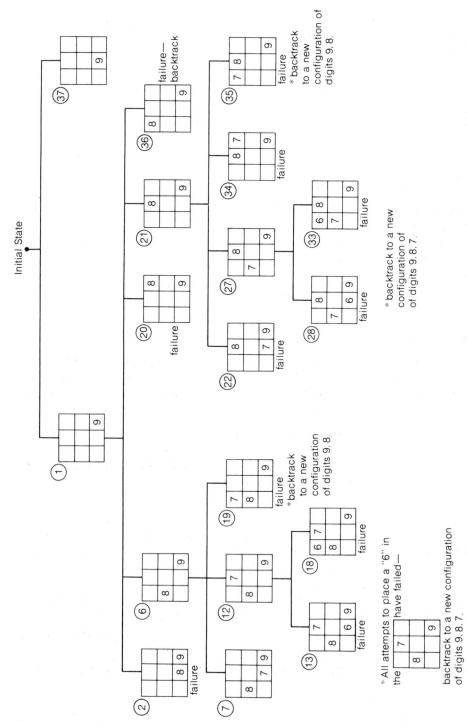

Figure 11.3:   Search and backtrack in the magic square problem

fail; the search moves back to node ⑥ and generates a state with digit 7 in a new position. Backtracking again occurs at node ⑲ when all attempts to place a 7 in the square

fail; here the search moves back to node ① and generates a state with digit 8 in a new position. Eventually, the solution

6	1	8
7	5	3
2	9	4

will be obtained.

Sum-free partition problem

A partition of a set is a division of the elements of the set into nonempty subsets. The sum-free partition consists of finding the smallest partition (the one with the fewest subsets) of a set of numbers such that if A and B are both elements of a subset, then their sum is not also an element of that subset.

For example, the set $\{1, 2, 3, 4, 5, 6, 7\}$ has as its sum-free partition the subsets $\{1, 3, 5, 7\}$, $\{2, 6\}$, $\{4\}$. Figure 11.4 illustrates the search for this solution. A state consists of the elements placed into subsets thus far. An operator (D, E) will place number D in subset E; operator $(\ )$ generates a new temporarily empty subset. We shall apply operators (D, E) in order from smallest to largest pair and use a depth-first search; the depth of the search is limited by the heuristic that a new subset not be generated unless it is impossible to obtain a sum-free partition with the existing number of subsets. Note that in Figure 11.4, nodes O, P, Q differ from nodes F, G, H in that three subsets can now be used to form the partition.

11.4   Game Playing

Game playing has intrigued many researchers in artificial intelligence. The concern is not with some particular game itself, but with the characteristics of certain games that make them good tools for research in problem solving.

A true game is nondeterminate in the sense that no easily utilized algorithm exists guaranteeing a win. Therefore, intelligent decision-making processes are essential for winning play. In essence, a game is a problem. The problem

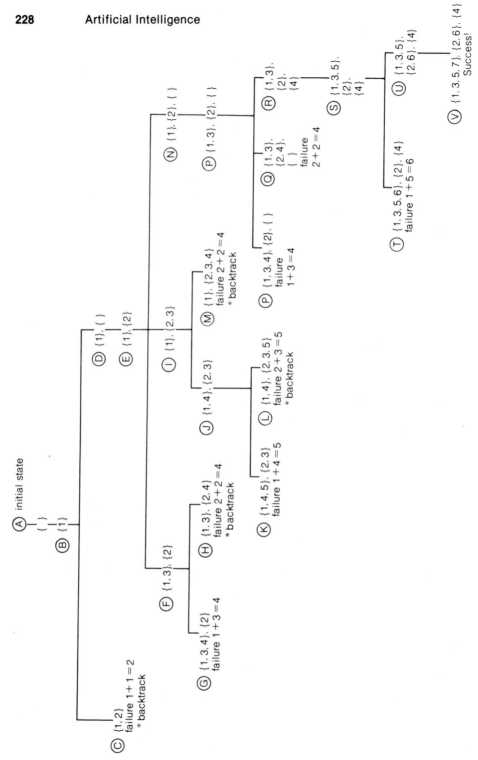

Figure 11.4: Search and backtracking in the sum-free partition problem

framework is the set of rules governing play of the game. The problem itself may be stated: "within the problem framework, devise a winning line of play." Actually, a game is several problems in one, since each move requires solution of the subproblem: "within the problem framework, determine the best move for the given game situation." The problem is correctly solved by the player winning the game.

Two important facets of problem-solving research are testing and evaluation of the mechanical problem solver. That a machine can solve one particular problem is no proof that it possesses good decision-making ability. A game provides a framework within which an extremely large number of different formulations of the same problem may be posed. The machine solution of each problem may be compared with various human solutions or with a store of "expert" play.

These qualities—the indeterminate nature of a game, its similarity to a problem environment, and its ease of testing and evaluation—have resulted in the construction of a number of successful game-playing programs.

The search tree

The major element of most game playing programs is search of a move tree— a tree of moves by player 1, then countermoves by player 2, etc. This search attempts to find the initial move that leads to a winning line of play for player 1. Such a tree search is called a *look-ahead procedure*, since it "looks ahead" in the game.

Consider the move tree shown in Figure 11.5. The move tree is expanded three moves and the final positions evaluated. Most two-person games are zero-sum games; that is, the goodness of a particular position to one player is necessarily a measure of the badness of this situation to his opponent. Accordingly, we have chosen to evaluate the final positions as +1 if player 1 wins, 0 if a tie, and −1 if player 1 loses. You might assume that if the current position of the game is represented by node A of the move tree, then player 1 should choose the move leading to node B, since this takes him along the path to nodes H and J which are winning positions. However, this is not true—at node B it is player 2's turn to move, and only a poor player will choose a move to node D from which player 1 can win; therefore player 2 will move to node E, and now player 1 can move only to nodes K and L which are losing positions.

Thus, the correct initial move by player 1 must be determined by "backing up" from the final positions in such a way that player 1 chooses the line of play that *max*imizes the value of the final position with player 2 always choosing moves that *min*imize it. This is called a *minimax procedure*.

As an example of minimaxing, consider again the move tree of Figure 11.5. At node D, player 1 will choose to maximize his advantage and will therefore select the move leading to a final position value of +1. Position D therefore

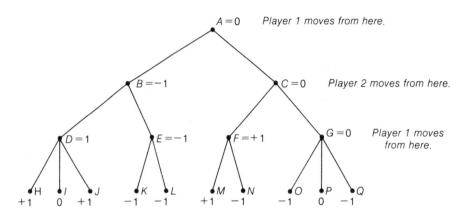

Figure 11.5:   A look-ahead move tree, with minimaxing

assumes the value +1 since it guarantees a win for player 1. Similarly nodes
E, F, and *G* receive values −1, +1, and 0 respectively. At node *B,* opponent 2
will move to maximize his advantage or, equivalently, to minimize the final
position value. Player 2 therefore chooses to move to node *E* since this makes
the final board value −1. Position *B* therefore assumes value −1; *C* assumes
value 0. Similarly player 1 will choose to move from node *A* to node *C,* guaranteeing that the final position value must be at least 0. The correct line of
play from node *A,* given that each player maximizes his advantage and assumes his opponent will do the same, is *C-G-P.* Thus, the correct initial move
for player 1 is the move leading to node *C.*

If you could look-ahead to any depth, you could consider all lines of play
until termination of the game and minimax to determine whether each initial
move for player 1 leads to a win, lose, or draw. However, for chess over 10^{120}
move continuations must be examined—an impossible situation. Therefore,
the move tree is expanded to a certain depth, an evaluation function used to
score the goodness of these final positions to player 1, and minimaxing used
to determine the best intial move. The basic premise here is that looking
ahead in the game and evaluating the results of a finite line of play is better
than merely applying an evaluation function to the possible initial moves.

The evaluation function depends on the game being played and may be linear
or nonlinear. Linear evaluation functions usually take the form of a polyno-
minal $f(P) = A_1 (T_1) + A_2 (T_2) + \ldots + A_n (T_n)$ where *P* is a position, T_i is the value
of a parameter, and A_i is an experimentally determined weight. For example,
in TIC-TAC-TOE, you might choose for the evaluation function

$$f(P) = T_1 + 10T_2 + 100000 \, T_3$$

where $T_i = $ (number of rows, columns, or diagonals in which player 1 has *I*
unblocked marks) − (number of rows, columns, or diagonals in
which player 2 has *I* unblocked marks).

Thus, the board position $P =$

	2
1	1
2	

would be evaluated as

$$f(P) = 1(T_1) + 10(T_2) + 100000\ (T_3)$$
$$= 1(2 - 3) + 10(1 - 0) + 100000(0 - 0)$$
$$= -1 + 10 = 9$$

Note that $f(P)$ is positive if the position favors player 1 and negative if it favors player 1 and negative if it favors player 2. Also note the large coefficient of T_3, since if $T_3 = 1$ player 1 wins; if $T_3 = -1$ player 1 loses—thus, this parameter must overshadow all others.

Nonlinear evaluation functions provide more accurate measures of the goodness of a position since they allow the machine to account for cases in which parameter T_J is of immense importance if parameter T_K has a large value but of negligible interest otherwise. However, such functions are more difficult to implement than linear evaluation functions.

Many other techniques are used to develop successful game playing programs. A few of these are the *alpha-beta* tree pruning algorithm to reduce the tree search, the use of heuristics to generate moves to be investigated, and the use of goals related to the current status of the game to guide the tree search.

11.5   Machine Learning

Learning is the "revision of opinion on the basis of experience." Intelligent beings are born not with knowledge and judgment ability, but with the capacity for acquiring them. Similarly, research in artificial intelligence has demonstrated that machines may be constructed with the capacity for improving their decision-making abilities by learning from experience.

As problems increase in complexity, this self-improvement of the machine's decision-making processes becomes significantly more important. Given a particular problem, the correct solution may be obtained from experts in the field. However, in many complex situations, it would be extremely difficult, if not impossible, to consider a sufficient number of problems in enough variation and detail to generalize these problem-solutions into a competent machine decision-making apparatus. Thus, methods must be devised for constructing machine decision-making frameworks that may be self-adjusted and self-altered as the machine's experience dictates, resulting in a complex, efficient, decision-making apparatus.

Types of learning

Two types of learning ability, rote and generalized, have been exhibited by recent machines. *Rote learning* is the cataloging in memory of specific instance-response or problem-solution pairs. Thus, if a particular problem has been encountered previously, the machine need only search its memory for the correct solution.

Rote learning produces several notable results. Solutions to recurrent problems are immediately available within the machine. The time saved by avoiding resolution of old problems may be used to examine other problems in greater depth than might otherwise be expedient. New problems may reduce to a set of previously learned subproblems and will be immediately solvable at the point of reduction. This occurs frequently in theorem proving and game playing. The more complex the problem under consideration, the more advantageous is this reduction. In many sufficiently complicated cases, the original problem would otherwise remain unsolvable.

Upon first glance, this rote learning may appear only to save computation time but to have little effect on the ability of the machine. This is not the case. For example, the depth of the look-ahead procedure in game-playing programs is severely limited for reasons of time and memory capacity; yet this limitation is a serious handicap. Rote learning allows the most significant moves to be analyzed in greater depth than would otherwise be possible.[*] This is accomplished in the following manner.

Given a particular game situation, an X-ply (expansion to depth X) look-ahead search is made to determine the best initial move and its "backed-up" score. Each correct initial move encountered during the game, and its associated score, is then rote-learned by the machine and stored in memory. Now, suppose one of the final positions generated during an X-ply look-ahead is found to be stored in memory as a result of rote learning. Its rote-learned evaluation is already at least an X-ply backed-up score. If minimaxing selects this position's evaluation as the score for the best initial move, the score has been backed-up at least $2 \times X$ plys instead of X plys.

Thus, moves that were encountered most often and which probably were most significant would have scores that had been analyzed to a depth many times greater than the X-ply limit.

Two factors restrict the widespread use of machine rote-learning. As the number of problem-solution pairs in the memory store increases, the search time expended quickly reduces the effectiveness of rote-learning as a time-saving device. More important, machine memory has a finite capacity that in most cases will be far exceeded by the problem-solution pairs and the data space necessary to sufficiently describe them.

---

[*]Samuel, A.L. "Some Studies in Machine Learning Using the Game of Checkers I." *Computers and Thought*, E. Feigenbaum & J. Feldman, eds. 1963.

Several attempts have been made to lessen those disadvantages. Larger and faster machines have been developed. The set of problem-solutions has been subdivided according to the peculiar characteristics of problem groups to eliminate the need to search the entire memory store. The utilization of this learning then assumes many of the aspects of a problem in pattern recognition. The memory store has been pruned at intervals to eliminate pairs of marginal utility. This has the effect both of reducing the store search time and of increasing the memory available for future problem-solution pairs.

However, as the complexity of problems for machine solution increases, the disadvantages of rote-learning become more significant. Rote-learning is quite effective for accurately learning small amounts of information, but it alone is not sufficient to enable machines to develop expert decision-making abilities.

Generalized learning is the "learning of solutions or methods of solution for general classes of problems." Closely aligned with this type of learning is the concept of reinforcement. To "reinforce" a behavioral instance is to increase the probability of eliciting a given response upon application of a particular set of stimuli. In generalized learning, the machine examines the characteristics of a particular problem and in some way reinforces the correct solution for this character set. For example, rote learning in TIC-TAC-TOE involves memorizing the best move for each possible board situation, whereas generalized learning involves generalizing each situation according to a set of parameters and learning the best move for each combination of parameter values. The parameters might include the unblocked one, two, and three in a row advantage used in the sample evaluation function, the number of corner positions held, etc. However, one set of values for the parameters will describe more than one TIC-TAC-TOE situation; thus, generalized learning cannot guarantee a correct solution for a given situation, but can only maximize the probability of a correct solution for situations represented by a given set of parameter values.

Several methods of "training" such a machine exist. A trainer may be used. The trainer either indicates the goodness of the machine's solution or presents the machine with the correct solution. In the former, the machine is left to find the correct solution independently, being told only when that solution is obtained and perhaps whether it is proceeding to steadily better solutions. In the latter case, the machine may proceed immediately to reinforce the correct response, which invariably leads to more rapid learning. If an indication of both success and failure is available within the problem itself, a trainer is not essential. Game playing and theorem proving often contain easily recognized success-failure stimuli.

Throughout this discussion, it has been assumed that the machine somehow found pertinent characteristics for generalizing problems. In all the learning machines designed so far, the characteristics or parameters have been generated by the programmer; the machine has been allowed to select and discard from this general set, but machine generation of parameters has not been accomplished. This looms as one of the major problems of learning machines and still appears a long way from solution. Generalized learning overcomes the time and space limitations of rote learning; however, it still has its own inherent difficulties. Generalized learning does not guarantee a correct solution even if the identical problem has been previously encountered. Better reinforcement techniques and learning schemes must be developed to increase the probability of correct responses. Machine generation of parameters would be a major step in this direction.

Rote and generalized learning each have peculiar characteristics that suit them to particular types of problems; in many cases, both are used, each to its particular advantage.

Summary

Although the notion of an "intelligent" machine still generates much controversy, recent developments indicate that machines can indeed exhibit behavior patterns that resemble human thought and decision-making. Research in language recognition, language generation, and vision has provided limited mechanical sensory capability. Recently the development of robot systems has been pursued with increased vigor, and it remains to be seen whether a robot will pass the Turing Test within this century.

References and Suggested Additional Readings

(1) Bobrow, D. and Raphael, B., "New Programming Languages for Artificial Intelligence," *Computing Surveys* 66. no. 3. (1974): 153–74.

(2) Elithorn, A. and Jones, D., eds, *Artificial and Human Thinking.* (New York: American Elsevier Publishing Co., 1973).

(3) Ernst, G.W. and Newell, A., "GPS: A Case Study in Generality and Problem Solving." (New York: Academic Press, 1969).

(4) Feigenbaum, E. and Feldman, J., *Computers and Thought.* (New York: McGraw-Hill, 1963).

(5) Findler, N. and Meltzer, B., *Artificial Intelligence and Heuristic Programming.* (New York: American Elsevier Publishing Co., 1971).

(6) Greenblatt, R., "Greenblatt Chess Program," 1967 Fall Joint Computer Conference.

(7) Jackson, P., *Introduction to Artificial Intelligence.* (New York: Petrocelli Books, 1974).

(8) Michie, D. et. al., eds, *Machine Intelligence.* Vol. 1–8, (New York: American Elsevier Publishing Co., 1968).

(9) Newell, A. and Shaw, J.C. and Simon, H.A., "Empirical Explorations of the Logic Theory Machine," Proceedings of the 1957 Western Joint Computer Conference.

(10) Nilsson, N.J., *Problem-Solving Methods in Artificial Intelligence.* (New York: McGraw-Hill, 1971).

(11) ——. "Artificial Intelligence," Proc. of International Federation of Informational Processing. (1974), pp. 778–801.

(12) Samuel, A.L., "Some Studies in Machine Learning Using the Game of Checkers I," *Computers and Thought,* E. Feigenbaum and J. Feldman, eds. (New York: McGraw-Hill, 1963). pp. 71–105.

(13) ——. "Some Studies in Machine Learning Using the Game of Checkers II. Recent Progress," *IBM Journal of Research and Development* 2, (November 1967): 601–17.

(14) Slagle, J.R., *Artificial Intelligence: The Heuristic Programming Approach.* (New York: McGraw-Hill, 1971).

(15) Smith, M., "A Learning Program Which Plays Partnership Dominoes," Communications of the Association for Computing Machinery 16, no. 8, (1973): 462–67.

(16) Turing, A.M., "Computing Machinery and Intelligence," *Mind,* 59, (October 1950): 433–60.

(17) Uhr, L., *Pattern Recognition, Learning, and Thought.* (Englewood Cliffs, N.J.: Prentice-Hall, 1973).

Problems

1. The following move tree is expanded two moves for player A and one move for player B. Final positions of positive value favor player A. Use minimaxing to determine the best initial move for player A.

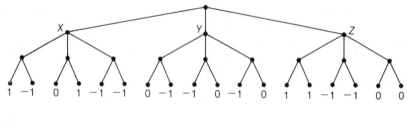

1 −1   0   1 −1 −1   0 −1 −1   0 −1   0   1   1 −1 −1   0   0

2. A Tic-Tac-Toe game looks as follows: 0 | X | 0

   (a) How many final positions would occur if the entire move tree for the remainder of the game were expanded to completion?
   (b) Expand the move tree two moves for player X and one move for player 0. Use the evaluation function given in the text to evaluate these final positions and minimax to determine the best initial move for player X.

3. List some activities that require trial-and-error search. Would you use a depth-first or breadth-first search, and why?

4. List some heuristics that you use in everyday activities. List some heuristics that you might use in writing a bridge-playing program.

5. Examine a game with which you are familiar (for example, chess, checkers, Go). What parameters would you include in a polynomial evaluation function for eval-

uating a board position in this game, and what relative weights would you assign each?

6. The missionaries and cannibals problem starts with 3 missionaries and 3 cannibals on one side of a river. There is a small boat that can carry only two passengers, and each person knows how to operate the boat. If at any time there are more cannibals than missionaries on one side of the river, the cannibals will eat the missionaries. The problem is to get all six persons across the river without any missionaries being eaten.

Using the state-space approach to problem solving,
(a) What are the states in this problem?
(b) What are the operators?
(c) What is the initial state?
(d) What is the goal state?

7. Draw a portion of the search space tree for problem 6. Search the tree for a solution.

8. Using the problem reduction approach to problem solving,
(a) How can the missionaries and cannibals problem be reduced to subproblems?
(b) How can the problem and subproblem descriptions be formulated?

9. Discuss appropriate data structures for use in representing states and operators in problem 6 and subproblem descriptions in problem 8.

10. Suppose you are designing a machine for proving theorems in plane geometry. What learning would be useful in such a machine and why?

11. Discuss an area of activity in which generalized learning is appropriate.

12. Complete the search through the state tree of the Magic Square Problem of Figure 11.3.

13. The NINE puzzle consists of a 3 × 3 square filled with eight 1 × 1 tiles and one empty space. The configuration of tiles can be changed by swapping the position of the blank space and a tile adjacent to it. Given an initial configuration and a goal configuration of the NINE puzzle, the problem is to find a sequence of moves transforming the former into the latter.
(a) Describe two states and operators for the NINE puzzle.
(b) Describe a heuristic to guide the search through the state tree.

Chapter 12

Computer Software

Introduction

The purpose of computer software is to make the preparation of programs easier. Perhaps in a future ideal situation, one might take programming assignments to the computer, and *say* to the computer, "Please solve these problems for me and notify me when you are done." The computer might then, ideally, be expected to satisfy the stated request.

The gap between this hypothetical ideal and our present status in computer science is large enough so that we do not anticipate this sort of computer usage in the foreseeable future, science-fiction novels notwithstanding. First, there is the problem of voice recognition which is itself difficult and not well understood. Second, even if the computer were able to reliably decipher spoken requests, the analysis of grammatical or quasi-grammatical English dialogue is also not yet formulated algorithmically. Third, the ability of the computer to read printed or handwritten text, possibly including figures, tables, and diagrams, is still very limited. Fourth, even assuming that all of the above problems could be solved, we do not know how to proceed from an arbitrarily stated problem to a computer program to solve that problem. Moreover, we know that in some cases there is *no* program to solve a given problem as discussed in Chapter 2.

Still, despite the difficulties of realizing our hypothetical problem solver, and it remains as an ideal objective that we would hope to achieve either in this generation, or in some succeeding generation, we hope to develop tools and techniques that will simplify the process of program preparation. There are many ways in which programming has been made easier in the hardware and software dimensions, as well as in the techniques.

Briefly, in the hardware area, input has been facilitated through the use of remote entry devices thus not requiring one to go to the computer, through the use of keyboard and cathode ray display terminals eliminating the need for punched cards, and in the enlarged storage media allowing one's programs to be stored in the computer rather than be repeatedly entered. Further, the increased computing power has allowed the computer to concurrently service many users, allowing for the development of time-sharing computing (discussed in the next chapter) which makes the computing resource more widely available.

In the software area, there have also been many advances making the computer easier to use, by having programs which do many of the algorithmically formulated tasks in program preparation. We have already seen how a richer set of control structures (Chapter 6) and data structures (Chapter 7) enhance a problem formulation language, and can in turn be algorithmically implemented in a processor for such a language. (In this chapter, we take a more comprehensive view of computer software, starting with an overview from the user's point of view of the "software menu". Then, we examine in some more detail some of the major types of software components—compilers, assemblers, and operating systems. We conclude the chapter with a discussion of the software hierarchy from several perspectives.)

We have also mentioned the development of programming techniques as a part of the software improvement process, and, indeed, in Chapters 2 and 3 we discussed programming methodology. Also, in Chapter 5 we briefly mentioned the study and analysis of algorithms, which try primarily to improve the running time or storage requirements of problems but also often have the effect of providing better descriptions of the algorithms. Further, in Chapter 11, we discussed some different problem solving strategies.

12.1   An Overview of Computer Software

The term computer software is used here to describe the collection of programs which a computer system might expect to have in its library. These programs, which are generally intended for a broad class of users, are either provided by the computer system vendor, obtained through a user's group, purchased from a software developer, or written by one's own systems programming group. Most of these programs are frequently used and, therefore, reside on a direct access device such as a disk pack where they are available to a user without the need for operator intervention to physically move the program medium. Of course, as additional software is developed the size of this resident system library of programs grows, but, fortunately, so does the amount of storage that is available in direct access devices.

The software "menu" that is provided for the user thus covers a large range of programs, and the effective use of the computer is enhanced through a familiarity with this system software library. In this section, a quick tour of the components of such a library is given, and in subsequent sections we look at several of the items in the library in more depth. We, then, summarize at the end of the chapter, an overall software perspective, in a framework which includes all of the components.

Application Packages

We start our discussion with the class of application packages. In general, these are programs which are intended for people with little or no knowledge of programming, which are custom designed to the needs of a particular set of users. Examples of such application packages are the engineering design packages—COGO and STRESS for civil engineers, ECAP for electrical engineers.

Usually application packages are programmed in a widely available algorithmic language, and for engineering calculations this might typically be FORTRAN, while for symbol manipulation programs LISP is frequently used. The components of the application package embody algorithms to solve frequently encountered problems, relieving the user of the need to program the algorithms. Also, the formats that are used to communicate with the user are in a vocabulary which the user understands, and thus are directly suitable for use in the application.

In many cases, since the application package is built on an algorithmic language, the users have the ability to extend the application package, by adding subroutines, if they know how to program in the language.

Algorithmic Language Support

Algorithmic languages, which allow one to conveniently describe a class of computations, and processors of algorithmic languages are one of the most important parts of computer software. In general, when a program is written in such an algorithmic language it must be translated to the language of the machine before it can carry out computations. There are a possible variety of processors to translate an algorithmic language, many of which may be available on a computer system for a language which the system supports.

The primary processor for many languages is a *compiler,* which is a translating program that transforms the user written program to the machine language. We shall discuss compilers in the next section, but a given algorithmic language may have many different compilers. One compiler may be a very fast translator which yields a translation at minimum cost, while another compiler may be an *optimized compiler* which takes a long time translating but tries to generate a very efficient machine program. Users may run a program through the fast compiler for debugging, and if the program is to be used repeatedly it may then be recompiled by the optimizing compiler.

Yet another common form of language translator is an *interpreter.* Essentially, the interpreter translates one line of the program at a time, running each line as soon as it is translated. A compiler, on the other hand, translates the complete program before running. An advantage of an interpreter is that, in case of an error, it is often possible to modify the source program and then reinterpret the corrected version, something that is not possible with compiler operation. However, interpreters are typically much slower running than compiled programs, making their use too expensive for many applications. Of course, reduced processor costs may make interpretation more attractive as a translator alternative.

Also, if a compiler is modular, then components of the compiler may be available for language processing. For example, the portion of the compiler that checks the syntax of the input program may be available for use to check the syntax of source programs.

Meta-machine support

At an even more primitive level than algorithmic languages, but still somewhat abstracted from the machine language, are assembly language and macros.

As we know, the only programming language that a computer really responds to is machine language. It consists of a vocabulary of binary numbers, each of which the machine interprets directly as an instruction. Each instruction is subdivided into fields. The contents of each field specify or modify an operation or an operand. A format of a typical instruction is shown below:

The intent of each operation code is determined by the computer circuitry. Table 12.1-1 provides a summary of a typical set of instructions for a hypothetical computer.

Functionally, we can divide the above set of instructions into four categories: arithmetic, control, input/output, and directives.

The instructions in Table 12.1-1 can thus be classified as follows:

(1) Arithmetic: Add, Subtract, Multiply and Divide
(2) Control: Load, Store, and the four jump instructions
(3) Input/Output: Read and Write
(4) Directives: Word, Halt, Start, and End

Since a machine-language program is executed by interpreting the contents of consecutive memory registers until the HALT instruction is met, you must specify where the program starts. This is realized by writing START address as the first instruction in the program. To make our ideas clearer, write a machine-language program to find the largest number in a set of three positive numbers. Such a program is flowcharted in Figure 12.1.

The machine language version of such a program might then be as given in Table 12.1-2, where we have even simplified the actual machine code by including symbolic operation code names, and added the annotations in the right hand column for ease of understanding. In a typical sample of actual machine code, all that one sees is a block of numbers. Because of this, absolute machine-language programming is a difficult task and prone to errors. The programmer has to remember the codes of the instructions and supply the numeric addresses. In addition, the process of correcting or modifying an existing program takes almost as long as writing a new program. For example, the task of inserting an instruction between two existing ones

Instruction	Symbolic Operation Code	Semantics
Load ⟨address⟩	LDA	Load accumulator with contents of indicated memory register.
Store ⟨address⟩	STA	Store contents of accumulator in indicated memory register.
Add ⟨address⟩	ADD	Add to the contents of accumulator the contents of the indicated memory register.
Subtract ⟩address⟩	SUB	Subtract from contents of accumulator the contents of indicated memory register.
Multiply ⟨address⟩	MLT	Multiply contents of accumulator by the contents of indicated memory register. The product replaces the contents of accumulator.
Divide	DIV	Divide the contents of accumulator by contents of indicated memory register; quotient replaces contents of accumulator.
JUMP ⟨address⟩	J	Take next instruction from indicated memory register.
JUMP ON POSITIVE ⟨address⟩	JPOS	If contents of accumulator is {greater than, equal to, less than} zero take next instruction from indicated memory register; otherwise execute next instruction in program.
JUMP ON ZERO ⟨address⟩		
JUMP ON NEGATIVE ⟨address⟩		
READ ⟨address⟩	RD	Read into indicated register a five digit decimal number from the input device.
PUT ⟨address⟩	PUT	Write on output device the contents of indicated memory register.
Directive	WORD	Reserve a memory register.
HALT	HALT	Terminate the current program.
START	STRT	Physical start of the program.
END	END	Physical end of the program.

Table 12.1-1 A typical instruction set

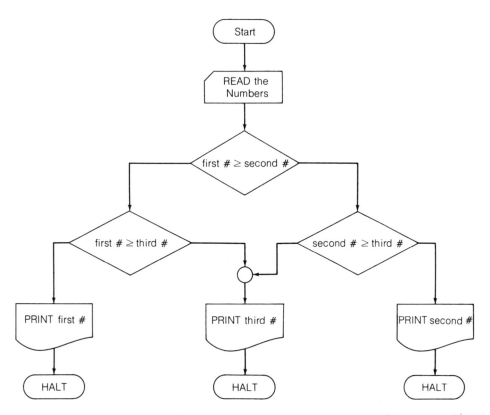

***Figure 12.1:   Program to find the largest number in a set of three positive
numbers.***

will involve changing the address parts of the instructions preceding the
insertion which reference the instructions after the insertion. To alleviate
these problems, symbolic rather than absolute memory addresses may be
used. The following program is a more symbolic version of the machine-
language program we have just written. Before this symbolic form can be
executed, it must be translated into a machine-language form by a translator
program called the *assembler*. The more symbolic language is usually called
an assembly language.

In the above program, each instruction has the format:

$$\{ < \text{Label} > \}_0 < \text{operation code} > \{ < \text{symbolic names} > \}_0{}^*$$

---

*{ }$_0$ indicates zero or more occurrences.

Storage Address of the Instruction	Operation Code	Address	Semantics
	STRT	100	Address of first instruction is 100.
100	RD	200	First number in location 200.
101	RD	201	Second number in location 201.
102	RD	202	Third number in location 202.
103	LDA	200	(AC ← first number.
104	SUB	201	(AC) ← difference between the first and second numbers.
105	JNG	111	Jump to location 111 if second number > first one.
106	LDA	200	(AC) ← first number.
107	SUB	202	(AC) ← first number minus third number.
108	JNG	116	Transfer to location 116 if third number largest.
109	PUT	200	Output first number.
110	HALT		Terminate run.
111	LDA	201	(AC) ← second number.
112	SUB	202	(AC) ← difference between second and third numbers.
113	JNG	116	Transfer to location 116 if third number is larger.
114	PUT	201	Output second number.
115	HALT		Terminate run.
116	PUT	202	Output third number.
117	HALT		Terminate run.
118	END		Physical end of program.

Table 12.1-2   Computer Program of Figure 12.1 in Machine Language

The translator assigns the addresses for both instructions and data. A typical assembly language version of the program just written is given in Table 12.1-3. The major advantages provided by the assembly language are:

symbolic addresses rather than actual machine locations may be used in the program, and the assembler assigns actual locations;

symbolic operation codes are used;

pseudo operations are available, such as instructions to the assembler to allocate storage.

```
              STRT
              RD A
              RD B
              RD C
              LDA A
              SUB B
              JNG SECOND
              LDA B
              SUB C
              JNG SEC
              PUT A
              J STOP
   SECOND     LDA B
              SUB C
              JNG SEC
              PUT B
              J STOP
   SEC        PUT C
   STOP       HALT
   A          WORD 0
   B          WORD 0
   C          WORD 0
              END
```

Table 12.1-3   Computer Program of Figure 12.1 in Assembly Language

An extension of assembly language which greatly enhances its useability is a *macro* facility. The macro facility allows the user to define operation codes which are not available in the machine—much like the definition of a subroutine in an algorithm high-level language. When the assembly program is translated to machine code, the call on the macro is first replaced by its definition. Macros are typically used to facilitate input/output programming in assembly language.

We mentioned that assembly language provides the facility for symbolic addressing, i.e., the address portion of the instruction can be a name. This is very restrictive since this will not permit program modification by computer during the running of the program. A facility is needed that provides for alteration of some of the instructions during the running of the program to create new ones that can be executed, with a consequent reduction of the number of instructions required for a program. You can imagine how long a program will be for computing the sum of a large number of elements in an array, say 1000 elements, without such a facility. Symbolic languages provide for program modification by permitting variations in the address field, as follows:

In the direct-addressing mode, the symbolic name appearing in the address field is the name of the memory register whose contents is the operand, i.e., the operand is located at that address. Indirect addressing refers to a method in which the computer interprets the address portion of the instruction as the address of the register containing the address of the operand. Indirect addressing is usually denoted by the addition of some symbol to the address field. In our case, we will indicate this by enclosing the symbolic address by a pair of parentheses. Thus, the instruction ADD (A) will add the contents of the register specified by the contents of the location whose symbolic name is A to the contents of the accumulator. In other words, we first go to location A to find the address of the operand. If the contents of this location is B, the above instruction is interpreted as ADD B. Indirect addressing is almost always used in connection with calling library routines.

Two other modes of addressing are provided for in almost every assembly language: literal and indexing. In the literal mode addressing, the actual operand appears in the address field preceded by an equal sign, e.g. $= 77$. The machine interprets such a symbol as the operand of the instruction. Thus, the instruction ADD $= 77$ means increase the contents of the register by the literal value 77.

Index mode addressing is specified by writing the symbolic name of an index register after the operand and separating them by a comma. Thus LDA A, X1 is an example of such an instruction. The contents of the selected register and the contents of the index register are added to form the address of the operand. The contents of the index register may be used as a base for calculating a series of addresses, thus allowing access to elements of data structures. They may also be used as counters for iterative control. We can summarize these modes as follows:

⟨op. code⟩ = ⟨number⟩   The literal appearing after "=" is the operand.

⟨op. code⟩ ⟨name⟩   The name specifies the location whose contents is the operand.

⟨op. code⟩ (⟨name⟩)   The name specifies the location whose contents is the address of the operand.

⟨op. code⟩ ⟨name⟩, ⟨xname⟩   The contents of the register specified by xname is added to the contents of register specified by name to specify the address of the operand.

Linkers and Loaders

The use of assembly language and symbolic addresses does, however, provide one additional important capability, since an assembly language program can be assembled to be run starting at any location in memory. In fact, the process of assembly language translation may decompose into two stages.

In the first stage, the program is translated into machine language, except that a part of the actual address is not fixed, its definition being deferred until the program is actually loaded into the machine at the time it is to be run. The *utility program* which does the actual loading and address adjustment (if necessary) is called a *loader*, and is simpler than an assembler. In fact, on most machines the assembler is now required to prepare *relocatable* code, which is machine code with added information to facilitate the loader's task.

Closely, related to the loader, is another utility to assist the assembly process called the *linkage editor*. The linkage editor allows independently written assembly language programs to share data and variables, by being "linked" together when they are to be loaded into computer memory to be run.

Utilities

In addition to supporting directly the translation of algorithmic and assembly language there are a variety of utility programs that are available to help the user in processing. These programs generally adjust the formats of information being transferred from one storage medium to another, or from one file organization to another. Thus if a user has a large program, or large set of data, and wants to avoid the use of cards, there is a utility to read in cards and catalog them on direct access storage. Conversely, if a program, or data, resides on disk and one wants to maintain a punched card copy, there is a utility to do this. These utilities are programs written by the systems programmers and stored on direct access devices in the public library portion of the computer system.

Another grouping of utility programs are the text editors. These can be subdivided into special purpose editors and general purpose editors. Special purpose editors are designed to facilitate program preparation, so that the program written by a user will be stored on a direct access device in a form which is acceptable to the translating program. General purpose editors are used to prepare and edit textual material for print media such as correspondence, books and articles.

Supervisory Programs

The supervisory programs, also known as the operating system, are a set of programs designed to assist the computer operator in providing services to users. In the early days of computer, it was usual for a programmer with a program to run to reserve the use of the computer for a fixed block of time. The initial portion of this block of time was used to set up the program, then the next segment of the block of time was used to check out and, if necessary, modify the program, and the last portion of the block of time was used to output results. As the speed of computers increased, and as it became possible to share the computer between a number of different programs, it became clear that one could no longer reserve time for manual set-up, and that the computer itself could be enlisted to help in managing the increasing number of resources at its disposal.

The supervisory programs now provide many essential services for controlling the flow of programs through the computer system, and for communicating with the computer operator when manual operations—such as loading tapes—are required. The supervisory programs decide in which order the programs that are ready to run should be executed, which input and output devices should be assigned to programs, and how much memory should be allotted to a program. Also, the supervisory program keeps records for both control and billing purposes.

With the availability of large resident files through the use of direct access devices, the supervisory programs also manage the files, keeping records on what files are available, and retrieving them as required by user programs.

The supervisory programs often use a significant amount of computer storage—typically tens of thousands of bytes—and time, and thus, represent a non-negligible overhead item in the computer system—sometimes on the order of 100%. However, they provide essential services, and, in a well-designed system, lead to lower overall costs of computation.

12.2   Compilers

Typically, a student's initial introduction to computer science and first programming experience is through the medium of a compiler. As we have noted, a compiler is a program which translates another program—the user's source program—from a high-level, algorithmic language to the language of the machine. In the process of using the compiler, other elements of the software hierarchy are necessarily involved since the whole job of reading, translating, and subsequently running one's program involves the use of the supervisory programs as well as a number of utility programs. In this section, we shall concentrate on the compiler itself.

A compiler is a complex program, and the construction of compilers has been the subject of extensive study. Thus an extensive technical literature on the subject of compiler design exists and is growing. Even the simplest of compilers is likely to include hundreds of lines of program, with commercial compilers being thousands of lines of program, and in order for such programs to work reliably, careful software design is essential.

In order to make the design of a compiler a manageable programming activity, it is necessary to decompose the compiler description into a simpler conceptual framework. The typical compiler may, therefore, be understood in terms of the block diagram shown in Figure 12.2. An actual compiler may not, in fact, have any identifiable subunit which could be labelled "lexical

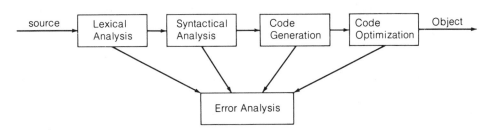

Figure 12.2:   Conceptual Block Diagram of a Compiler.

analysis" but the function indicated by lexical analysis is present in each compiler. Similar remarks apply to all the other components of Figure 12.2.

The functions indicated in Figure 12.2 are as follows:

lexical analysis—In lexical analysis the program text is organized into a uniform representation, where all names, numbers, and operators are designated by symbols of fixed length, called tokens, and some preliminary syntactic decisions are made.

Example. The arithmetic expression 1.3333*PI*R**3 occurring in the source text of an algorithmic language might be shown at the end of the lexical analysis phase as NO1-OP1-NM1-OP1-NM2-OP2-NO2 where NO1, NO2, NM1, and NM2 are indices for retrieving the constant or variable data from tables generated by the compiler, and OP1 and OP2 are designators used by the compiler for the operations of multiplication and exponentiation, respectively.

syntactical analysis—During syntactical analysis, the grammatical structure of the program is checked, and this structure is organized for subsequent processing in the code generation phases of the compiler.

Example. The output of the syntactic analyzer for the arithmetic expression would be a representation of the arithmetic tree:

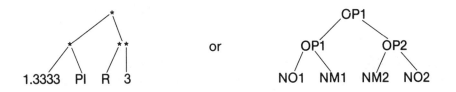

This representation indicates that the computations 1.3333*PI and R**3 are to be performed before the results of the computations are to be multiplied.

code generation—In code generation the machine code is prepared from the output of the syntactical analyzer.

Example. Continuing with the arithmetic expression the machine code may look like:

```
LDA    NO1          1.3333 to the accumulator
MPY    NM1          times PI
STO    TEMP1        store 1.3333*PI in TEMP1
LDA    NM2          R to the accumulator
MPY    NM2          R*R
MPY    NM2          R*R*R
STO    TEMP2        store R**3 in TEMP2
LDA    TEMP1        Recall 1.3333*PI
MPY    TEMP2        compute (1.3333*PI)*(R**3)
```

code optimization—The machine code which would be generated by very simple translation rules can often be vastly improved by a code improvement phase, known as code optimization. Strictly this is a misnomer, since no compiler ever tries to produce the optimum machine language program, but it is an abuse of language that is well established. The purpose of code optimization is to reduce the running time or memory requirement of the program.

Example. Even in our small example, several code optimization opportunities exist. First, if PI is indeed a constant whose value never changes from its initial assignment in the program, then 1.3333*PI is also a constant, say NO3. In that case, the tree may be shown as:

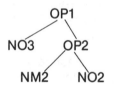

Further, if multiplication is commutative, x*y is equal to y*x, the tree may be rearranged to the form:

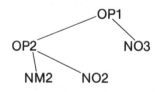

The use of the commutative property of multiplication can reduce, or, in this case, eliminate storage needed for temporary results. With these code improvements, the machine code becomes:

```
LDA        NM2
MPY        NM2
MPY        NM2
MPY        NO3
```

Error Analysis—In case the source program is syntactically incorrect, or in some other way violates the requirements of a good program, information is provided to the error analysis phase which generates an appropriate message to the user.

12.3   Assemblers and Macro Processors

The language of the computer is a sequence of binary digits. Programming in such a language is an error-prone activity, because the binary representations of the operation codes do not suggest to the programmer what operation is to be performed. Also, in machine language the management of memory must be explicitly performed by the programmer, and when the number of variables stored is large the programmer has a large amount of bookkeeping to do. The function of assembly language programming is to facilitate the programming task by performing these two functions of providing symbolic instruction names, and symbolic variable names.

It is, indeed, the case that an algorithmic language also provides these functions, and thus the exact boundary between assembly and algorithmic languages is not always clear. However, as a general rule the assembly language instructions correspond to the machine language instructions and mirror the structure of the machine.

The sample program given earlier in Table 12.1-3 illustrates these features of assembly language. The assembly language mnemonic instructions LDA, SUB, JNG whose effect is, respectively, to load the accumulator, subtract from the accumulator, and jump if the result in the accumulator is negative, correspond exactly to machine instructions which are specified in machine language as strings of binary digits. The symbolic names of variables A,B,C, are available in assembly language, because the assembly language instruction WORD O, is an instruction to the assembler to reserve a word of memory and to initialize its value to 0; labelling these instructions to reserve words is, then, the assembly language form of variable declaration and initialization. The labels SEC, SECOND, and STOP are used by the assembler as symbolic addresses, so that the assembler performs the clerical tasks of keeping track of the memory location corresponding to an instruction. STRT and END, which occur at the beginning and end of the assembly language program are instructions to the assembler to start and terminate the preparation of machine code for this segment of the program. Finally, the instructions RD and PUT are assembly language instructions which are to be translated into sequences of machine language instructions to perform the somewhat more complicated operations of entering and recording data.

In order to actually run an assembly language program, it must first be translated by an assembler to machine language, and then be loaded into the machine and run. Figure 12.3 is a block diagram describing the program assembly and execution.

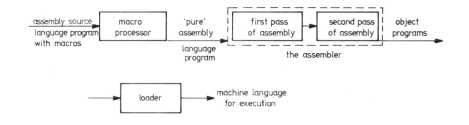

Figure 12.3:   *Block diagram of the assembly process.*

The macro-processor front end of the assembly process allows assembly source language to include instruction codes that do not meet the usual assembly language criteria: the macro instructions do not correspond to machine language instructions and do not necessarily correspond to the structure of the machine. Rather, a macro-instruction is an instruction which is replaced by a sequence of assembly source statements before the rest of the assembly process. The process of replacing a macro instruction by a sequence of source statements is known as *macro expansion*. If the macro expansion itself introduces new macro instructions, then the macro expansion process continues until only "pure" assembly language is left.

In the source language, to be processed by the macro processor, the programmer may define macro instructions for subsequent use. The macro language provides, in general, formal parameters and conditional control structures so that much of the programming can be kept implicit in the macro definitions. The programmer may thus use the macro language to define additional control and data structures and the macro instructions to operate on these.

There are generally a set of utility macros provided by the systems programmers for the management of input/output and for communication with peripheral storage. These utility macros allow the programmer to use GET and PUT instructions in assembly language programming, and avoid the detailed considerations of the hardware addressing and control sequences associated with the handling of these peripheral devices.

The assembly process itself is most easily understood as a two phase process, in which the source program is read twice by the assembler; each phase is thus called a *pass*. In the first pass, the assembler constructs a table of symbolic names (called *symbol table*) used in the program and the storage locations of these addresses. The storage location is generally computed as the location relative to the beginning of storage of the part of the program being assembled. Then, in the second pass, the assembler constructs machine code replacing each symbolic instruction with the corresponding machine instruction, and replacing each symbolic name with the corresponding machine address.

When all parts of the program have been assembled into object program form, and the program is to be run, the loader combines these object programs, loads them into the main memory of the computer, and initiates machine execution of the program. The details of the linking and loading operations are somewhat more dependent on the specific features of the machine organization.

12.4   Operating Systems

An operating system is a set of programs designed to assist in the management and operation of a computing facility. These programs have largely replaced manual operations in the running of computer programs because the speed of computers have made manual set up uneconomical. Suppose that a manual changeover from one computing job to another takes five minutes—to set up the input and output devices, and to connect any temporary files—and the computing job itself takes t minutes. Then the efficiency of the system may be computed as:

$$\text{efficiency} = \frac{\text{compute time}}{\text{compute time \& set up time}} = \frac{t}{t + 5}$$

As the compute time decreases from one hour, to five minutes, and then to one minute, the efficiency goes from 92% to 50% and then to 16% respectively.

Consider a typical student job to compile a source program written in an algorithmic language, load the object program into memory, and perform the required computation with a given set of input data. Assume that the job is submitted in the form of a card deck and that the results are to be printed out on a high-speed printer. The operating system will read the source deck from the card reader onto a secondary storage device before any further processing occurs. Once the source deck is stored on secondary storage it will be examined by the operating system for those instructions to the operating system which are included within the source deck. The instructions included in the source deck will allow the operating system to estimate what sources are needed to perform the requested job and what priority is to be assigned to the job. The operating system acting as a resource manager, within the limits of parameters set by the human operator, then determines the appropriate scheduling and resource allocation for the job, which may either preempt lower priority items or be deferred because of higher priority items.

When the first part of the job is to be initiated, the operating system must load the appropriate compiler using the program portion of the source deck as its data. The first part of the job will only be initiated when sufficient high speed memory can be reserved for the compiler to operate effectively. Also, the operating system must set up files in secondary storage for the object program which is generated by the compiler, and for error and diagnostic messages if the compilation should fail because of errors in the source program. When the first part of the job has been completed, the operating system must either initiate a printout of error and diagnostic messages if the compilation was unsuccessful, or continue to process the job if compilation was successful.

The second part of the job begins with the loading of the object program. Here the operating system must call upon the loading program to load the object program which was generated by the compiler. During the execution of the object program, the operating system must provide input to the program from the source data provided by the user, and must accumulate any output generated by the program for subsequent printout. During the second part of the job, if there is any error which causes the program to abort, the operating system must generate appropriate error and diagnostic messages.

When the object program has completed execution, the operating system must schedule the printout of the output files which were generated for the user on the job.

This overview of one job, as it is processed by the operating system, gives an indication of the range of activities that the operating system must schedule and keep a record of the progress of each job as it proceeds through the computing system. In general, many jobs may be proceeding simultaneously. The operating system is expected to provide input and output services to the user in a convenient form. The operating system must handle any file processing, including the allocation and release of temporary files needed for the particular job. And, all of these functions, and others, must be performed efficiently, and maintaining the security of each user.

In order to provide this large range of services, the operating system must be able to call on the many programs in the software hierarchy that we have described, but in addition, the operating system itself requires a set of its own programs. We shall only briefly review some of the major components of typical operating systems.

The central program of the operating system, known as the supervisor or monitor, maintains overall control of the computer system and coordinates the activities of the other components of the operating system. The memory manager controls the use of high speed and secondary memory, allocating memory to programs which require additional memory, or reclaiming memory when the program is terminated. The file manager controls the storage of files or secondary memory, and ensures that access to files is granted only to authorized programs. Input/output or device managers control the access to and sequencing of peripheral devices.

When contrasted with the fairly standardized decomposition of compilers, the organization of operating systems appears very ad hoc. Indeed this is a fair assessment.

12.5   Software Hierarchy

Computer software, that is, all the programs associated with a computer, is usually organized into a well-disciplined hierarchy. The discipline enforced on a software hierarchy varies considerably in terms of the constraints it places on the user and the protection provided to the user. The design and description of the software hierarchy is highly dependent on the individual's point of view of the system. This situation is quite analogous to a similar phenomenon in human organization wherein every individual views himself as the center of all activity.

From the user's point of view, the software of a computer system is organized in strata of support levels. The first line of support is often packaged programs for specific applications (i.e., linear programming, numerical integration, symbolic differentiation, etc.). These programs are in turn supported by procedure-oriented languages such as ALGOL or FORTRAN. As we have seen in section 12.2, these languages must be translated into a machine-acceptable form by translators. A software system such as a translator is quite large, both physically and in terms of the amount of effort needed to create it. Consequently, we would like to implement them according to certain criteria: portability, clarity of system structure, and higher programmer productivity. To achieve these goals, several systems-programming languages have been designed specifically for system implementation. These are usually algebraic in form but oriented toward a family of machines, e.g., PL360. From this point of view, the complete software hierarchy of a computer system is illustrated in Figure 12.4. A user is likely to judge the performance of overall systems by the performance and convenience of the applications packages. As the user becomes more sophisticated in the use of computers, he will probably wish to by-pass some of the support levels provided in such a hierarchy. He will most likely find some features in the

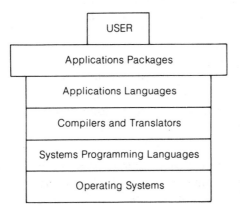

Figure 12.4:   Software hierarchy from the user's point of view.

other support levels which were previously hidden to him, but which also must be used with some degree of caution. The user soon finds himself deeply engrossed in the exploration and discovery of the various levels of support, sometimes losing sight of the fact that he is not participating in discovery at all. Instead he is really on a treasure hunt for things that have been intentionally hidden from him.

At the other extreme of viewpoints is the machine designer. The computing machine is viewed as a primitive but complete set of operations and an associated interpretation cycle. All software is then viewed as successive redefinition of the machine. Some of the operations are combined into single, easier to use operations such as input/output handler, interrupt handler, and memory allocator.

Remember, the operating system controls the allocations of the central processing unit among several programs so as to maximize the use of the whole computer. Typically a program works as follows:

> initiate an operation
>
> compute as long as data is available
>
> idle while required information is being transferred
>
> repeat the above steps when ready.

Information may be transferred to or from the auxiliary memory or through input/output statements in the program. Many systems cannot afford to keep the central processor idle while the movement of information is taking place. Consequently, computers use a special mechanism called an interrupt system to alleviate this problem. When transfer of information is requested, an interrupt signal is sent to the central processor. This signal causes the central processor to stop the execution of the current instruction sequence and to start executing an instruction sequence, called the interrupt handler, at a predefined location that is equal to the select code for the interrupting process. The interrupt handler, in turn, will activate the proper procedure to deal with the process that initiated the interrupt. Examples of this sort of procedure: the memory allocator that finds space in the main memory and the input/output subprogram that turns over control to the device requested. This primitive interpretation cycle may be extended to include stack or queue management. This process continues until the user interacts with what is known as a virtual machine designed specifically for his application. Software has been the tool for redefining the original machine to be the desired machine. (See Figure 12.5.)

When viewed as successive machine redefinition, software has a natural hierarchical structure imposed on it. Such a viewpoint has been suggested as the best basis for the design of software. All of the software of a computer system is organized into a tree structure. The parentage of any stage

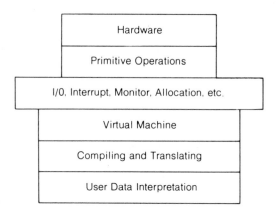

Figure 12.5:   *Software hierarchy from the machine definition point of view.*

of definition is clearly specified. When changes are contemplated at any level in the definition tree, the propagation of the change through the tree is also clearly specified. (See Figure 12.6.) This structure usually constrains the control and data flow of the system to be along the branches of the tree. Thus, the user of a compiler cannot initiate bulk file management except through the operating system.

A third point of view is now emerging amongst software designers that relates the hierarchy of software to the data and control base of each part. A precise yet machine-independent discipline is imposed on the data and control interactions of various parts of the software system. The essential

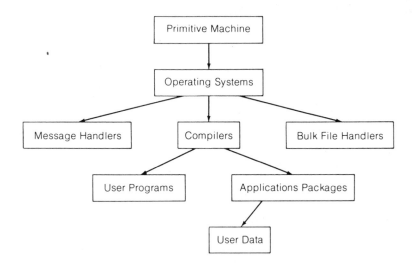

Figure 12.6:   *Software hierarchy as a tree structure.*

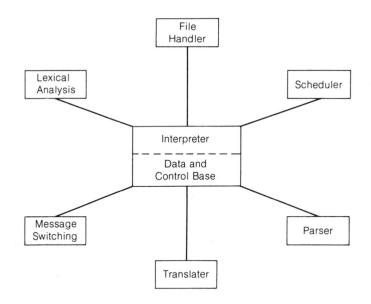

Figure 12.7:   Structured software.

semantics of the interaction and the data and control environment are describable in terms rigorous enough to permit all levels of software to interact with each other. Most nonuser software is implemented at a single level, eliminating the layering of the various programs.

The precise control of interactions between computer programs has become a subject of intense study in computer science. The foundation of this new subject has been discussed in Chapter 3.

Summary

Software, as with many evolved methodologies, bears some of the characteristics of an artform. Issues of style, motivation, point of view, and abstraction become dominant concerns in construction of good software. The analogy to an artform is even more apparent in the progression of the tools of the trade. From the most primitive of machine languages, and assemblers, the tools of software construction have advanced in the number of possible modes of expression as well as in the subtlety of expression. This evolution of software construction technique has had a profound effect on the style and expressiveness of the resulting software.

As the scale of software developments continues to increase, the analytic point of view, wherein the whole is understood in terms of its parts, becomes inadequate as a point from which to understand or design software. An overview in terms of a hierarchy is usually imposed to simplify the interactions between parts of large-scale software. This hierarchy may take many forms, all with the same purpose of enforcing a discipline on the interaction between the components of a large program.

References and Suggested Additional Readings

Ullman, J.D. *Fundamental Concepts of Programming Systems*, Addison Wesley, 1975.

Kernighan, B.W. and Plauger, J.D. *Software Tools,* Addison Wesley, 1976.

Aho, A.V., and Ullman, J.D. *Principles of Compiler Design*, Addison Wesley, 1977.

Donovan, J.J. *Systems Programming*, McGraw Hill, 1972.

Tsichritzis, D.C., and Bernstein, P.A. *Operating Systems*, Academic Press, 1974.

Graham, R.M. *Principles of Systems Programming*, John Wiley & Sons, Inc., 1975.

Problems

1. Define the following terms:

   a) Assembler
   b) Compiler
   c) Batch Processing
   d) Multiprocessing
   e) Multiprogramming
   f) Time-sharing
   g) Monitor
   h) Loader
   i) Lexical Analysis
   j) Syntax Analysis

2. Enumerate the advantages of procedure-oriented languages programming.

3. How do assembler languages reflect the structure of the computer for which they are designed?

4. Write a machine-language program to find the median of five positive numbers.

5. Write an assembly-language program that will find the number of nonnegative numbers in a set of N numbers.

6. Find a description of the software hierarchy of a particular computer. Discuss the data and control interactions between the various parts.

7. Discuss the thesis that the principal goal of computer software is to make explicit those techniques that have been used implicitly to solve problems.

8. Using the literature, determine the use of the term "firmware". How does firmware differ from software?

Chapter 13

Interactive Computation

Interactive computation

Technology makes a variety of languages and means of communicating with the computer available. In this chapter we will be concerned with interactive systems.

We might best begin the discussion of interactive computation by trying to imagine different classes of computer usage and the way in which the user and the computer communicate. An *interactive computation* is one in which a sequence of intermediate results are presented to the user and additional inputs dependent on these intermediate results are then provided by the user. The overall computation proceeds by a sequence of interleaved input-computation-intermediate output.

(1) Computer-aided instruction—Here the computer is communicating with a student according to some programmed instruction schema (possibly one that allows adjustment for the variable student learning rate) and presenting the student with information and queries. The student in turn is responding, and the responses are to be communicated to the computer. In a somewhat more ambitious system, the student might also interrogate the computer and receive responses to certain questions.

(2) Airline reservation system—Here the computer is communicating with a ticket agent. The agent might request information from the computer on availability of seating on certain flights. The computer could furnish this information to the ticket agent, who, in turn, could reserve seats that were available.

(3) Engineering design—An engineer, communicating with the computer, might attempt to calculate the feasibility of a specific design. An elaborate system of programs associated with different design techniques might be available to the engineer together with a variety of handbook data, suitably arranged for automated information retrieval, and the facility for performing quick "slide rule" calculations.

From these different cases, which are certainly not exhaustive, it should be clear that the kinds of information passing between the user and the computer will vary from one application to another, and the speed of response will be different as well. The documentation required by the user as a record of the computation depends on the application, as does the size of the data base to which the user must have access. A tentative list of entry devices for the user might include:

> card punch and reader
> remote special keyboard device
> remote teletypewriter keyboard
> cathode ray tube and light pen

Linkage of the input and output devices with the computer may be hard wired or proceed via telephone connection. Output from the computer to the user may be from any of a number of devices, including:

special keyboard printer
audio response
teletypewriter output
cathode-ray tube
high-speed line printer

In the usage of the computer, the user may operate in a very simple "desk calculation mode" or have access to large data bases, or execute programs that the user or others have developed. The purpose of this chapter is to consider the interactive mode of computer usage. You would expect such usage to be prevalent in tactical situations such as computer-aided instruction and airline reservation systems. Interactive computation is playing an increasingly important role in situations where time is less critical but where direct user-computer communication is an aid in problem solving. Although one user does not dominate the computer's activity, the computer clearly holds and dominates the user's attention. Time becomes a critical consideration in being sure that the user is sufficiently stimulated that his attention does not wander.

In the next section, we discuss one of the better known general purpose interactive languages. The language features will be described, but it should be understood that each implementation of APL will have file facilities for storage of user programs or data, procedures for editing, and correcting input. These aspects will vary from one system to another.

Communication with the computer using APL generally proceeds from a keyboard device provided with a special purpose APL type symbol set. The typewriter is used for both input and output; signals to and from the computer are sent via normal telephone lines.

13.1   Features of Interactive Languages

It should be clear from the preceding discussion that the interactive mode of computation is distinguishable from more conventional "batch" computation. However, the distinction does not lend itself to formal analysis because of the close interplay of psychological factors with technical ones. A number of successful interactive languages have been designed and implemented and their important features are identifiable.

In interactive computations there is nearly a one-to-one correspondence between physical lines and programs. Most of the thought, program construction, and error removal is performed a line at a time. Once the line is complete, it should be possible to translate and perhaps execute it. The span of attention of the user seldom exceeds a few lines of program. Since this limited program context is a common feature of successful interactive languages, it is not surprising that such languages have a minimum of declarations. Environments and data types are highly dynamic features in interactive languages.

Because of the need to hold the user's attention on the problem-solving task, any use of a language reference manual during interactive computation would be most undesirable. As a result, interactive languages tend to have very simple syntax and semantics. The user should be able to commit the important linguistic features to memory. APL even eliminates all precedence between operators in order to simplify the semantic description of the language.

As mentioned before, most error removal in interactive computation is performed one line at a time. The program-editing facilities usually include deletion or insertion of text within a single line. The interactive language is provided with facilities for backing up in a line to perform such editing functions.

13.2   Examples of Interactive Languages

APL

APL, an acronym for *A Programming Language*, is an interactive programming language based on the work of Iverson*. A key ingredient of APL is a set of primitive data structures and operators on these data structures.

APL has two data types: numbers and literal strings. No distinction is made between fixed and floating point numbers. A literal string is any quoted string of valid characters. The following are numbers:

$$4 \quad 2.3 \quad 3.2E^-15 \quad 26E^-2$$

They stand for 4, 2.3, 3.2×10^{-15}, and 26×10^{-2}.

The following are literal strings:

$$\textit{"A"} \quad \textit{"CAT"} \quad \textit{"12AX} \uparrow \square \textit{"}$$

The character set of APL is a specially designed character set, implemented by using a replaceable type-ball on an electric typewriter. The character set contains capital letters, decimal digits, and many special characters used to denote primitive operators in APL.

The basic data structure in APL is the array. APL arrays are similar to arrays in other languages—an array is an *n*-dimensional arrangement of homogeneous elements in which each component element can be accessed by giving its *n* indices. Arrays of 1 dimension are called *vectors,* and arrays of 2 dimensions are called *matrices.* (Numbers are called *scalars,* i.e., arrays of 0 dimensions). An example of a matrix is

$$M: \quad 1. \quad 2. \quad 3.4$$
$$4. \quad 6.1 \quad 2.E^-5$$

---

*Iverson, K.E. *A Programming Language.* (New York: Wiley & Sons, 1963).

The components of M may be specified by giving two indices in M; thus, $M[1; 3]$ is 3.4, $M[2; 2]$ is 6.1. (The origin of the subscripts is taken to be 1.)

Assignment in APL is specified by a variable name, followed by $\leftarrow$, followed by an expression. The value of the variable becomes the value of the expression.

Example:

$$X \leftarrow 3.4$$

gives X a value of 3.4.

$$Y \leftarrow 1 \quad 2 \quad 3$$

gives Y a value of a 1-dimensional vector, whose elements are 1, 2, and 3 respectively.

$Y[1]$ is 1 after the assignment statement is executed.

If X is a variable whose current value is a vector, then the assignment statement $Y \leftarrow X$ will make the value of Y a copy of the vector, X. Similarly, for arrays of any number of dimensions, the assignment operation makes the value of the variable immediately on its left the copy of the value of the expression on its right.

Expressions in APL are evaluated strictly on a right-to-left basis, with no precedence of operators, except that parentheses have precedence for bracketing terms. Thus, in an expression being scanned from right to left, if θ is a binary operator and β is the expression to the right of θ, and α is the term immediately to the left of θ, the value of $\alpha\theta\beta$ will be value $(\alpha)\theta$ value (β). Several examples may help to clarify these semantic rules:

(1) $3 + 4 - 5 + 2$ first becomes $3 + 4 - 7$, then $3 + (-3)$, then 0. Each expression is successively evaluated from right to left.

(2) $(3 \times 5) - 4$ is 11. Here the term immediately to the left of the minus sign is (3×5) because of the parentheses. The value of the expression $3 \times 5 - 4$ is 3, without the parentheses.

(3) $(3 + 5 \div 4 - 2 + 6) - 3$ evaluates to -1.25 using the rules given above.

Assignment, denoted "$\leftarrow$", is a binary operator whose left hand operand must be a variable name; the value of the expression $\alpha \leftarrow \beta$, is the value of α. Hence, the expression $Z \leftarrow 3 + Y \leftarrow 2$ makes the value of Y become 2 and then makes the value of Z become 5.

Most unary and binary operators in APL are extended to vectors, termwise. *Termwise addition* means if A and B are arrays of the same dimensions, then $A + B$ adds correspondingly indexed elements of A and B. Thus, after $C \leftarrow 3$ $4\ 5 + 2\ 5\ 8$ is executed, C has a value of 5 9 13. Similarly $D \leftarrow 2\ 4\ 3 \times 1\ 2\ 3$ gives D a value 2 8 9; and $E \leftarrow 1\ 2\ 5\ 9 \div 1\ 4\ 8\ 3$ gives E a value 1 .5 .625 3.0.

In addition to the binary operations extended to vectors, there are vector and array operations defined only for vectors or arrays. We mention only three of these here: the ravel operation, a unary operation denoted by ",", on any array yields a vector of the components array row by row. Suppose the value of B is

$$\begin{bmatrix} 1 & 2 \\ 3 & 4 \end{bmatrix}$$

then the value of B is 1 2 3 4. The reduction operation, "/", is a binary pseudooperator that applies the binary operation to the element of an array as follows: If θ is any binary operator, and V is any vector, then the value of θ/V is the value of $V[1]\theta V[2] \ldots \theta V[N]$ where N is the rank of V (i.e., is the number of elements in V). Example: $+/1$ 2 3 is 6; $-/1$ 2 3 4 5 is 3. The restructure operation on vectors, denoted ρ, forms arrays as follows: if X and Y are vectors then the value of $X\rho V$ is an array of dimension X formed from the elements of V. $A \leftarrow 2$ 3 ρ 1 2 3 4 5 6 gives A a value of

$$\begin{bmatrix} 1 & 2 & 3 \\ 4 & 5 & 6 \end{bmatrix}$$

Additional array operations in APL may be found by consulting Table 13.1-1 below. (Note: If A, B are conformable matrices, $A+ . \times B$ is the coding in APL for "usual matrix multiplication.")

Table 13.1-1   APL operators and functions

I. Unary Operators

Symbol	Name	Semantics
$-$	NEGATIVE	$-A \longleftrightarrow 0-A$
$+$	POSITIVE	$+A \longleftrightarrow 0+A$
$\div$	RECIPROCAL	$\div A \longleftrightarrow 1 \div A$
$\times$	SIGNUM	$\times A \longleftrightarrow (A>0)-(A<0)$
ι	INDEX GENERATOR	$\iota S \longleftrightarrow$ VECTOR OF FIRST S INTEGERS; $\iota 0 \longleftrightarrow$ EMPTY VECTOR
$?$	ROLL	$?S \longleftrightarrow$ RANDOM CHOICE FROM ιS
ρ	SIZE	$\rho V \longleftrightarrow$ NUMBER OF ELEMENTS IN V; $\rho M \longleftrightarrow$ VECTOR OF SIZES OF EACH DIMENSION OF M
$\sim$	NOT	$\sim 0 \longleftrightarrow 1; \sim 1 \longleftrightarrow 0$
$\bigcirc$	PI TIMES	$\bigcirc A \longleftrightarrow PI \times A$
ϕ	REVERSAL	$\phi X \longleftrightarrow \begin{matrix} 4 & 3 & 2 & 1 \\ 8 & 7 & 6 & 5 \\ 12 & 11 & 10 & 9 \end{matrix}$
$\otimes$	TRANSPOSE	$\otimes X \longleftrightarrow \begin{matrix} 1 & 5 & 9 \\ 2 & 6 & 10 \\ 3 & 7 & 11 \\ 4 & 8 & 12 \end{matrix}$

Symbol	Name	Semantics
*	EXPONENTIAL	$*A \longleftrightarrow e^A$
⍟	NATURAL LOGARITHM	$⍟A \longleftrightarrow LN\ A$
⌈	CEILING	$\lceil 3.5 \longleftrightarrow 4;\ \lceil ^-3.5 \longleftrightarrow {}^-3$
⌊	FLOOR	$\lfloor 3.5 \longleftrightarrow 3;\ \lfloor ^-3.5 \longleftrightarrow {}^-4$
⍋	GRADE UP	$⍋V \longleftrightarrow$ PERMUTATIONS WHICH WOULD ORDER V ASCENDINGLY.
⍒	GRADE DOWN	$⍒V \longleftrightarrow$ PERMUTATIONS WHICH WOULD ORDER V DESCENDINGLY.
!	FACTORIAL	$!S \longleftrightarrow S \times (!S - 1)$ $!0 \longleftrightarrow 1$
[ ]	SUBSCRIPTING	$X[2;4] \longleftrightarrow 8;\ X[;3] \longleftrightarrow 3\ 7\ 11$ $X[2;] \longleftrightarrow 5\ 6\ 7\ 8$
|	ABSOLUTE VALUE	$\|A \longleftrightarrow \|A\|$
,	RAVEL	$,A \longleftrightarrow (\times/\rho A)\rho A$

II. Binary Operators

Symbol	Name	Semantics
<	LESS THAN	
≤	LESS THAN OR EQUAL	
=	EQUAL	RESULT IS 1 *IF* THE RELATION HOLDS; 0 OTHERWISE
≥	GREATER THAN OR EQUAL	
>	GREATER THAN	
≠	NOT EQUAL	
−	MINUS	$A - B$
+	PLUS	$A + B$
÷	DIVIDE	$A \div B$
×	MULTIPLY	$A \times B$
∧	AND	$S \wedge S1 \longleftrightarrow 1$ IF S AND $S1$ ARE 1; 0 OTHERWISE.
∨	OR	$S \vee S1 \longleftrightarrow 1$ IF S OR $S1$ ARE 1; 0 OTHERWISE.
⍲	NAND	$S ⍲ S1 \longleftrightarrow \sim S \wedge S1$
⍱	NOR	$S ⍱ S1 \longleftrightarrow \sim S \vee S1$
?	DEAL	$S\ ?\ S1 \longleftrightarrow$ RANDOM DEAL OF S ELEMENTS FROM $\iota S1$.
∊	MEMBER	$S \in V \longleftrightarrow 1$ IF S IS A MEMBER OF THE SET V; 0 OTHERWISE.
ρ	RESTRUCTURE	$V \rho V1 \longleftrightarrow$ RESHAPE $V1$ TO HAVE DIMENSIONS V.
↑	TAKE	$S \uparrow V \longleftrightarrow$ VECTOR OF THE FIRST S ELEMENTS OF V.
↓	DROP	$S \downarrow V \longleftrightarrow$ VECTOR OF THE LAST $(\rho V) - S$ ELEMENTS OF V.
ι	INDEX OF	$V \iota S \longleftrightarrow$ LEAST INDEX OF S IN V.
○	CIRCULAR FUNCTION	$S \bigcirc A \longleftrightarrow$ TRIGONOMETRIC OF HYPERBOLIC FUNCTIONS; $0 \le S \le 7$.

Symbol	Name	Semantics
ϕ	ROTATE	$S \phi V \longleftrightarrow$ SHIFTS V S PLACES, END AROUND.
$*$	POWER	$S * S1 \longleftrightarrow S^{S1}$
$\circledast$	LOG TO A BASE	$S \circledast S1 \longleftrightarrow$ LOG $S1$ BASE S ˙
$\lceil$	MAXIMUM	$3 \lceil 5 \longleftrightarrow 5$
$\lfloor$	MINIMUM	$3 \lfloor 5 \longleftrightarrow 3$
$!$	BINOMIAL COEFFICIENT	$S ! S1 \longleftrightarrow (!S1) \div (!S) \times ! S1 - S$
$\perp$	DECODE	$S \perp S1 \longleftrightarrow$ EXPRESS $S1$ IN RADIX S
$\top$	ENCODE	$S \top S1 \longleftrightarrow$ ENCODES $S1$ IN RADIX S
$\mid$	RESIDUE	$S \mid S1 \longleftrightarrow S1 - (\mid S) \times \lfloor S1 \div \mid S$ IF $S \neq 0$; ELSE ERROR.
$,$	CATENATE	$(1\ 2\ 3), (4\ 5\ 6) \longleftrightarrow 1\ 2\ 3\ 4\ 5\ 6$
$f/$	REDUCTION	$f/V \longleftrightarrow V[1]fV[2] \ldots fV[N]$
$/$	COMPRESSION	$V / V1 \longleftrightarrow$ ELEMENTS OF $V1$ FOR WHICH CORRESPONDING ELEMENTS OF V ARE 1.
$\backslash$	EXPANSION	$V \backslash V1 \longleftrightarrow$ ELEMENTS OF $V1$ AND 0'S WITH THE ELEMENTS OF $V1$ FILLING THE POSITIONS OF THE RESULT CORRESPONDING TO $V[N] = 1$.
$\circ.f$	OUTER PRODUCT	
$f.g$	INNER PRODUCT	

Notation used in Table 13.1-1

Symbol	Use
A	ANY
S $S1$	SCALARS
V $V1$	VECTORS
M	MATRIX
X	1 2 3 4
	5 6 7 8
	9 10 11 12

We have emphasized arrays because they are the basic data structure in APL. Moreover, the effect of unary and binary operations being extended to vectors and arrays is that limited iterative control is provided. The other control structures in APL are functions, which correspond to a block structure, and a form of computed branch.

Before we discuss branching, let us observe how a statement may be named in APL. *Labeling* is achieved by starting the statement with its name and terminating it with a colon character which is a separator from the body of the statement. Thus, JEAN is the name of the following statement:

$$JEAN: X \leftarrow 2\ 3\ \rho\ 1\ 2\ 3\ 4\ 5\ 6$$

As we know, each branch statement specifies a statement to be executed if a certain condition is satisfied. Consequently, each branch statement should contain a label and may contain the condition to be tested. In APL some legal branch statements are:

Form	Semantics
→ o	exit from program.
→ e	branch unconditionally to statement labelled with the value of expression, e. If e is a vector or matrix, then use the first element of e.
→ ι0	(i.e., empty vector) proceed to the next statement in sequence.

Labels, and thus branch statements, are only possible within function definitions (i.e., within the body of subroutine definitions). Numerical labels are assigned to each line of a function definition. Symbolic labels, such as *JEAN* in the example above, take on numerical values corresponding to the statement number. This numerical value is assigned during translation of the function. Iterative control is achievable as illustrated by the following program segment, which corresponds to the flowchart of Figure 13.1.

$$[i-1] \quad I \leftarrow 1$$
$$[i] \quad START: (I \le M) \downarrow (,EXIT)$$

Body

$$[j] \quad I \leftarrow I+1$$
$$[j+1] \quad \rightarrow START$$
$$[j+2] \quad EXIT:$$

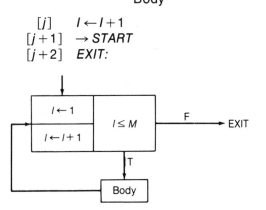

Figure 13.1:   Example of iterative control

Functions serve to define the scope of variables. Any variable name not declared to be local to a block is global to that block. Within each function the expressions are numbered in sequence as in any APL program. We note that since the assignment operator ← is considered a binary infix operator, each assignment operation is an expression; while the transfer of control operator → with → α causing a branch to the expression whose line number or name, is the value of α or the label α.

In APL, as in any other procedure-oriented language, a function consists of a name, formal parameters, and a body. The function head starts with the symbol ∇ followed by the name of the function and may also contain one or two formal parameters and possibly a result variable (i.e., the value returned) as shown in the following table.

Function Head	Semantics
∇ RAT	no explicit result; no arguments
∇ RAT X	no explicit result; one local argument
∇ Y RAT X	no explicit result; two local arguments
∇ $Y \leftarrow$ RAT X	an explicit result; one local argument
∇ $Z \leftarrow Y$ RAT X	an explicit result; two local arguments
∇ RAT $A; B; C; D; E$	no explicit result; one argument and additional local variables.

The body of the function is APL program and its termination is the symbol ∇. We shall illustrate the use of functions by a simple example. Let us consider writing a sort algorithm as a function. It will have the following format:

$$\nabla A \leftarrow \text{SORT } X$$

```
[1]    A ← ι0
[2]    START: (0 ≠ ρX) ↓ (,0)
[3]    A ← A, (X = ⌊ / X)/X
[4]    X ← (X ≠ ⌊ / X)/X
[5]    → START
[6]    ∇
```

The algorithm's call will involve writing the name of the function followed by the elements to be ordered, i.e., *SORT* 3 1 2 7. It should be noted that the sort can also be accomplished by primitive operations; $X[\uparrow X]$.

Readers interested in learning APL are advised to read Gilman and Rose. More detailed specification of APL/360 is given in Pakin. A more mathematical treatment of APL, as an algorithmic—as opposed to a programming language is given in Iverson.

13.3   Other Interactive Languages

Sammet* discusses the following interactive systems:

> JOSS
> BASIC
> QUIKTRAN
> CPS

---

*Sammet, Jean. *Programming Language: History and Fundamentals.* (Englewood Cliffs, N.J.: Prentice-Hall, 1969), pp. 215–265.

        MAP
        LINCOLN RECKONER
        APL
        PAT
        CULLER-FRIED SYSTEM
        DIALOG
        AMTRAN

Of these languages, the most commonly available are QUIKTRAN and BASIC. QUIKTRAN is a FORTRAN-like language. The user may either operate in a mode whereby each statement is executed when entered or may enter complete programs for execution. Thus, QUIKTRAN may be used either as a desk calculator or for program development.

BASIC* is a FORTRAN-like language, developed primarily as an introductory programming tool. The arithmetic assignment statement is:

$$\text{LET } X = E$$

where E is an arithmetic expression. Output statement is PRINT. An example of its usage is:

$$\text{PRINT ``}X\text{ IS''}; X$$

which will print X IS 10, when the value of X is 10.

Control structures in BASIC include an IF ... THEN statement, iterative control provided by a FOR ... NEXT loop, limited recursive subroutine capability, an arithmetic function statement, and some iterative control provided by limited matrix operations.

Input may be read from a terminal during program execution using the INPUT statement. When the program is executing and an input statement is encountered, the computer prints a "?" and waits for a typed response, followed by a RETURN button depression.

BASIC is very widely available, very easy to learn, and should serve the needs of most casual computer users.

The authors experience is that a class of students familiar with any algorithmic language having an algebraic flavor similar to BASIC can begin programming in BASIC after reading a short summary of the language statements, and a one page introduction to system commands and editing.

References and Suggested Additional Readings

(1) Gilman, L. and Rose, A.J. *APL/360, An Interactive Approach.* New York: John Wiley & Sons, 1970.

---

*Sammet, Jean. *Programming Language: History and Fundamentals.*

(2) Gross, J.L. and Braimerd, W.J. *Fundamental Programming Concepts.* New York: Harper & Row, 1972. A good programming text using BASIC.

(3) Iverson, K.E. *A Programming Language.* New York: John Wiley & Sons, 1963.

(4) Pakin, S. *APL/360 Reference Manual.* Chicago: SRA, 1968.

(5) Sammet, Jean. *Programming Language: History and Fundamentals.* Englewood Cliffs, N.J.: Prentice-Hall, 1969.

(6) Singer, B. M. *Programming in Basic, with Applications.* McGraw Hill, 1973.

Problems

1. Evaluate the following APL statements by hand. Assume $A = 2$; $B = 4, 10, -2, 5$; $C = 3$.

$$D \leftarrow C \times 2 + A \times 2 + A \times C$$
$$D \leftarrow (C \times 2) + (A \times 2) \times A \times C$$
$$D \leftarrow (A > C) \wedge (C \neq 6 \div 2)$$
$$D \leftarrow L/B$$
$$D \leftarrow A \times C$$

2. Write an APL function for multiplying of two matrices A and B and storing the result in a matrix C, i.e.,

$$C_{ij} = \sum_k A_{ik} B_{kj} \qquad i = i, \ldots m; j = i, \ldots, m$$

3. As you would expect of an interactive language, APL encourages the programmer to put as much as possible on a single line. APL programmers often take great pride in their "one liners." Discuss "one line" programming in consideration of the points raised in the chapter of Programming Methodology (chapter 3). Develop an APL program to find the median value of the elements of a vector.

4. If you have been learning to program in an algorithmic language similar to BASIC, rewrite one or more of your programs in BASIC.

Chapter 14

Mathematical Models of Machines

We have emphasized that one of the central concerns of computer science is with the algorithmic process and its implementation. One manifestation of this is our treatment of the linguistic aspects of computer science and the specification of the syntax and semantics of our programming languages. As programming languages become better understood, it becomes clearer that they must have a well-specified syntax and semantics to facilitate use by people and interpretation by machine.

Similarly, in developing programs, a structure discipline that is algorithmic in nature must be used to achieve comprehensible, error-free, and efficient programs. Ad hoc programming methods have been shown to be unworkable. Moreover, theoretically, a program developed in an ad hoc method cannot be easily proven to be correct, and, usually, turns out to be incorrect.

Our programs are run on a computing machine, so we need a precise description of the action of the computer. In the case of machines, as with programs, the structural complexity of the typical computer exceeds the mental capability of the users and designers. The computer is the most intricate of all machines conceived by man. The functioning of our computers is required to be an algorithmic process.

A theory of algorithmic machines—known as *automata theory*—once developed, should enable us to describe how structurally complex a machine needs to be to accomplish a given computation. Conversely, given a mathematical—i.e., algorithmic—description of the structure of the machine, we might ask what its capability is.

Both questions on the relation of structure and function are of interest to scientists in other disciplines. For example, biologists are interested in the type of description required of the cellular mechanism to explain the systematic patterns of development of large complexes of these elemental cells into complex organisms.

In this chapter, we will discuss two types of abstract computers. The more complicated of these—the *Turing machine*—is believed to be a completely general abstract computer. It is conjectured that no algorithmic process could be developed that could not be modeled in a Turing machine; this claim is known as *Church's thesis*. We do know that our present computers are exactly as powerful as Turing machines.

The second, and simpler, abstract computer is the so-called *finite state machine*. The finite state machine is useful both as a model of a computer of limited capability—and as a building block of more powerful abstract computers. An example of one of the tasks a finite state machine can perform is the lexical scanning phase of a compiler which, among other computations, checks the syntax of names in a program.

14.1   An Overview of Mathematical Models

We want to obtain mathematical models of different types of machines. Such a model will view the machine as a black box containing logic and storage elements; the exact configuration of these elements is of no concern to us. The input to our black box represents external information supplied to the system; the output from our black box represents observable results supplied by the system. In any but the very simplest machine, the output is a function not only of the current input but also of past inputs. Thus, our machine must possess a type of memory. We shall use a set of machine "states" to represent a system's memory, each state corresponding to the remembrance of a different set of information. Thus, the greater the number of "states," the greater will be the machine's memory capacity. Figure 14.1 illustrates this "black box" view of a machine.

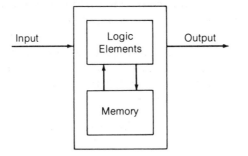

Figure 14.1:   Black box representation of a computing machine

Our mathematical model should use the machine's input and current state to determine its output and next state; such a model would then provide a precise specification of the external behavior of the machine when supplied with any input sequence.

Many mathematical models take the form of a set of differential equations relating the input and output characteristics of the system. This is the case when the variables take on a continuous range of values. In our case, we are interested in systems in which the parameters assume only discrete values; for example, our input might consist of only 0 and 1 (as in the case of binary numbers). Such systems require discrete state transition functions for their representation.

14.2   Finite State Machines

Our finite state machines are a rather abstract model of a machine with a fixed memory size and no auxiliary memory. The "state" of the machine at any given time is the contents of its memory. If the memory can store 10,000 words of 30 bits each, then a total of $30 \times 10{,}000$ bits can be stored. Consequently, the total number of different memory contents that such a machine might hold is $_2 10{,}000 \times 30$, and so this astronomical number is the number of states of the machine. Actually, whenever we design a finite state machine for an algorithmic task, the number of states will usually be less than 100, and we will denote them by:

$$S = \{S_1, S_2, S_3 \ldots\}$$

The input to the machine at any time is one of a finite number of inputs selected from a designated input alphabet, I. For example, in the case of binary numbers, our input alphabet might consist of two symbols, 0 and 1. At each step, the machine proceeds from its state before an input is received to a new state that depends only on the current input symbol and current state. A computation of the machine is taken to be the response of the machine to a finite sequence of inputs from I. The machine produces an output symbol at each step of the computation. This output symbol is selected from a designated finite set of output symbols; the exact symbol output depends only on the current input symbol and current state. This dependency of both the output and next state upon the current input symbol and current state is often represented by the two equations:

$$S' = g(i, S)$$
$$Z = r(i, S)$$

where i and S are the current input and current state respectively, S' is the new state determined by the "next state function" g, and Z is the output symbol determined by the "output function" r.

A finite state machine is completely specified or "modelled" by its next state function g and its output function r. Once these are defined for each combination of input symbol and current state, we can trace through the response of the machine to any input sequence.

Representation of finite state machines

Two methods of representing the next state and output functions are the *transition table* and the *transition diagram*. In the transition table, the relationships are specified in tabular form. The states are listed along the left side of the table, with each state corresponding to a row of the table; the inputs are listed along the top, with each input corresponding to a column of the table. At the intersection of each row and column is found the next state and output, in the form S'/Z resulting from that row's current state and that column's input.

Figure 14.2 shows the transition table for a parity machine. The input to this machine consists of a sequence of 0's and 1's. The machine is started in state S_1; it outputs a "1" if the total number of 1's received as input is even, and outputs a "0" otherwise. Consider the machine's response to the input sequence 101. The first input of 1 causes the machine to change to state S_2 (indicating it has received an odd number of 1's) and output a "0."

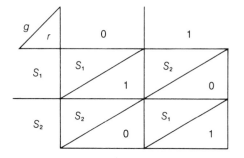

Figure 14.2:   Transition table for parity machine

The next input of 0 causes the machine to remain in state S_2 and again output a "0." The next input of 1 results in a change to state S_1 (indicating it has received an even number of 1's) and an output of "1."

Often the machine's structure is more easily visualized in graphic form. Such graphs are called *transition diagrams.* The nodes of the graph are labelled with the states which they represent. The branches between states are labelled with the input symbol that causes the transition and the resultant output symbol, in the form *i/Z.* Following usual practice, we show an arrowhead in at the starting state. Figure 14.3 shows the transition diagram for the parity machine of Figure 14.2.

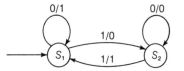

Figure 14.3:   Transition diagram for parity machine

Transducers and recognizers

The "result" of a machine computation may take one of two forms. In the first type of machine, called a *transducer,* we interpret the sequence of output symbols produced by the machine as our answer. Computations performed by such finite state transducers include determining the complement of a binary number and adding and subtracting numbers.

Exercise 14.2-1   Addition of Binary Numbers

Draw the transition diagram for a finite state machine that adds two binary numbers and outputs their sum.

Solution: Our input alphabet will consist of four symbols: 0, 1, 2, 3. We shall input the digits of the two binary numbers as pairs beginning with the least significant digit of each number. The pair (0, 0) will be presented by the input symbol 0, and the pairs (0, 1), (1, 0), and (1, 1) by the input symbols 1, 2, and 3 respectively. The end of both numbers will be followed by a 0 input symbol. Thus, the binary numbers 101 and 011 would be input as the three symbols 3, 1, 2. The finite state machine, adding the binary representations of 5 and 3, will produce as output the binary representation of 8, least significant digit first: 0, 0, 0, 1.

	State	Input	Output
Starting State	S_1		
		3	
	S_2		0
		1	
	S_2		0
		2	
	S_2		0
		0	
	S_1		1

Table 14.2-1:   Sequence of States and Outputs of Finite State Machine Adding $(101)_2$ and $(011)_2$ (proceeding from top of table to bottom).

Figure 14.4 illustrates the transition diagram for a finite state machine that adds two such numbers and outputs the sum. State S_1 is the initial state; it represents the situation in which we do not have a "carry" of 1 from the sum of the preceeding digits. When the machine is in state S_1, inputs of 0, 1, or 2, representing the binary pairs (0, 0), (0, 1) or (1, 0), result in an output of 0, 1, or 1 respectively and the machine remains in state S_1. However, an input of 3, representing the binary pair (1, 1) produces an output of 0 with a carry of 1. Thus, the machine must move to state S_2, the "carry" state, to remember to add 1 to the sum of the next two binary digits. In state S_2, an input of 1, 2, or 3 results in an output of 0, 0, or 1 and the machine remains in state S_2 since we again have a "carry." However, an input of 0 produces an output of 1 with no "carry" and the machine moves back to state S_1.

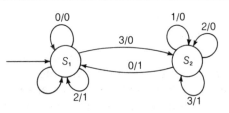

Figure 14.4:   Finite state machine to add two binary numbers

In the second type of machine, called an *acceptor,* output is ignored and the result of a computation depends only on the state in which the machine resides after the entire input sequence is processed. For this purpose, we partition the states into two groups: the first group we call the *set of accepting*

states the second group we call the *set of rejecting states.* Overall, an acceptor receives, as input, sequences of symbols, and it either accepts or rejects
each sequence. The transition diagram for an acceptor indicates the accepting states by double circles.

The machine in Figure 14.5 can be interpreted as a simple lexical scanner. If
we take L to be any letter, D to be any digit, and X to be any other input symbol such as * or +, then this machine will accept exactly those sequences
consisting of letters and digits, whose first character is a letter. The set of
sequences accepted or recognized by this machine are precisely the set of
valid identifiers in most programming languages. Figure 14.6 shows the
finite state machine to accept the same set of sequences when proceeding
from right to left.

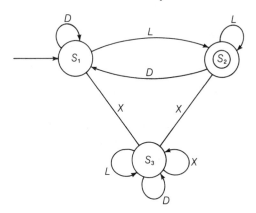

Figure 14.5:   Finite state machine to accept valid variable names

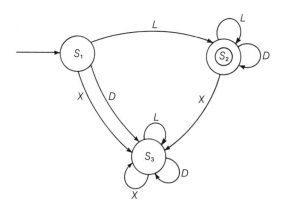

Figure 14.6:   Finite state machine to accept valid identifiers

Exercise 14.2

Draw the transition diagram for an acceptor that accepts all binary numbers in
which no 1 is immediately preceded *and* followed by a 0.

Solution: Our input alphabet will be 0, 1. In Figure 14.7, our machine starts in state S_1. An input sequence containing 010 will cause the machine to enter rejecting state S_4, which it will never leave. All other states are accepting states.

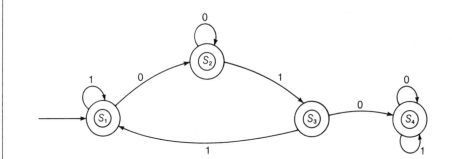

Figure 14.7: **Finite state machine to accept a subset of binary numbers**

Exercise 14.2-3

Draw the transition diagram for an acceptor that accepts all real numbers between 10 and 90. (Assume the numbers do not have a leading 0.)

Solution: We shall let D be any digit other than 0 or 9 and X be any nonnumeric symbol other than a decimal point. In Figure 14.8, our machine starts in state S_1. Any input other than digits 1 through 9 causes it to move to reject state S_5 which it will never leave. In state S_1 we must distinguish between digits 1 through 8 and the digit 9 since an input of 9 must be followed by a 0 if the number is to be accepted. Thus, an input of 9 moves us to state S_2 and, if followed by a 0, to state S_4. An input of digits 1 through 8 moves us to state S_3 and, if followed by a second digit, to state S_4. State S_4 is an accepting state since it is entered on input of a two digit number between 10 and 90. Once in state S_4, any input other than a decimal point moves us to reject state S_5 since the input sequence is either not a valid number or the number is too large. Input of a decimal point in state S_4 moves us to accepting state S_7; input of any digit in state S_7 causes us to remain in that state since the input sequence still is a valid number between 10 and 90.

Transducers and acceptors are really just two different ways of viewing a finite state machine computation. We use a transducer when the output sequence is interpreted as the answer and an acceptor when we want a YES (accept) or NO (reject) answer.

Capabilities of finite state machines

We are interested in the capabilities of finite state machines—what computations they can perform and what their limitations are. We have already seen several examples of problems within the range of a finite state machine. In this section we shall investigate the limitations of these machines.

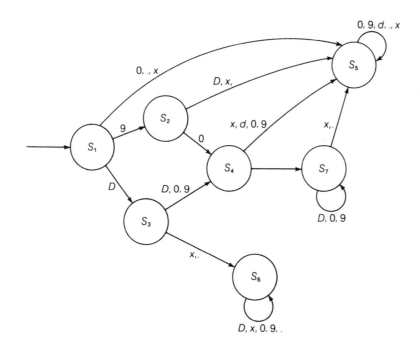

Figure 14.8: **Finite state machine to accept real numbers between 10 and 90**

Exercise 14.2-4   Limitations on Counting

Show that a finite state machine cannot count arbitrarily high.

Solution: First, what do we mean by count? In the case of a finite state machine, we shall consider that it "counts" if it can recognize the number of inputs it has received and can designate the answer by its current state. We could, in addition, have the machine output an appropriate symbol from that state, say the symbol "6" if it has received six inputs. Figure 14.9 illustrates a finite state machine capable of counting to 4.

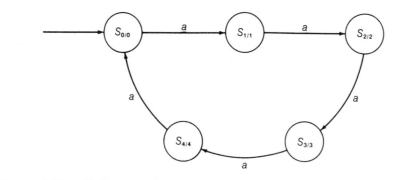

Figure 14.9: **Finite state counting machine**

However, notice that once we reach state S_4, we must now return to a previously used state on receiving another input. Thus, this machine really "counts modulo 5"; that is, the output at the end of computation is "the remainder upon dividing the number of inputs by 5".

Thus, an arbitrary machine with n states can count no higher than $n - 1$ because it can distinguish the number of inputs only up to $n - 1$ such inputs, at which point the next input must send it to a previously used state.

Exercise 14.2-5 *Limitations on Languages Accepted by Finite State Machines*

Show that a finite state machine cannot accept precisely the sentences of the language generated by the BNF grammar:

$$\langle S \rangle ::= a \langle S \rangle \, a \,|\, b$$

Solution: Suppose such an n-state machine exists. If it is presented with an input sequence of the form $a^k b a^L$, it must accept the sequence if the number of a's preceeding the b is the same as the number following it and reject it otherwise. Thus, the machine must count the sequence of a's preceding the b as they are input. However, in Exercise 14.2-4 we showed that an n-state machine can count no higher than $n - 1$. Thus this problem cannot be solved for all sequences of the form $a^k b a^L$. Therefore, a finite state machine cannot accept precisely the sentences of the language generated by the BNF grammar $\langle S \rangle ::= a \langle S \rangle \, a \,|\, b$.

An important and similar result concerns the periodic behavior of a finite state machine under constant input. With any input sequence and a finite number n of states, we must eventually enter some state S_K a second time. Since there are only n distinct states through which the machine can pass, this repetition must occur as a result of one of the first n inputs to the machine. If the input is constant (that is, the same symbol is input all the time), then we repeat from state S_K the same sequence of states and same output sequence as when we left S_K the first time. The period of this sequence is at most n, since there are at most n states through which we can pass before repeating a state. Thus, any finite state machine with n states and constant input will, within the first n inputs, result in a periodic output and state sequence, of period at most n.

Figure 14.10 shows a finite state machine with three states. If constant input of 0 is applied, the resulting state sequence is

$$\underbrace{S_1 \, S_3 \, S_2} \ \ \underbrace{S_1 \, S_3 \, S_2} \ \ \underbrace{S_1} \ldots$$

and the output sequence is

$$\underbrace{0 \, 1 \, 1} \ \ \underbrace{0 \, 1 \, 1} \ \ \underbrace{0} \ldots$$

In this case periodic behavior sets in immediately and the period is three. Under a constant input of 1, the resulting state sequence is

$$S_1 \ \underbrace{S_2 \, S_3} \ \ \underbrace{S_2 \, S_3} \ \ \underbrace{S_2 \, S_3} \ \ldots$$

and the output sequence is

$$1 \quad \underbrace{0 \ 1} \quad \underbrace{0 \ 1} \quad \underbrace{0 \ 1} \quad \ldots$$

In this case, periodic behavior begins after the first input and the period of the sequence is two.

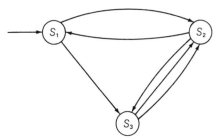

Figure 14.10:   Finite state machine showing periodic behavior

Although this periodicity of the finite state machine under constant input is relatively simple to show, it forms the basis of our proofs of more complex phenomenon.

Exercise 14.2-6   Limitations on Squares

Show that a finite state machine cannot square an arbitrary number.

Solution: We shall represent our number in binary and input the digits from least to most significant. When the first digit is received, the rightmost digit of the answer can be output; similarly when the kth digit is input, the kth rightmost digit of the answer can be output. Notice that this is the only part of the answer that can be determined until the entire number has been input; for a k-digit number, all but the $k - 1$ rightmost digits of its square require carrys and sums computed from all the digits.

Now suppose our machine to square numbers has n states. We shall ask the machine to square the number 2^{2n}. Once the entire number has been input, the rightmost $2n$ digits of the answer, namely $2n$ zeroes, will have been output. However, we showed that a finite state machine under constant input enters, within the first n inputs, a periodic output sequence with period at most n. An output sequence of $2n$ zeroes followed by a 1 does not meet this criteria and therefore cannot be produced by this machine.

Since an n state machine cannot square the number 2^{2n}, we conclude it cannot square an arbitrary number.

Exercise 14.2-7   Limitations on Acceptors

Show that a finite state machine cannot accept precisely the set of perfect squares.

Solution: We shall input numbers as sequences of 1's; such as a 5 is input as 11111.

> Our input to the machine is constant, always 1. Thus, our state sequence must eventually become periodic. Upon receiving 1, 4, 9, 16, 25, . . . or any perfect square number of 1's, our machine should be in an "accept" state; if our input terminates at this point, the machine must accept this sequence. In all other cases the machine must be in a "reject" state since the sequence input thus far is not a perfect square. But such a sequence of states through which the machine passes can never become periodic; this is because the sequence of states through which the machine passes between each entry to an "accept" state is continually increasing. Thus, a finite state machine to accept perfect squares does not exist.

Another example of a set of sequences a finite state machine cannot accept is the set of all syntactically valid sentences specified by BNF grammar. [Note, however, that if a set of sequences contains only finitely many sequences, you can always synthesize a finite state machine to accept exactly the sequences in that set.]

We have seen that there are computations a finite state machine cannot perform. This inability is due to the limited memory of such machines. Next, we shall investigate a machine model with unlimited memory.

14.3   Turing Machines

A *Turing machine* is a finite state machine with a working tape marked off in squares. There is no limit on the amount of tape available to the machine, as much being added as is required by the computation. The sequence to be fed into the finite state machine is recorded on the tape, one symbol per square; the rest of the tape is blank. The finite state machine is connected to a tape head that can read and write. Initially the machine is reading the leftmost nonblank tape square. In a single move the symbol on the tape is read, and depending on the state of the finite state machine and the symbol being read, a new symbol is recorded. The tape head is moved one square left, one square right, or not moved, and the finite state machine moves to a new state. Some of the states of the finite state machines are designated as terminal states. A computation is concluded only when a terminal state is reached, at which time the machine halts. The result of a computation is represented by the contents of the tape when the machine stops. In the case of a transducer, this result is the answer; in the case of an acceptor, the result will be 0 or nonzero depending on whether the tape input sequence is accepted or rejected respectively.

Representation of Turing Machines

Turing machines are easily represented in tabular form as (q_i, x, y, q_j, M) where q_i and x are the current state and symbol read, y and q_j are the symbol written and next state, and M specifies a Right (R), Left (L), or stationary (S) move.

Exercise 14.3-1 Turing Machine for Subtraction

Design a Turing Machine to perform subtraction of two numbers represented as strings of 1's separated by a single 0. Assume the first number is always larger than the second.

Solution: The computation $x - y$ where $x = 5$ and $y = 2$, would be represented on our tape as 11111011, a string of five 1's and a string of two 1's separated by a 0. Figure 14.11 shows a Turing machine to subtract two such numbers x and y; the answer on the tape will be represented by a string of 1's.

The Turing machine starts in state q_0 and moves right searching for the 0 separating the two numbers. When this 0 is found the machine moves to state q_1. It now searches for a 1 in the subtrahend y; if a blank is encountered first, the machine moves to terminal state q_3 and stops with the answer on the tape. On finding a 1 in the subtrahend y, the machine zeroes it, moves to state q_2, and searches to the left for a 1 to zero out (subtract) from the minuend x. Once this is completed, the machine moves to state q_0 and repeats this procedure. The configurations assumed by the TM during the execution of the program of Figure 14.11 are illustrated in Table 14.11.

Executed Instruction	New Machine Configuration	New State
Starting Configuration	$\underset{\blacktriangle}{1}1111011$	
$q_0, 1, 1, q , R$	$1\underset{\blacktriangle}{1}111011$	q_0
$q_0, 1, 1, q_0, R$	$11\underset{\blacktriangle}{1}11011$	q_0
$q_0, 1, 1, q_0, R$	$111\underset{\blacktriangle}{1}1011$	q_0
$q_0, 1, 1, q_0, R$	$1111\underset{\blacktriangle}{1}011$	q_0
$q_0, 1, 1, q_0, R$	$11111\underset{\blacktriangle}{0}11$	q_0
$q_0, 0, 0, q_1, R$	$111110\underset{\blacktriangle}{1}1$	q_1
$q_1, 1, 0, q_2, L$	$11111\underset{\blacktriangle}{0}01$	q_2
$q_2, 0, 0, q_2, L$	$1111\underset{\blacktriangle}{1}001$	q_2
$q_2, 1, 0, q_0, R$	$11110\underset{\blacktriangle}{0}01$	q_0
$q_0, 0, 0, q_1, R$	$111100\underset{\blacktriangle}{0}1$	q_1
$q_1, 0, 0, q_1, R$	$1111000\underset{\blacktriangle}{1}$	q_1
$q_1, 1, 0, q_2, L$	$111100\underset{\blacktriangle}{0}0$	q_2
$q_2, 0, 0, q_2, L$	$11110\underset{\blacktriangle}{0}00$	q_2
$q_2, 0, 0, q_2, L$	$1111\underset{\blacktriangle}{0}000$	q_2
$q_2, 0, 0, q_2, L$	$111\underset{\blacktriangle}{1}0000$	q_2
$q_2, 1, 0, q_0, R$	$1110\underset{\blacktriangle}{0}000$	q_0
$q_0, 0, 0, q_1, R$	$11000\underset{\blacktriangle}{0}00$	q_1
$q_1, 0, 0, q_1, R$	$111000\underset{\blacktriangle}{0}0$	q_1
$q_1, 0, 0, q_1, R$	$1110000\underset{\blacktriangle}{0}$	q_1
$q_1, 0, 0, q_1, R$	$11100000\underset{\blacktriangle}{}$	q_1
$q_1, , , q_3, S$	$11100000\underset{\blacktriangle}{}$	q_3

Table 14.11: Configuration of turing machine for subtraction

Current State	Current Symbol	Symbol Written	Next State	Move
q_0	0	0	q_1	R
q_0	1	1	q_0	R
q_1	0	0	q_1	R
q_1	1	0	q_2	L
q_1	—	—	q_3	S
q_2	0	0	q_2	L
q_2	1	0	q_0	R

Terminal state is q_3.

Figure 14.11:   *Turing machine for subtraction*

Exercise 14.3-2   *Turing Machine Acceptor for a Language*

Design a Turing machine to accept the sentences of the language generated by the BNF grammar $\langle S \rangle ::= a \langle S \rangle\, a | b$

Solution: The input sequence on the tape is preceded and followed by blanks. Figure 14.12 gives a Turing machine that accepts this language. The machine starts in state q_0 and moves right searching for an "*a.*" If none is found before "*b*" is read, then the machine moves to state q_5.

Current State	Current Symbol	Symbol Written	Next State	Move
q_0	a	-	q_1	R
q_0	b	b	q_5	R
q_1	a	a	q_1	R
q_1	b	b	q_1	R
q_1	-	-	q_2	L
q_2	a	-	q_3	L
q_2	b	b	q_4	-
q_3	a	a	q_3	L
q_3	b	b	q_3	L
q_3	-	-	q_0	R
q_5	a	a	q_4	-
q_5	-	-	q_6	-
q_5	b	b	q_4	-
q_6	b	0	q_4	-

Terminal state is q_4.

Figure 14.12:   *Turing machine to accept sentences of the form* $\langle S \rangle ::= a \langle S \rangle\, a | b$

If no "*a*" follows the "*b*," then the sequence is accepted, the "*b*" is overwritten with a "0," and the machine stops. However, if an "*a*" is found while in state q_0, then the machine overwrites it with a blank, moves to state q_1, and searches for the last symbol of the input sequence. If this symbol is a "*b*," the sequence is rejected; if the last symbol is an "*a*," it is also overwritten with a blank. The machine has now matched and erased the first and last *a*'s of the input sequence; it moves to state q_3, searches left for the beginning of the remainder of the sequence, and repeats this entire process on it.

Turing machine computations

Exercise 14.3-2 is an example of a computation within the capability of a Turing machine, but not a finite state machine (Exercise 14.2-5). With their essentially infinite tape memory, Turing machines have the ability to perform and remember the results of extensive intermediate calculations. Therefore, although the set of "instructions" would be quite lengthy, Turing machines can square binary numbers and accept the set of perfect squares.

We have seen that Turing machines have greater capability than finite state machines. Our next section concerns the capability and limitations of Turing machines.

We now summarize some known facts about Turing machines. If a Turing machine never writes on its tape but may scan back and forth, its computation can be performed by some finite state machine which is only presented with the symbols on the tape in sequence—without repetition. If a Turing machine is provided with several working tapes, it cannot carry out any algorithmic process that could not be simulated by a Turing machine having only one tape. There is no algorithmic process for determining if a given Turing machine started with a given sequence recorded on its tape will ever reach a halting state.

Effective procedure

By an *effective procedure*, we mean a precise, unambiguous step-by-step set of rules for performing a task. We would like to know the set of tasks for which effective procedures exist. More significantly, we would like to know whether there are tasks that can be performed but whose performance cannot be described by an effective procedure. Such tasks would be outside the capability of machines. These questions have been the subject of much discussion but as yet there is no satisfactory answer.

In 1936, A.M. Turing formulated the mathematical model we call a Turing machine. He postulated that any effective procedure could be carried out by such a machine. Since we do not know precisely which processes fall into the category of "effective procedures," we cannot prove this statement. However, every process that is universally accepted as an effective procedure has been shown to be within the capability of a Turing machine. In addition, other intuitively acceptable models of "effective procedure" formulated more recently have been shown to be equivalent. Thus, it is generally agreed that no algorithmic or effective procedure can be developed that could not be modelled by a Turing machine. This postulate is often called *Church's thesis* after the logician Alonzo Church, who did extensive research in this area.

We state without proof that the computational capability, in terms of specifying algorithms, of Turing machines, and flowcharts is the same. As an indication of why this is so, we will show how to develop a flowchart to simulate a Turing machine.

Assume first that there is an array T capable of storing one symbol per cell and that T has no fixed upper or lower limit.* Let i be the address of the current cell of the array on which the computation is being carried out. The array T is a model of the Turing machine tape.

Each state q_j corresponds to a label in the program. If the action specified by the Turing machine in state q_j is

$$q_j \quad a \quad b \quad q_e \quad R$$
$$q_j \quad b \quad a \quad q_k \quad L$$
$$q_j \quad c \quad a \quad q_j \quad —$$

then the corresponding flowchart segment will be that shown in Figure 14.13.

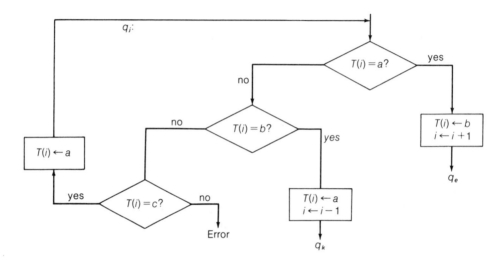

Figure 14.13: Flowchart Segment Corresponding to Subset of Turing Machine Instructions

A flowchart segment can be constructed modelling the action of the Turing machine in each of its states; the individual segments are connected via their labels derived from the current state they represent. The overall flowchart simulates the Turing machine.

The construction in the other direction, i.e., developing a Turing machine for a given flowchart, is more complicated. Essentially, it requires the development of Turing machine models for each flowchart component and a methodology for interconnecting these components.

Universal Turing machines

The specification of a Turing machine to carry out a specific computation required a listing of the elemental actions of the machine for each combina-

---

*If T has a fixed upper *and* lower limit, then the resulting machine will be no more powerful than a finite state machine.

tion of tape symbol and state. The problem data are represented by the contents of the tape at the beginning of the computation and the problem result is represented by the tape contents at the end of the computation.

If we accept Church's thesis, does this mean we will need a different Turing machine for each effective procedure? Or can we design one Turing machine that can perform any effective procedure, no matter how complex?

We can build a Universal Turing Machine T_M which can simulate any other Turing machine. The tape input to T_M will include not only the problem input data for the machine T being simulated, but also a specification of that machine's structure. Using this two-fold input, T_M will run the computation, simulating at each step the action of T and generating the same result as T, if any.

The construction of a Universal Turing Machine is facilitated using the fact, cited earlier, that a multitape Turing machine is "no more powerful" than a one-tape Turing machine; i.e., for any multitape machine, there is an equivalent one-tape Turing machine with some way of arranging the computations to be carried out on it.

The machine T_M can be constructed using three tapes. Tape No. 1 will be problem data for T. Tape No. 2 will record the structure of "program" of T. Tape No. 3 will be used to store, in T_M, the current state of the machine T being simulated. At each step of the computation in T, T_M will search through Tape No. 2 to find the new symbol, new state, and motion of T, and make the appropriate corrections to tapes No. 1 and No. 3.

T may have many more states and tape symbols than T_M, but T_M can encode this information and take many steps for each step of T. Because T_M can model any algorithmic computation when provided with the program and data, T_M is called a *Universal Turing Machine*.

Summary

In this chapter, we have presented briefly some theoretical machine models. At the simple end of the machine spectrum are the finite state machines. We introduced two types of finite state machines, the transducer and the acceptor. These two types are essentially equivalent; they differ only in the manner in which the result of a computation is interpreted. The transducer interprets the output sequence as the "answer;" the acceptor accepts or rejects the input sequence as a member of a set, depending on the state of the machine when the computation is completed.

The capability of finite state machines is restricted by their limited memory. These machines are equivalent to programs without dynamic storage allocation. For such machines, the theory does not preclude a development of techniques for the halting and correctness problems—in fact, they can be solved, in theory, by exhaustive enumeration.

At the complex end of machine capability, we have presented the Turing machine. Although these machines are structurally much simpler than the computers with which we are familiar, you can simulate any general purpose digital computer on a Turing machine. In fact, according to Church's thesis, any effective procedure can be carried out on a Turing machine. We also described a Universal Turing Machine that, on receiving as input both the problem input data and a description of a Turing machine's structure, simulates that machine's action on the problem. Thus, we have a single Turing machine capable of performing any effective computation.

References and Suggested Additional Readings

(1) Hennie, Frederick C. *Finite State Models for Logical Machines.* New York: John Wiley & Sons, 1968.
(2) Hopcroft, John E. and Jeffrey Ullman. *Formal Languages and their Relation to Automata.* Reading, Mass.: Addison-Wesley, 1969.
(3) Kain, Richard Y. *Automata Theory: Machines and Languages.* New York: McGraw-Hill, 1972.
(4) Minsky, Marvin L. *Computation: Finite and Infinite Machines.* Englewood Cliffs, N.J.: Prentice-Hall, 1967.

Problems

1. Design a finite state machine that will accept all strings of *a*'s and *b*'s having an even number of *a*'s.
2. Design a Turing machine that will accept all strings of *a*'s and *b*'s having an even number of *a*'s.
3. Design an acceptor for valid variable names in some programming language.
4. Design a Turing machine to perform addition of two numbers represented by strings of 1's separated by a 0.
5. Design a finite state machine that will accept all strings of *a*'s and *b*'s in which the difference between the number of *a*'s and the number of *b*'s is a multiple of 3.
6. Design a finite state machine to perform subtraction of two binary numbers.
7. Design a finite state machine that accepts all real numbers between 9.63 and 20.72.
8. Design a Turing machine that accepts any string of *a*'s whose length is a perfect square.
9. Show that a finite state machine cannot accept precisely the set of strings whose length is a prime number.
10. Design a Turing Machine to accept precisely the set of strings whose length is a prime number.
11. Show that a finite state machine cannot accept precisely the set of strings whose length is a power of 2.

12. Design a Turing machine to accept precisely the set of strings whose length is a power of 2.

13. Show that a finite state machine cannot accept precisely the sentences of the language generated by the BNF grammar:

$$\langle s \rangle ::= a \, \langle s \rangle \, b \mid aaa$$

14. Design a Turing Machine to accept precisely the sentences of the languages generated by the BNF grammar:

$$\langle s \rangle ::= a \, \langle s \rangle \, b \mid aaa$$

Chapter 15

Programming a Pocket Calculator

The pocket calculator is already established as an increasingly important tool in many areas. We can predict confidently that the slide rule will soon be obsolete, as mechanical and electromechanical desk calculators already are. Further, we can foresee an expanding heirarchy of capabilities among pocket calculators.

With the great availability of such calculators and their ever-increasing application, many more people will be doing some programming as a part of their job. If programming is approached in a systematic (i.e., algorithmic) method, it requires much less effort, and is much less error prone, than otherwise. If programming is not done according to a disciplined approach, the limits of human competence interfere with the programming process. (This has been discussed in greater length in chapter 3.)

The method described here for programming a pocket calculator is a specialization of the techniques that have been emphasized throughout this book. Start with an algorithm, described in standard form by a flowchart. Use a computational procedure to translate the flowchart to the language of the machine. Use further algorithms applied at various stages of the translation process to improve the efficiency of the generated machine language.

In subsequent sections we will describe an idealized pocket calculator, then a method for translating a flowchart. The translation is broken down into three phases: In the first phase, the flowchart is transformed into a tree-structured program. Next is an optional phase, in which the tree is improved so that a more efficient program will result. Finally, the tree program is transcribed to the language of the calculator.

15.1   Description of a Calculator

The calculator that will be used as the model for this exposition of programming methods is the Hewlett-Packard, HP-65, shown in Figure 15.1. The HP-65 is a small (1 in × 3 in × 6 in) programmable computer. The HP-65 can be used in one of two modes:

(1) By using the keys on the keyboard other than those the top row, the HP-65 will carry out built-in operations. A sequence of such operations can then be used to solve a problem.

(2) The keys on the top row of the keyboard initiate programs stored in the memory of the HP-65. A program consists of a sequence of steps, and is the equivalent of a sequence of keyboard operations. The difference between an automatically run program and a sequence of keyboard actuations is that the automatic program runs at high speed and eliminates potential errors. Thus, it is faster, easier, and more accurate.

The HP-65 can store 100 instructions in its memory. The memory can be reloaded with other programs stored on 1/2 in × 3 in magnetic cards. These

Figure 15.1-1:   HP-65 programmable calculator
By permission of Hewlett-Packard.

other programs can either be written by a user, obtained by pooling resources with other users, or bought from the manufacturer. If the user pre-
pares his own programs, he can enter them directly into memory via the
keyboard and subsequently record the program onto a blank magnetic card.

In the remainder of this chapter we shall use a subset of the HP-65 reper-
toire to simplify the discussion. To avoid confusion, the subset will be referred to as sHP-65.

A. Variable Storage

The sHP-65 has a *stack* of four registers, X, Y, Z, T. Data keyed from the
keyboard are stored in X and displayed. The ENTER ↑ operation is equivalent to the following program:

$$T \leftarrow Z$$
$$Z \leftarrow Y$$
$$Y \leftarrow X$$

The old contents of T, before the ENTER ↑ operation, are lost. T stores what
was in Z. Z stores what was in Y. Y stores what was in X. X retains old value,
but now keying in new data will alter the contents of X. Most operations,
described below, use X and Y as operands.

In addition to the stack, there is a set of nine registers $R1, R2, \ldots, R9$. These
registers are used to store other data that can be brought to the stack as
needed.

15.2   Arithmetic Operations

Arithmetic operations fall into two sets: unary operations and binary operations. Unary operations replace x with the result of the operation and do not
affect other storage.*

Example:

	Replaces x with:
$1/x$	Reciprocal of x.
ABS	Absolute Value of x.
CHS	$-x$.
INT	The integer part of x.
$\sqrt{x}$	The square root of x.
SIN, COS, TAN	The respective trignometric functions.**
ln	The natural logarithm of x.
log	The base_{10} (or common) logarithm of x.

Binary operations use the x and y data as operands and have an effect equivalent to the following program; assuming that θ is the binary operation:

$$x \leftarrow y\,\theta\,x$$
$$y \leftarrow z$$
$$z \leftarrow T$$

The contents of x are replaced by $y\,\theta\,x$. If θ is a commutative operation, such
as $+$ (meaning that $x + y = y + x$), the order is not important. But for noncommutative operations such as subtraction, division, and exponentiation,
the order is significant. The contents of y are replaced by z, and the contents
of z by T. T also retains its old value.

Example:

	Replaces x with:
$+$	$y + x$
$\times$	$y \times x$
$-$	$y - x$
$\div$	$y \div x$
y^x	$y \uparrow x$ (y raised to the power x)

A.   Other Operations on the Stack

$x \leftrightarrows y$ interchanges the contents of the x and y registers. This may be useful for noncommutative operations.

---

*In the HP-65, as opposed to the sHP-65, there is a register called LST x.

**In sHP-65, we assume that x is in radians, and that no register other than x is affected by the
computation. In the HP-65, neither assumption is valid.

CLx clears the x register. The effect is that of $x \leftarrow 0$.

π causes its numerical value to be in x. CLEAR STK clears the whole stack; i.e.,

$$x \leftarrow 0$$
$$y \leftarrow 0$$
$$z \leftarrow 0$$
$$T \leftarrow 0$$

No explicit POP stack instruction is provided.* A stack (see chapter 6) POP operation should be equivalent to:

$$x \leftarrow y$$
$$y \leftarrow z$$
$$z \leftarrow T$$

The effect can be achieved by the following sequence of two instructions:

$$\text{CL}x$$
$$+$$

The first instruction sets x to 0, and the second instruction adds y to x, which leaves y in x since x had been set to 0.

B. Register Transfer Instruction

Two register transfer instructions are provided:

STO i has the effect $R_i \leftarrow x$. The contents of R_i are replaced by the contents of x; the contents of x are not affected.**

RCL i has the effect $x \leftarrow R_i$. The contents of the stack are pushed down, and the contents of x are replaced by the contents of R_i. The contents of R_i are unaffected.

C. Flags

Flags are variables whose domain is $\{0, 1\}$; i.e., a flag variable can assume one of two values, 0 or 1. Two flags, F_1 and F_2, are available. The following flag instructions are used to assign flag values:

$$\text{SF}_i, \text{ set } F_i. \text{ The effect is } F_i \leftarrow 1.$$
$$\text{RF}_i, \text{ reset } F_i. \text{ The effect is } F_i \leftarrow 0.***$$

---

*The HP-65 has some additional stack "roll" operations which cyclically permute x, y, z, T, but not a POP instruction.

**In the HP-65, there are also instructions of the form STO θn where θ is a binary operation. The effect is $R_i \leftarrow R_i \theta x$.

***In the HP-65, SF$_i$ is performed by keying $\boxed{f}$ followed by $\boxed{\text{SF}_1}$ of $\boxed{\text{SF}_2}$. RF$_i$ is performed by keying $\boxed{f^{-1}}$ followed by $\boxed{\text{SF}_1}$ or $\boxed{\text{SF}_2}$.

D. Control Structures

The control structures of the sHP-65 include sequential control, conditional and unconditional branching, and nonimbedded subroutine calls.* No parameter passing is provided, as all variables are global. Similarly, no block structure is provided.

Any instruction may be labelled 0, 1, . . . , 9 or *A, B, C, D, E. A, B, C, . . . E,* are subroutine names. A call to the subroutine labelled *A* causes a transfer of control to the instruction labelled *A.* (The subroutine *A* is called by using the instruction *A.*) Control proceeds from *A* until a RTN instruction is encountered. Control then returns to the instruction immediately following the call to *A.*

Any label can also be used in an unconditional transfer instruction. GTO 1 causes a transfer of control to the instruction labelled 1, where 1 is a label.

The conditional transfers of control test a condition, *C.* If *C* is true, then the next instruction performed is the one that immediately follows the test. If *C* is not true, then the next instruction performed is the instruction occurring two positions beyond the test instruction. The two items that are executed only if the test succeeds may be inserted. In particular, the most commonly inserted items are GTO ⟨LABEL⟩.

The following table summarizes the test conditions:

$$x \neq y$$
$$x \leq y$$
$$x = y$$
$$x > y$$
$$F_1 = 1$$
$$F_1 = 0$$
$$F_2 = 1$$
$$F_2 = 0$$

Table 15.1:   Test Conditions Provided in sHP-65 Instructions.

Finally, the R/S (run/stop) instruction switches the machine between keyboard and program mode. In the program mode, an R/S instruction causes the machine to stop, allowing data to be entered. In the keyboard mode, R/S causes the program to be entered.

---

*The HP-65 has a special iterative control in the DSz instruction. This instruction uses R_8 as an iteration control counter, decreasing it by 1 each time until R_8 is zero, at which time a branch occurs. This is similar to iteration control on such computers as the IBM/360 or 370, in which the B x LE instruction uses a register with automatic increment for iteration control.

Program structure

In this section, we describe how an algorithm may algorithmically be prepared for programming on the sHP-65. The algorithm is presented in two stages. In the first stage we apply the algorithm to an arithmetic expression. In the second stage we generalize the algorithm to make it applicable to a flowchart.

E. Tree of an Expression

Each arithmetic expression can be uniquely represented as a tree. The simplest way to proceed is to first fully parenthesize the given expression. If θ is a binary operator, it must occur in the context $(x\theta y)$ where x and y are the left and right operands, respectively. If θ is a unary operator then θ must occur in the context $\theta(x)$ where x is its operand. Some examples:

Expression	Completely Parenthesized Expression
$x + y \times z - u \div v$	$((x + (y \times z)) - (u \div v))$
$x + \sqrt{2} \times \ln y$	$(x + (\sqrt{(2)} \times \ln\ (y)))$
$\sin\ (x + y^2)$	$\sin\ (x + (y \uparrow 2))$
$Ax^2 + Bx + C$	$(((A \times (x \uparrow 2)) + (B \times x)) + c)$

Next, if the whole expression is a completely parenthesized binary expression, it must be of the form $(x\,\theta y)$ where x and y are expressions and θ is the principal connective. If so, we may develop the tree as:

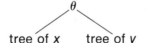

$$\theta$$
tree of x tree of y

If the whole expression starts with a unary operator, then it is of the form $\theta(x)$ and we may develop the tree as:

$$\theta$$

tree of x

If the whole expression is of neither of these forms, then it must be a simple operand, i.e., a variable, or a constant. In which case, the tree is:

$$x$$

Applying this procedure to some of our examples, we have:

Tree of $((x + (y \times z)) - (u \div v))$ is

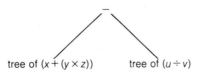

tree of $(x + (y \times z))$ tree of $(u \div v)$

which is

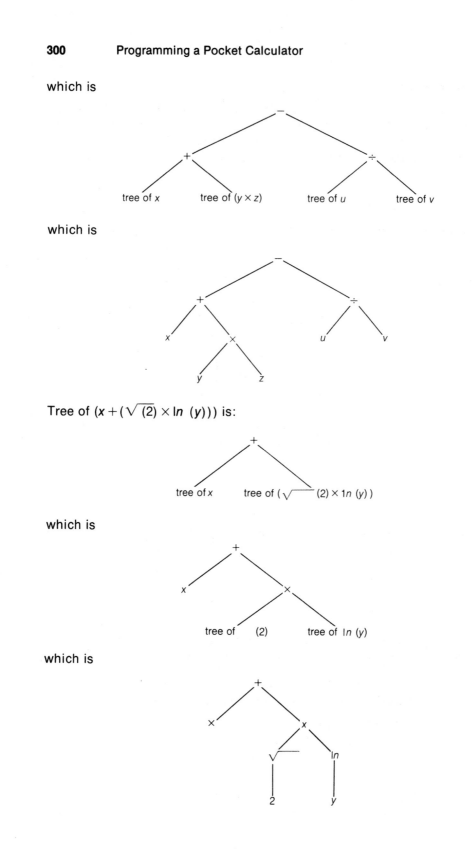

which is

Tree of $(x + (\sqrt{(2)} \times \ln{(y)}))$ is:

which is

which is

The tree of sin $(x + (y \uparrow 2))$ similarly is:

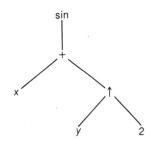

The tree of $(((A \times (x \uparrow 2)) + (B \times x)) + c)$ likewise is:

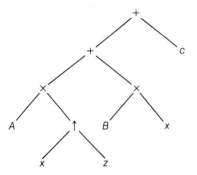

A formal grammar in BNF for our completely parenthesized arithmetic expression language is:

⟨EXPRESSION⟩ ::= (⟨EXPRESSION⟩ ⟨BIN–OP⟩ ⟨EXPRESSION⟩) |
         ⟨UN–OP⟩ (⟨EXPRESSION⟩) | ⟨VAR⟩ | ⟨CONST⟩ |
         ⟨LABEL⟩

with rules for

       ⟨BIN–OP⟩ ::= + | − | × | ÷ | ↑
       ⟨UN–OP⟩ ::= (⟨CONDITION⟩) | √ | ln | INT | log | sin
       ⟨CONST⟩ ::= π | ⟨number⟩
       ⟨VAR⟩

The tree of an arithmetic expression is very closely related to the derivation tree of the BNF grammar. The difference is that whereas

    ⟨EXPRESSION⟩ ::= (⟨EXPRESSION⟩ ⟨BIN–OP⟩ ⟨EXPRESSION⟩)

is diagrammed as

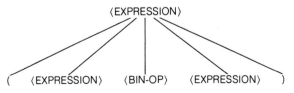

in a derivation tree; it is diagrammed as

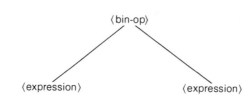

in an arithmetic tree (similarly for unary operators).

Finally, having an arithmetic tree for the expression, we read off the tree as follows:

Procedure: End-order scan (see chapter 7.)

(1) If there are one or more trees below the topmost symbol, use this end-order procedure scan to read them off in left to right order.

(2) Read off the top-most symbol.

Example: (Abbreviating end-order scan as EO)

EO

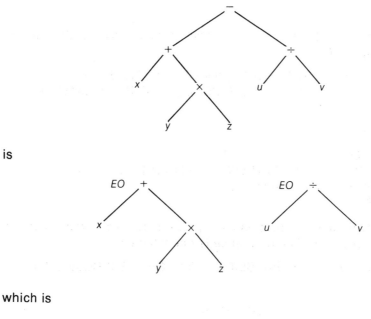

is

which is

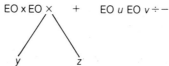

which is

$$x\ y\ z\times+u\ v\div-$$

The end-order scans for the remaining examples are:

$$x\ 2\ \sqrt{y}\ 1n\times+$$
$$x\ y\ 2\uparrow+\sin$$
$$A\ x\ 2\uparrow\times B\ x\times+c+$$

The result of the end-order scan can also be written down from right to left by following a maze tracing route. Start at top. Proceed downward always branching to the right. When you cannot go downward any more, back up to the last branch point in which there is an alternate path which has not been followed and proceed down it. While proceeding in this way, record each symbol the first time it is encountered.

Example: Maze Tracing Post-Order Scan

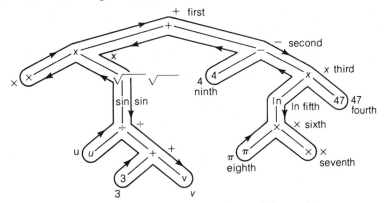

The sequence of symbols encountered is, from right to left:

$$x\ u\ 3\ v\ +\div\sin\ \sqrt{\ }\times 4\ \pi\ x\times 1n\ 47\times-+$$

F. Tree of a Program

The algorithms for which we will construct trees are assumed to be presented in the form of flowcharts. We may assume that our flowcharts consist of the components described in chapter 2: tests, merges, input, output, and computation. Further, we may assume that the computation block consists of a sequence of assignment statements. We consider first the tree of a computation block.

Each statement in a computation block is of the form $x \leftarrow E$ where E is an arithmetic expression. The tree of $x \leftarrow E$ is:

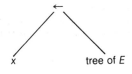

tree of E

so that the statement $x \leftarrow y^2 + \sin (5 \times u)$ has the tree:

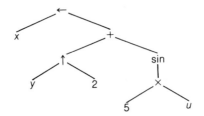

If $s_1, s_2, s_3, \ldots$ are the sequence of statements in a computation block, then we may imagine the commas as operators, and the complete parenthesization of the sequence is $(\ldots((S_1, S_2), \ldots)$. The tree is then developed as usual. (It turns out that the effect of this parenthesization and tree structure is to yield a post-fix form for the sequence which is the sequence of post-fix forms of the individual statements separated by commas.)*

In the case of conditional transfers of control, the test and transfer operations will be treated as a single unary operation according to the following example:

$$\text{if } c \text{ then GO TO } \alpha$$

becomes

$$(c)(\alpha)$$

which is represented by the following tree:

$$c$$
$$|$$
$$\alpha$$

The choices of c are given in Table 15.1-1. The label α is used to mark the starting point of the true branch of the flowchart decomposition discussed below.

Finally, we consider the tree of a complete flowchart. First, modify the flowchart by labelling each merger node. Also, label the *true* exit from each test node. Next, trace a path starting at the START node and proceeding via the *false* exit from each test node. If this path ever completes a loop by returning to a node it had visited, the loop will be completed at a merger node. Disconnect this second entry to the merger node and have it enter a block la-

---

*Note that the comma is an associative operator, so that $(s_1, (s_2, s_3)) = ((s_1, s_2), s_3)$. Since the comma is a control operator, it also imposes a *left branch first* evaluation discipline upon the tree.

belled GO TO x where x is the label of the entry node. Otherwise, continue until the STOP node is reached (*).

If every node in the flowchart has been visited by our algorithm, we are done. Otherwise, start at the true exit of a test point along an edge that has not yet been traversed and proceed, as above, until the current path enters a merger node that has been visited on some path or reaches the STOP node. If we reach a previously visited merger node, treat it as above. Continue the algorithm at (*).

The algorithm just described constructs a sequence of paths $s_1, s_2, s_3, \ldots$. We use the same trick that was used for the sequence of statements in a computation block to form a single tree.

(The preceding description of the algorithm essentially combined two steps of the decomposition, thus violating our own dictum about proceeding in the simplest sequence of elaborations of the programs. This was done to follow most closely the algorithm of chapter 2.)

Consider the following example:

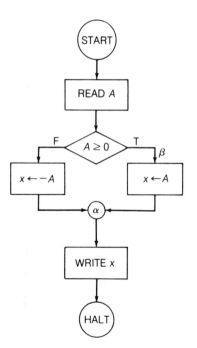

which is just $x \leftarrow ABS(A)$ programmed as an illustration. A tree for this program would be:

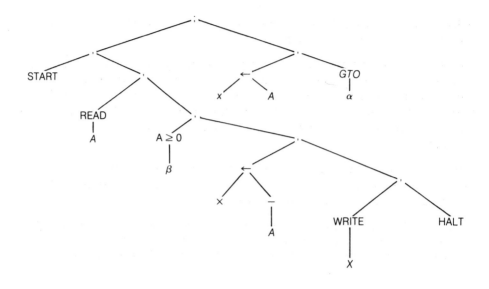

Consider the flowchart for solutions of a quadratic equation (Figure 15.2). This is a slight variation on an algorithm that is available in the Standard-Pac of the HP-65.

(1) START
(2) READ a, b, c
(3) $(a=0)(\delta)$
(4) $z \leftarrow -b/2a,\ y \leftarrow z^2,\ x \leftarrow c$
(5) $(x \le y)(\alpha)$
(6) WRITE -1
(7) $y \leftarrow \sqrt{x-y},\ x \leftarrow z$
(8) γ: WRITE x, y
(9) HALT
(10) δ: WRITE 0
(11) HALT
(12) α: WRITE 1
(13) $x \leftarrow \sqrt{y-x}$
(14) $(z \ge 0)(\varepsilon)$
(15) $x \leftarrow z - x$
(16) β: $y \leftarrow c/(a \times x)$
(17) GTO γ
(18) ε: $x \leftarrow z + x$
(19) GTO β

Table 15.1-2:   Intermediate Program for Solutions of a Quadratic Equation

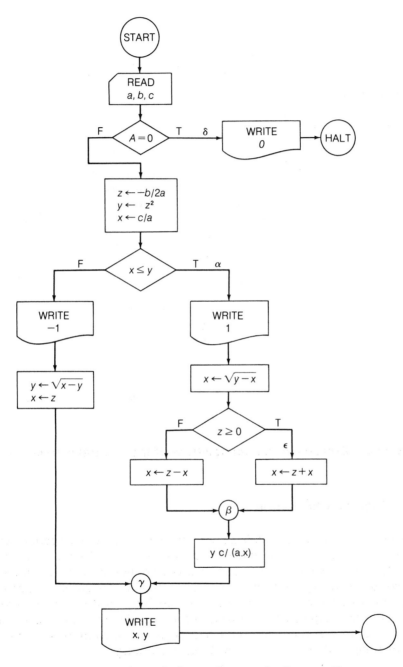

Figure 15.2:   Flowchart for solutions of a quadratic equation.

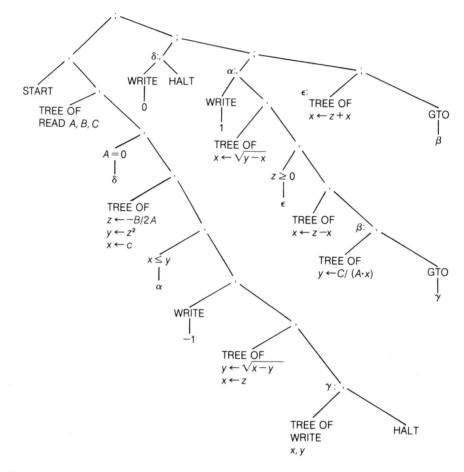

Figure 15.3: Expression tree for solutions of the quadratic equation

15.3   Compiling the Program

We have set up the basis for this section in the preceding two sections of this chapter. In section 15.1, the machine structure of the HP-65 was described with a few simplifying assumptions to avoid unnecessary detail. In section 15.2, we showed how arithmetic expressions and assignment statements can be translated into tree forms and then into Polish suffix form. Further, the whole algorithm expressed in flowchart form can be linearized, as shown in section 15.2, so that it consists of a sequence of a small number of different types of statements in an intermediate level language.

In this section, we show that this intermediate language can be directly compiled into the machine instructions to yield a running program. The code for the quadratic equation program is given in Table 15.1-3.

1: LBL	5: $g\ x \leq y$	14: $g\ x \rightleftarrows y$
E	GTO	0
f	1	$g\ x \leq y$
STK	6: 1	GTO
f	CHS	5
REG	R/S	15: CLx
R/S	7: CLx	+
2: LBL	+	$g\ x \rightleftarrows y$
A	$g\ x \rightleftarrows y$	−
STO 1	−	16: LBL
RTN	f	2
LBL	$\sqrt{}$	↑
B	$g\ x \rightleftarrows y$	↑
STO 2	8: LBL	RCL 1
RTN	3	×
LBL	R/S	RCL 3
C	$g\ x \rightleftarrows y$	$g\ x\ y$
STO 3	R/S	÷
3: RCL 1	9: RTN	$g\ x \rightleftarrows y$
0	10: LBL	17: GTO
$g\ x = y$	4	3
GTO	0	18: LBL
4	R/S	5
4: RCL 2	11: RTN	CLx
CHS	12: LBL	+
RCL 1	1	+
↑	1	19: GTO
+	R/S	2
÷	13: CLx	
↑	+	
↑	−	
×	f	
RCL 3	$\sqrt{}$	
RCL 1		
÷		

Table 15.1-3: HP-65 program for solutions of the quadratic equation

Notes on table 15.1-3

(1) The sequence of Greek letters was used to derive the number labels in the program; namely,

$$\alpha \longleftrightarrow 1$$
$$\beta \longleftrightarrow 2$$
$$\gamma \longleftrightarrow 3$$
$$\delta \longleftrightarrow 4$$
$$\epsilon \longleftrightarrow 5$$

(2) The decision was made to retain as much information in the stack as possible. This is particularly evident in the compiled code of steps 7 and 16 (among others).

(3) Data are entered in step No. 2. The constant a is entered and then A is depressed; b is entered and B is depressed; c is entered and C is depressed.

(4) If a = 0, the equation may have a real root but we ignore it and return a 0 (step 4) as an indication that the program does not cover this case. Similarly, in steps 6 and 12, −1 or +1 is presented as an indication that the roots are complex, or real, respectively.

(5) Stack management requires that the display indications of step 6 be removed (by popping stack) in step 7. Similarly, in steps 12 and 13.

The method for generating the code illustrated by this example is always applicable. Starting with the flowchart, an intermediate level code is obtained. Both the flowchart and the intermediate level code are quite understandable so the correctness of the algorithm can be assured. The intermediate level code is translated into the code of the machine so that the sections of the machine code corresponding to the intermediate code are clearly identifiable and can be checked separately.

Optimizing the computation

Once a machine executable form of the program has been generated, the question of optimizing that program will arise. The object of the optimization may be to reduce the number of program steps, or reduce the physical size of the program, or both.

Some optimization was already performed in the flowchart by ensuring that identical computations are not repeated. Notice, for instance, that the computation of b/2a is performed once and used twice in the flowchart. Most of the movement of computations from one block to another in order to eliminate common computations is most easily performed on the flowchart.

The remaining optimizations involve finding the best use of the machine registers and the elimination of unnecessary transfer operations. These optimizations would be performed on the machine instructions (e.g. Table 15.1-3) since they would exploit the particular control structures and stack management features of the machine.

Summary

A programmable pocket calculator provides a good vehicle for the application of the algorithmic method to the development of programs, since the resources provided by the calculator are sparse enough to motivate a disciplined approach to program development.

The method described starts with a flowcharted algorithm. The flowchart is then linearized into a sequence of statements in an intermediate language. Each arithmetic statement in the intermediate language is translated into machine language via the tree of the statement and its Polish suffix representation. Other statements in the intermediate language are similarly translated.

References and Suggested Additional Readings

(1) Aho, A.V. and Ullman, J.D. "The Theory of Parsing Translation, and Compiling." (Englewood Cliffs, N.J.: Prentice-Hall, 1973), Vol. II: Compiling, Chapter 11, Code Optimization, p. 844–960.

(2) Freiburghouse, R.A. "Register Allocation Via Usage Counts." CACM 17, (November 1974): 638–642.

(3) Gries, D., *Compiler Construction for Digital Computers.* (New York: Wiley & Sons 1971), Chapter 18. Code Optimization, p. 375–412.

(4) Pollack, B.W. *Compiler Techniques.* Philadelphia: Auerbach, 1972, p. 211–247. This book is essentially a collection of articles:

    (a) Gear, C.W. "High-Speed Compilation of Efficient Object Code." CACM 8, (August 1965): 483–488.

    (b) McKeeman, W.M. "Peephole Optimization." CACM 8, (July 1965): 443–444.

    (c) Sethi, R. and Ullman, J.D. "The Generation of Optimal Code for Arithmetic Expressions." JACM, 17 (October 1970): 715–728.

Problems

1. Assume that you have a calculator at your disposal. Outline a method for estimating the execution speeds of operations. (They are typical 10 ms to 100 ms.)

2. Which is more important in programming a pocket calculator—memory or speed? Explain your answer.

3. Develop the trees of the following arithmetic expressions.
   (a) $x^3 + 5x^2y + 37xy^2 + 4x^3y^3 + 5 \sin (x + 2y)$
   (b) $e^{(x^2 + 5y)} \{ \ln (4x + y) + \sqrt{x} + 37/y \}$

4. Develop the Polish suffix forms of the trees in problem 3.

5. Define a uniform binary tree as a tree all of whose terminal nodes are on the same level. Some examples are:

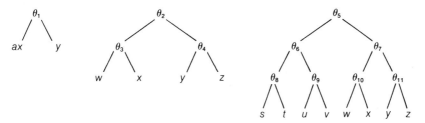

having depth 1, 2, and 3 respectively. What is the size of the smallest stack that can be used to evaluate a depth 2 tree? A depth 3 tree? A depth k tree?

6. Assuming that the tree of your arithmetic expression exceeds the capacity of your stack, how do you proceed in the case of a uniform tree?

7. In evaluating the Polish suffix expression $a\ b\ c\ d\ e\ +++ +$, a depth 5 stack is apparently required. What is the best one can do using associativity? Which operators are associative?

8. In chapter 2, a program for computing Fibonacci numbers is given. Develop a program for the HP-65 which will calculate the nth Fibonacci number.

9. What improvements would you like to see in pocket calculators? Be specific in the areas of processing, storage capacity, and input-output.

10. What improvements to the sHP-65 would most enhance its programmability?

11. What heuristics are appropriate in developing the flowchart of a program so that when reduced to HP-65 code it will require the smallest program storage? Register storage?

12. What algorithmic techniques might you use to optimize the program? Consult the references.

13. In developing the code for the quadratic equation program, stack management is one of the major tasks. Discuss how you keep track of the stack during code development.

14. Reconsider the coding of the quadratic equation program, using the stack primarily for evaluating expressions and the registers for temporary results whenever possible. Compare the coding with that given in Table 15.1-3, both with respect to efficiency and programming ease.

Project

Design and program an HP-65 simulator in a higher level language of your choice.

Index